W9-BOO-134

BEST-PRACTICE
APPROACHES TO
INTERNAL
AUDITING

BEST-PRACTICE APPROACHES TO
INTERNAL AUDITING

BLOOMSBURY

Copyright © Bloomsbury Information Ltd, 2011

First published in 2011 by
Bloomsbury Information Ltd
36 Soho Square
London
W1D 3QY
United Kingdom

All rights reserved; no part of this publication may be reproduced, stored in a retrieval system, or transmitted by any means, electronic, mechanical, photocopying, or otherwise, without the prior written permission of the publisher.

The information contained in this book is for general information purposes only. It does not constitute investment, financial, legal, or other advice, and should not be relied upon as such. No representation or warranty, express or implied, is made as to the accuracy or completeness of the contents. The publisher and the authors disclaim any warranty or liability for actions taken (or not taken) on the basis of information contained herein.

The views and opinions of the publisher may not necessarily coincide with some of the views and opinions expressed in this book, which are entirely those of the authors. No endorsement of them by the publisher should be inferred.

Every reasonable effort has been made to trace copyright holders of material reproduced in this book, but if any have been inadvertently overlooked then the publisher would be glad to hear from them.

A CIP record for this book is available from the British Library.

Standard edition
ISBN-10: 1-84930-023-2
ISBN-13: 978-1-84930-023-0

Middle East edition
ISBN-10: 1-84930-024-0
ISBN-13: 978-1-84930-024-7

This book is produced using paper that is made from wood grown in managed, sustainable forests. It is natural, renewable and recyclable. The logging and manufacturing processes conform to the environmental regulations of the country of origin.

Project Director: Conrad Gardner
Project Manager: Ben Hickling
Assistant Project Manager: Sarah Latham

Cover design by Suna Cristall
Page design by Fiona Pike, Pike Design, Winchester, UK
Typeset by Marsh Typesetting, West Sussex, UK
Printed in the UK by CPI William Clowes, Beccles, NR34 7TL

Contents

Best-Practice Approaches to Internal Auditing

Contributors

Ilias G. Basioudis is senior lecturer in financial accounting and auditing at Aston Business School. He is also chairman of the Auditing Special Interest Group of the British Accounting Association, a fellow of the UK Academy of Higher Education, and an adjunct senior lecturer at the University of South Australia. Dr Basioudis has published widely in academic and professional journals and his textbook Financial Accounting: a Practical Introduction is recently published by Pearson. His research interests lie primarily in the area of empirical auditing, corporate governance, and accounting education. He is a member of various international accounting associations and is on the editorial board of the *International Journal of Auditing*.

Richard E. Cascarino is CEO of Richard Cascarino & Associates, based in Colorado, with over 26 years' experience in audit training and consultancy. Well known in international auditing circles as one of the most knowledgeable practitioners in the field, he is a regular speaker at national and international conferences and has presented courses throughout Africa, Europe, the Middle East, and the United States. He is a past president of the Institute of Internal Auditors (IIA) in South Africa, was the founding regional director of the Southern African Region of the IIA, and is a member of ISACA and the American Institute of Certified Fraud Examiners. He is also a visiting lecturer at the University of the Witwatersrand.

Andrew Chambers works for Management Audit LLP advising on corporate governance and internal auditing, and is also a professor at London South Bank and Birmingham City universities. Described in an editorial in The Times (September 15, 2006) as "a worldwide authority on corporate governance," until 2010 he chaired the Corporate Governance and Risk Management Committee of the Association of Chartered Certified Accountants. Professor Chambers was dean of what is now the Cass Business School, London where he is professor emeritus. He is a member of The Institute of Internal Auditors' international Internal Audit Standards Board.

Andrew Cox is a corporate governance professional who currently works as an independent consultant, primarily in Australia and the United Arab Emirates. His specialty areas are internal audit, quality assessment of internal audit functions, risk management, business continuity and IT disaster recovery planning. His professional experience also covers other areas including project management, change and capacity building programs, security, strategic planning, IT planning, and industrial relations. His career includes roles as chief audit executive at high profile organizations. He has given presentations on auditing in forums both in Australia and internationally, and has taught auditing in Australia and overseas.

Simon D'Arcy was until recently head of internal audit for a joint venture between two global banks. He began his career in internal auditing in 1986 with the UK Department of the Environment. Later he joined Abbey National, where he spent 14 years fulfilling a variety of roles. In 2003 he left Abbey National to become associate director, audit services, for the Portman Building Society, where he remained until its merger with Nationwide. D'Arcy has been a volunteer member of the Institute of Internal Auditors UK and Ireland (IIA) since 1996, and he was president of the IIA in 2007/08. He regularly speaks on a range of governance, risk management, and internal audit subjects and contributes on the same topics to professional publications and periodicals.

David A. Doney is vice-president of internal audit for SIRVA, Inc., a global moving and relocation services company, where he oversees the audit team and is the coordinator for the company's Sarbanes– Oxley (SOX) compliance efforts. Prior to SIRVA, Doney led the SOX assessment efforts for Bally Total Fitness from 2004 to 2007. He has also worked for Sears, Roebuck & Company in the internal audit and financial planning areas, and for Ingersoll-Rand Company as a financial management trainee. He is a frequent speaker at the MIS Training Institute on internal audit and SOX and gave presentations at the Institute of Internal Auditors' international conferences in 2002 and 2008. Doney is a registered Certified Public Accountant (CPA) and a Certified Internal Auditor (CIA).

Ian Fraser is professor of accounting at the University of Stirling, Scotland, and he has previously held academic posts at the University of Strathclyde and Glasgow Caledonian University. He trained for membership of the Institute of Chartered Accountants of Scotland

(ICAS) with Thomson Mclintock & Co. (one of the predecessor firms of KPMG). Professor Fraser has wide-ranging research interests in the fields of auditing, financial reporting, and corporate governance, and he has published on these areas in many academic journals. He has a particular interest in the interfaces between auditing, risk, and risk management. He is currently carrying out a major funded research project on the audit of narrative corporate reporting.

Gail Harden is internal audit manager with Specialized Technology Resources, Inc. (STR). She created the internal audit function at both STR and her previous employer, United Natural Foods, Inc. Harden has been the sole internal auditor at each company, utilizing creative and insightful ways to meet the demands and standards of the internal audit profession with limited resources. At United Natural Foods she was responsible for implementing the Sarbanes–Oxley compliance process. Gail has seven years' experience in internal audit and 13 years' experience in accounting. She holds a bachelor's degree in accounting and MS in business administration and is a certified internal auditor (CIA).

Andrew Higson is a lecturer in accounting and financial management at the Business School, Loughborough University. After qualifying as a chartered accountant, he studied for a PhD. Dr Higson's research has covered a wide range of topics, including accounting theory, the conceptual framework of financial reporting, the expectations gap in financial statements, external auditing, and fraud. He is on the editorial board of the *Icfai University Journal of Audit Practice*, which is based in Hyderabad, India.

Christopher Humphrey is a professor of accounting in the Manchester Accounting and Finance Group (MAFG) at Manchester Business School. His main research interests are in the areas of auditing, international financial regulation, public sector financial management, accounting education, and qualitative research methodologies. He is an associate editor of the *European Accounting Review* and sits on a number of editorial boards for international academic journals in accounting, business, and management. He is a co-opted academic member of the Council of the Institute of Chartered Accountants in England and Wales and is currently writing the official history of the International

Federation of Accountants (IFAC) (jointly with Anne Loft, Lund University, Sweden).

Anne Loft is professor of accounting at Lund University in Sweden. Gaining a PhD from the London Business School in 1986, she moved to Denmark, becoming professor of auditing there in 1997, moving to Lund University in 2005. She was one of the founder editors of the *European Accounting Review* (1992–2000), and is currently an editor of the *International Journal of Auditing*. At present she is writing the official history of the International Federation of accountants (IFAC) jointly with Christopher Humphrey. Her main research interests are in the accounting profession and in auditing regulation—from both historical and contemporary perspectives

Norman Marks, is vice president, governance, risk, and compliance at SAP, focusing on thought leadership around internal audit, governance, risk management, compliance, enterprise performance, and business intelligence. Marks has been chief audit executive of major global corporations since 1990 and is a recognized thought leader in the profession of internal auditing. He is the author of two of the most downloaded Institute of Internal Auditors (IIA) products: a guide for management on Sarbanes–Oxley s. 404 and the GAIT methodology for defining the scope for Sarbanes–Oxley of IT general controls. He is the editor of the corporate governance column in the IIA's *Internal Auditing* magazine, a member of the review boards of several audit and risk management publications, a frequent speaker internationally, the author of several award-winning articles, and a prolific blogger. He is a fellow of the Open Compliance and Ethics Group.

Michael Parkinson, CIA, CISA, is an internal auditor of more than 20 years' experience. While working as a government employee he was the chief audit executive of three different government agencies. He is currently a director in the government services practice of KPMG Canberra. Parkinson joined the board of the Institute of Internal Auditors Australia (IIA-Australia) in 1996, was elected vice-president in 1998, and became national president in 1999, serving until 2001. He has served as the International Secretary of IIA Inc since May 2009. He is a respected educator and author in internal auditing. He currently serves on the Standards Australia OB-007 Risk Management Committee.

Robin Pritchard is Professor of Internal Audit, Governance and Risk Management at Birmingham City University and a Non-Executive Director with a number of UK Government Agencies. He is Chairman of Severnside Housing and a specialist advisor to three further Audit Committees. Robin has developed a number of outsourced internal audit practices and was UK public sector internal audit partner with Arthur Andersen. Recognizing that there is a diverse understanding of what represents good governance and world class internal audit Robin has recently started his own consultancy business providing external quality assessment of internal audit teams and governance reviews in association with the Governance Forum.

Sridhar Ramamoorti is an associate professor at the School of Accountancy and director of the Center for Corporate Governance at Kennesaw State University, Georgia, United States. He has a combined background as an academic and practitioner spanning over 25 years of academic, auditing, and consulting experience. He was a member of the accountancy faculty at the University of Illinois before returning to professional practice with Arthur Andersen, Ernst & Young, and most recently as a corporate governance partner with Grant Thornton. Ramamoorti was co-chair in 2008–11 of the Institute of Internal Auditors' (IIA) 2010 global common body of knowledge (CBOK) study. Widely published, he is a coauthor of the best-selling IIA textbook on internal auditing, as well as of *The Audit Committee Handbook* (2010). Ramamoorti has presented at conferences in more than a dozen countries, serves on numerous boards, and has received awards for teaching and research.

Philip Ratcliffe left Oxford University to start his life-long career in internal audit with Unilever, where he qualified as a chartered management accountant. He later became head of internal audit at a number of large multinational companies involved in manufacturing, distribution, and natural resources. He is currently chief audit executive at a publicly quoted UK paper and packaging company. A long-term member and fellow of the Institute of Internal Auditors (in the United Kingdom, Brazil, and Belgium), Ratcliffe joined the council of the IIA, UK and Ireland, in 2006, becoming its president for 2008/09.

Jeffrey Ridley is visiting professor of auditing at the London South Bank University. He teaches and researches internal auditing, corporate governance, corporate social responsibility, and quality management. His experience spans both the public and private sectors over 40 years. Formerly he was manager of internal auditing at Kodak UK, an operational auditor at Vauxhall Motors, and a member of the British colonial audit service in Nigeria. He is a past president of the Chartered Institute of Internal Auditors—UK and Ireland, serving on many of its committees, and in 2010 was awarded its distinguished service award. He has been a member of the IIA's international board of regents and of its international committee on quality. Currently he is a member of the IIA Research Foundation's board of research advisers and also of the editorial advisory board for the IIA's journal *Internal Auditor*. He is an honorary member of the Charities Internal Audit Network and the Housing Association Internal Audit Forum in the United Kingdom. Ridley's books include *Leading Edge Internal Auditing* (coauthor) and *Cutting Edge Internal Auditing*.

Peter Tickner is sole director of Peter Tickner Associates, Ltd, and has 38 years' experience as a public sector auditor. In his early career he was an external auditor for the National Health Service in the United Kingdom. From 1988 to 1995 he was head of internal audit at Her Majesty's Treasury, and was then director of internal audit for the Metropolitan Police (Scotland Yard), London, between 1995 and 2009. He also spent five years as a lecturer in internal audit at the Civil Service College. Tickner is the author of *How to be a Successful Frauditor*, published by Wiley in 2010.

Bruce Turner has been chief internal auditor at the Australian Taxation Office since February 2007. As chief audit executive at one of Australia's largest and most prestigious public sector agencies, he provides strategic leadership for the Tax Office's internal audit activities and works closely with the audit committee. He has extensive experience in leading and managing internal audit areas, having previously held chief audit executive roles in the energy and transport sectors in Australia. In 2008 the Institute of Internal Auditors Australia presented him with the Bob McDonald Award in recognition of his contribution to internal audit services and the profession.

Contributors

Sheryl Vacca is the senior vice president/chief compliance and audit officer at the University of California (UC). Previous to UC, she served as the West Coast practice leader and national lead for internal audit, life sciences and healthcare. She was also the vice president of internal audit and corporate compliance officer for a large healthcare system in northern California. Vacca has published and presented nationally in the fields of healthcare compliance and internal audit to professional organizations such as the Institute of Internal Auditors, Health Care Compliance Association, Healthcare Financial Management Association, and the Practising Law Institute.

Best Practice
Core Principles

Best Practices in Risk-Based Internal Auditing by Sheryl Vacca

EXECUTIVE SUMMARY

- Agree on a common framework for the risk-based auditing and monitoring program.
- Assess risks across the enterprise and then prioritize them by looking at the likelihood of occurrence and impact for the organization.
- Develop a risk-based auditing and monitoring plan from the identified risk priorities.
- Execute a corrective action plan developed by management to mitigate risks and/or resolve risks.
- Assess the auditing and monitoring process for effectiveness.

GETTING STARTED

In designing risk-based auditing and monitoring activities, it is important that the internal auditor works closely with the organization's senior leadership and the board, or committee of the board, to gain a clear understanding of auditing and monitoring expectations and how these activities can be leveraged together to help minimize and mitigate risks for the organization. These discussions should also include leadership from the legal, compliance, and risk management functions, if they are not already a part of the senior leadership team.

This process should include performing periodic audits to determine compliance with respect to applicable regulatory and legal requirements, and to provide assurance that management controls are in place for the detection and/or prevention of noncompliant behavior. Additionally, risk-based auditing and monitoring should include mechanisms to determine that management has implemented corrective action through an ongoing performance management process to address any noncompliance.

Once the common framework for the risk-based auditing and monitoring program has been established, four key tasks must be performed:

1. Assessment and prioritization of risks, conducted enterprise-wide;
2. Development of a risk-based auditing and monitoring plan;
3. Execution of a corrective action plan developed by management to mitigate risks and/or resolve risks;
4. Periodic assessment of the overall process for effectiveness.

RISK ASSESSMENT

The Committee of Sponsoring Organizations of the Treadway Commission (COSO) helped to define "risk" as any event that can keep an organization from achieving its objectives.[1] According to the COSO model, risk is viewed in four major areas:

- operational (processes and procedures);
- financial (data rolling up to internal/external statements);
- regulatory (federal, state, local, organizational policy);
- reputation (institutional).

There are several ways in which risk assessments in these areas can be conducted. These include the use of:

- focus groups to assist in the identification of risks;
- interviews of key leadership and the board;
- surveys;
- reviews of previous audit findings, external audits conducted in the organization, and identifying what is occurring within the industry and the local market, etc.

Once risks have been identified, a prioritization process is needed to identify the likelihood of the risk occurring, the ability of management to mitigate risk (i.e. are there controls in place for risk, regardless of the likelihood of those risks of occurring?), and the impact of risk on the organization. Risk prioritization is an ongoing process and should include periodic reviews during the year to ensure that previous prioritization methods, when applied in real time, are still applicable for the risk.

It is important that senior leadership participate in, and agree with, the determination of the high-risk priorities for the audit and monitoring plan. This will ensure management buy-in and focus on risk priorities. Also, with managers involved at the development stage of the plan, they will be educated as to the type of activities being planned and the resources needed to conduct these activities. Hence, during the plan year, if there are changes, management will understand the need for additional resources or a change in focus in the plan as the business environment and priorities may change.

DEVELOPING THE PLAN

The International Standards for the Professional Practice of Internal Audit (IIA), Standard 2120 says "The internal audit activity must evaluate the effectiveness and contribute to the improvement of the risk management processes."[2]

This is done through the development and execution of the risk-based auditing and monitoring plan.

Risk assessments and prioritization are important elements in the development of your risk-based auditing and monitoring plan. Considerations related to the plan should also include:

- Review of other business areas in the organization which may be conducting an audit or monitoring activity in this area:
  - If so, could you leverage this resource for assistance in completing the stated activity, or utilize their activity and integrate the results into the overall plan?
- Resources available to implement the plan:
  - Do you have the appropriate resources for the subject matter as needed within your department? (If not, is there subject matter expertise somewhere else in the organization?)
  - If subject matter requires outsourcing, budget considerations and overall risk priorities may need to be re-evaluated.
- Hours needed to complete the plan.
- Projected timeframes.
- Defined auditing or monitoring activities and determination as to whether they are outcome or process oriented.
- Flexibility incorporated into the plan to address changes in risk priorities and possibly unplanned compliance risks/crises which may need an immediate audit or monitoring to occur.

IIA Standard 2120.A1 identifies the focus of the risk assessment process: "The internal audit activity must evaluate risk exposures related to the organization's governance, operations, and information systems regarding the:

- Reliability and integrity of financial and operational information;
- Effectiveness and efficiency of operations;
- Safeguarding of assets;
- Compliance with laws, regulations, and contracts."

The process of risk assessment continues through the execution of the plan where the engagement objectives would reflect the results of the risk assessment. Risk-based auditing and monitoring is ongoing and dynamic with the needs of the organization.

EXECUTION OF THE PLAN—MAKING IT HAPPEN

Each activity should have a defined framework which will provide management with an understanding of the overall expectations and approach as you execute the plan. The framework for your activities should include the following actions:

- Set the purpose and goal for the activity (audit or monitoring):
  - Identify the scope from the purpose or goal, but make sure that it is objective, measurable, and concise.
  - Before conducting activities in high-risk priority areas, it is important to consider whether legal advice may be needed in establishing the approach to the activity.
- Conduct initial discussion with the business area for input related to audit attributes, timing, and process:
  - Concurrent vs retrospective status may be determined at this point. (Concurrent is "real time" and before the end point of what you are looking at has occurred. Retrospective is after the end point has occurred, i.e. the claim has been submitted or the research has concluded, etc. Milestones should be determined for rationale as to how far back to go, for example, new law, new system, etc.).
- Finalize the approach and attributes:
  - Sampling methodology will be determined largely by the scope (purpose and goal) of your activity. For example, the sample used in self reporting a risk area to an outside enforcement agency may be predetermined by the precedent that the enforcement agency has set in industry; to determine if education is needed in a risk area, a small sample only may be needed, etc.
  - Consider the audience frame of reference that will receive the results of activity, and then develop an appropriate format for reporting.
- Conduct the activity.
- Identify preliminary findings and observations.
- Provide an opportunity for findings and observations to be validated by the business area.

4

- Finalize the report.
- Identify processes for the follow-up after management has taken corrective action related to activity findings and observations.
  - Data collection and tracking are critical because they provide trend analysis and measurement of progress.
- Determine the key points of activity that may be provided to leadership and/or in reporting to the board.

The overall process of developing the audit and monitoring plan should be documented. This would include a description of how the risk assessment was conducted and the methodology for prioritization of risks. Working papers to support the audit findings, reports, and corrective action plans should be documented and filed appropriately. Prior to the audit activity, be sure to define and document what should be considered as part of the working papers.

At the end of each plan year, it is important to conduct an evaluation of the overall effectiveness of the plan. Questions to consider may include:

- Was the plan fully executed?
- Were appropriate resources utilized for the plan's execution?
- Were the activities conducted in a timely manner?
- Did the plan "make a difference" in regard to the organization's strategy and business?
- Did the plan reach the goal of detecting, deterring, and/or preventing compliance research risks from occurring?

Annual evaluations may be conducted through self reviews or independently of the internal audit function by a third party, i.e. peer review conducted with auditors from other organizations, Quality Assessment Review conducted according to IIA standards (every 5 years), etc. However, while self reviews are less resource intensive, it is recommended that a independent review be conducted at least every other year to assess the effectiveness of your auditing and monitoring efforts. Figure 1 helps to identify the benefits of an effectively executed risk-based auditing and monitoring plan.

Figure 1. Benefits of an effectively executed risk-based auditing and monitoring plan

NO BIG SURPRISES

Early warning systems
- ◆ Systematically identify, assess, and prioritize risks.
- ◆ Avoid unrewarded risks and protect assets in place.

Integrated infrastructure
- ◆ Ensure that bad news travels fast internally first —have early warning systems in place.
- ◆ Prevent and respond rapidly to potential catastrophic failures.
- ◆ Improve ability to anticipate and prepare for change.
- ◆ Establish a risk-based culture.
- ◆ Provide assurance that key risks and exposures are understood and mitigated.

 **NO BIG MISTAKES**

NO BIG MISSED OPPORTUNITIES

Comprehensive policies and procedures
- ◆ Seek growth, but ensure that strategic and tactical risks are mitigated.
- ◆ Maximize chances of success of achieving business plan goals.
- ◆ Accelerate ability to respond to change and opportunities.

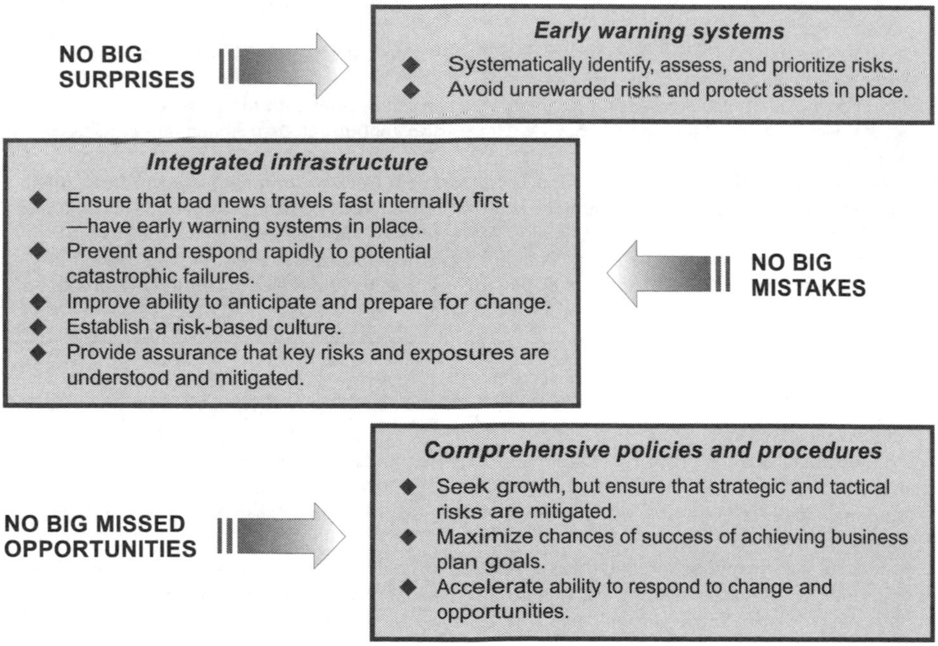

In summary, effectiveness in the development and execution of the risk-based audit and monitoring plan will be determined by the integrity and characteristics of the overall audit and monitoring process. Effective audit and monitoring activities will assist in the identification of weaknesses in controls, management's action to correct those weaknesses, and follow-up to ensure that timely mechanisms have been put in place to strengthen controls for mitigating the business risks. Additionally, risks will be detected, deterred and/or prevented with effective auditing and monitoring activities.

CASE STUDY

Scenario: An organization with multiple businesses in several geographic locations is conducting an enterprise-wide risk assessment. It is noted during the risk assessment that, due to recent financial losses, the organization is going through a consolidation of business units and reduction in workforce. This has been identified as a high-risk priority area for the auditing and monitoring plan for the next fiscal year.

In planning the audit on the risk area of business consolidation, the following considerations should be included:

- The business consolidation could be impacting the organization in various ways—customer base loss, reduced finances, loss of reputation, loss of workforce resulting in loss of controls, etc.
- The risk-based audit will focus on areas of greatest impact: loss of controls in financial areas due to the reduction in workforce.
- The timing of the audit will be negotiated to bring the most value to the organization. This might involve having a two-part audit. Part I could take place after the business consolidation and reduction in workforce have occurred. This would include assessing the consolidated business unit to determine if there are any gaps in the financial controls. For instance, segregation of duties is commonly found in situations with loss of people and consolidation of functions. Any gaps identified would become actions for management to correct before the Part II audit took place.
- Management may also want to set up its own monitoring system to ensure that its corrective actions have resolved any of the gaps identified.
- Part II of the audit would occur after a negotiated period of time with management and would allow the corrective actions to have been in place long enough for their effectiveness to be determined.

The overall purpose of this type of risk-based auditing is to work with management in "real time," to add value to the organization in regard to its strategic and best business interest, and to provide input on processes before they become "fixed." After management believes it has the "fixes" in place, then the second part of the audit will help to provide assurances that the risks identified are no longer risks and that no new gaps or lack of controls have developed around the process of business consolidation and reduction in workforce.

MAKING IT HAPPEN

The development of an effective risk-based auditing and monitoring program includes several key elements:

1 Performing an enterprise-wide risk assessment that includes operational, financial, regulatory, and reputational risk (1-IIA).
2 Prioritizing risks identified through measures such as likelihood and impact for the organization.
3 Developing a risk-based auditing and monitoring plan from the identified risk priorities.
4 Determining that corrective action plans which have been developed by management to mitigate priority risks or ensure controls are in place to lower the risk level for the organization.
5 Conducting follow-up activities that validate, monitor, or audit corrective actions to mitigate and/ or resolve the identified risks.

6 Re-evaluating risks on an annual basis through a risk assessment process to ensure that the priority risks of the organization have been addressed.
7 Conducting a periodic third-party review of the risk-based auditing and monitoring plan to assess whether:
  a processes are in place to identify risks;
  b appropriate resources are utilized to audit and/or monitor risks;
  c a commitment to reinforcing the need for management to execute plans to mitigate risks is demonstrated by the board and senior management.

MORE INFO

Websites:

Federal Sentencing Guidelines, Chapter 8. US Sentencing Commission's webpages at www.ussc.gov/general.htm (history and overview of the guidelines) and www.ussc.gov/guidelin.htm (guidelines and manuals). Chapter 8's provisions can be found at www.ussc.gov/2004guid/tabconchapt8.htm

General Accounting Office (GAO): www.gao.gov

Institute of Internal Auditors (IIA): www.theiia.org

Public Company Accounting Oversight Board (PCAOB): www.pcaobus.org

Sarbanes–Oxley Act 2002: www.soxlaw.com

Securities and Exchange Commission (SEC; US): www.sec.gov

Society of Corporate Compliance and Ethics (SCCE): www.corporatecompliance.org

NOTES

1 Committee of Sponsoring Organizations of the Treadway Commission. *Enterprise Risk Management Framework: Draft (2003)*. Published in 2004 as *Enterprise Risk Management—Integrated Framework* and available from www.coso.org

2 Institute of Internal Auditors. *Professional Practice Standards. 2120—Risk Management*, Section A1. January 2009.

World-Class Internal Audit
by Robin Pritchard

EXECUTIVE SUMMARY

- To be able to contribute and add value, internal audit must have the full backing of the board based on a sound understanding of what the service should deliver.
- There is a need for internal audit to ensure that it is in touch with the highest-profile control and risk environment within the organization and its relationship to industry and world events.
- Internal audit planning must be focused so that reporting is timely and properly directed toward critical organizational and business issues.
- To be regarded as world class, internal audit has to have the capability, skills, and confidence to influence the provision of assurance within the context of the increasing call for independent assurance from stakeholders.

THE AWARENESS DILEMMA

The world in which we live and work today has the most complex, diverse, and challenging demographics ever known to man. Not only have we developed an appetite for travel, trade, and communication across all boundaries, but the technological advancement, awareness of the dimensions of security, and the conflicts arising from political direction and change represent a demanding challenge for everyone. This encompasses both issues that are recognized as traditional risks to governance processes across all sectors of the economy and new threats that provide a constant and changing challenge to management to deliver on corporate objectives. A well-known Chinese proverb advises: "If you must play, decide on three things first: the rules of the game, the stakes, and the time to quit."

If in addition we map across this landscape the impact of the global financial crisis and the subsequent recession—which may yet in 2011 bring still further turmoil to financial markets, particularly in the eurozone—we have an environment in which world-class internal auditors can demonstrate the worth of their profession because, put simply, management cannot deal with the implications for their organization alone.

There is an increasing call for assurance that organizational expectations will be achieved, and, although this has historically reflected a financial focus, there is emerging evidence that a wider view is now much more appropriate to deal with the issues being faced by organizations. Interestingly, this voice does not come only from executive management but increasingly from stakeholders, who will, one assumes, expect nonexecutive directors to fulfil their responsibilities and provide protection of wider interests beyond share value or a balanced budget.

Clearly, there are many forms of assurance by which the board and executive management can be informed, either through the governance process or independently from external sources; however, an intrinsic aspect of the assurance framework must be a potentially enhanced role for internal audit. If organizations choose to use the independence of the internal auditor as the primary vehicle that informs the governance process, to satisfy national or global governance reporting requirements, then there is a significant challenge for internal audit to respond to the elevated transparency of an assurance agenda.

THE DEFINITION OF INTERNAL AUDIT

The Institute of Internal Auditors (IIA) has some 170,000 members, many of whom would pledge recognition of a global standard through their own professional bodies, but the number who do so is manifestly dwarfed by those who would claim to be an internal auditor but pay no regard to standards issued by the IIA, and this would include many who hold a professional accounting qualification. It is no wonder, therefore, that organizations have vastly different views on what constitutes internal audit, let alone something that reflects a world-class standard.

The definitive guidance for the delivery of internal audit is now widely recognized to be that published by the IIA and consisting of the International Standards for the Professional Practice of Internal Auditing and the Code of Ethics, supported by other advice relating to best professional practice. A significant part of this advice supports the definition of internal audit contained in the IPPF:

Core Principles • Best Practice

CASE STUDY: PART ONE

Following a tender exercise in which providers of outsourced internal audit services were invited to provide a professional view of the need for internal audit services for the United Kingdom's National Patients Safety Agency (NPSA), KPMG was appointed on a three-year contract.

The distinguishing elements of KPMG's tender reflected a significantly better understanding of the NPSA's strategic objectives and the risks associated with the delivery of services within the anticipated agenda of cuts in public sector expenditure following the UK general election in May 2010. The proposed plan contained a full reflection of the operational activity of the Agency, with a reduced but appropriate degree of attention to key financial controls.

Additionally, KPMG proposed a 40% reduction in the days to be committed to internal audit, a higher skill mix than other providers, a significant commitment to the contract from the partner/manager team, and a clear understanding of the *International Professional Practices Framework (IPPF)* issued by the Institute of Internal Auditors (2009).

"Internal auditing is an independent, objective assurance and consulting activity designed to add value and improve an organization's operations. It helps an organization accomplish its objectives by bringing a systematic, disciplined approach to evaluate and improve the effectiveness of risk management, control, and governance processes."[1]

While it is true that this is now widely regarded as a modern view of the profession, there remain two distinct issues:

- The permutations as to how to implement such a broad statement are endless, and as a result the manner in which internal audit is delivered, even by members of the professional body, varies both by organization and within an organization, resulting in the possibility that internal audit may not ask the "polite but nevertheless unwanted questions."[2]
- The extent to which the definition is recognized and adopted by the spectrum of interested people who presume to be internal auditors and by bodies involved in the provision or receipt of internal audit is unknown.

The task, therefore, of defining what world-class internal audit looks like presents a near-impossible challenge, as it reflects both the need to adopt the professional guidance and yet still satisfy the requirements of the host organization, no matter whether or not these are compatible.

As a client, the issue of assessing whether a world-class internal audit has been received by either the audit committee or the auditee is therefore probably more easily addressed in terms of recognizing what it feels like not to receive a world-class service than it is to satisfy a precise definition of what should be expected. Performance problems reflecting a lack of recognition of the client organization and

its objectives, poor communication, untimely reporting, and recommendations that are detached from the risk profile or appetite of the organization are familiar indicators of poor-quality delivery. My assertion would be that there is significant tolerance of "uninspiring" internal audit between the two extremes.

Another issue that may also not help in recognizing world-class internal audit is that the guidance contained in the IPPF, its standards and the definition, is largely focused at a practitioner level, whereas the response to the issues contained in the introduction to the present article reflect the need for internal audit to engage at a strategic level, locked into the corporate objectives of the organization, mindful of the risk environment in which it operates, and confident of delivering both assurance and consultancy advice within the agenda of the board and executive team.

In this respect I would encourage the professional body and other parties to elevate the definition to a level that prescribes for the boardroom the contribution that internal audit should make in terms of supporting the governance statements in the annual report and financial accounts by drawing a specific link between a chief audit executive's annual internal audit report, the audit committee's annual report, and the governance statement.

CRITICAL COMPONENTS

I believe therefore that world-class internal audit comprises three critical components: *perception*, *people*, and *professionalism*. If all three are effectively engaged and integrated into a unified product that is recognized and understood throughout the organization, then there is a realistic chance that a service that reflects "world-class" accreditation will be received.

QFINANCE

Best Practice • Core Principles

Perception concerns an awareness of the role that world-class internal audit should play in good governance and the responsibilities of each of the players within the governance agenda—particularly the board in complying with appropriate legislation and regulatory standards, but also executive management and all assurance providers. Underpinning this awareness is recognition of their responsibility to stakeholders for the delivery of expectations that satisfy the nature of the interest.

The *people* dimension represents a need for each of the participants to fulfil their role to the best of their ability, with particular emphasis on the internal auditor not only to deliver a world-class service on a consistent basis, but also to facilitate a better understanding of the role of internal audit in helping organizations to achieve high standards of governance and the role of internal audit within that agenda.

Professionalism is a fundamental aspect of the delivery of world-class internal audit, as it places a responsibility on the internal auditor, whether a member of the professional body itself or otherwise, to adhere to the expectations of the IPPF. The backcloth to this statement is a commitment to the full definition of internal audit and the focus of its operational scope throughout the organization. It may be beneficial for the whole profession to reflect on the fact that financial impact is for the most part a consequence of every other aspect of organizational activity and should possibly demand less attention than strategic, operational, or administrative risk features.

The combination of these three components is critical if world-class internal audit status is to be achieved. However, it is essential that we recognize that a universal model is unlikely to emerge and therefore it is for each organization to define in precise terms its expectations with regard to its understanding of the role of internal audit, the skill set, experience, and qualities it requires in terms of staffing its internal audit service, and the professionalism that it expects from it not only in terms of standards but also in terms of personal commitment to the Code of Ethics.

This may appear to be an oversimplification of the complexity of delivering a world-class internal audit service. Indeed, my personal experience would show that there are more organizations that fail to achieve such a standard than there are that approach anything like a world-class service. In reality, this may be a consequence of a lack of understanding of the role and a failure to commit sufficient resources to the service, thereby resulting in talented and career-minded individuals choosing other professions, including management consultancy—a service that is often confused quite appropriately with internal audit, given current definitions of internal audit that pursue an interest in both assurance and consultancy services.

Boards or audit committees may acquire independent and expert opinion to help them to decide on the nature of the internal audit service that would benefit them, its makeup, and the level of investment that may be required. There is value here in recalling the words of Donald Rumsfeld in 2002 concerning the "things we know we don't know,"[3] which represents the knowledge dilemma, and some assurance that internal audit is focusing on the most appropriate areas in the most effective manner is invaluable.

CASE STUDY: PART TWO
One outcome of the British government's comprehensive spending review (CSR) in 2010 was the abolition of the NPSA. Its three core departments were to be dispersed to other agencies or government departments, with a combination of significant reductions in staff costs and other expenditure, as well as an emphasis for one department's future being dependent on becoming self-financing. This was all to be achieved within the current financial year.

The immediate reaction of KPMG was to propose to the NPSA's audit and risk committee (ARC) that the internal audit plan, which had been accepted in a refined form following the award of the contract, should now be restructured to focus on the new risk profile of the NPSA, the critical aspects of which were now aimed at delivery of an effective closure in line with government instructions.

The KPMG recommendations that were endorsed by the ARC retained delivery of assurance relating to key financial controls but now also provided for a "watchdog" role over adherence to the closure program and additional attention to human resources, IT, and security of information and assets. It was envisaged that this would allow the board, on the recommendation of the ARC, to deliver a clean governance statement in the annual report.

QFINANCE

INTERNAL AUDIT REPORTING

A critical aspect of a movement to give greater status to the internal audit function would be the recognition of the meaning of two particular standards within the IPPF.

IPPF Internal Audit Standard 2050 defines the need for the chief audit executive (CAE) to take into account the sources of assurance that are available within the organization. This places a clear responsibility on the CAE to be aware of the risk profile of the organization, the significant control measures that are in place, and their vulnerabilities as well as the gaps in control that remain or are being addressed. This represents a massive agenda for the CAE, and it is therefore incumbent on the CAE to seek to rely on other forms of assurance with expertise beyond his or her own capability, while recognizing that trust must also be placed in the professionalism of each of these sources. Where there is doubt, inevitably the CAE should seek to recruit sufficient skills to provide assurance in his or her own name.

IPPF Internal Audit Standard 2060 requires the CAE to ensure that effective action is taken to report these concerns to the appropriate level, with further standards supporting the reporting of such findings outside of the organization in circumstances where the organization is not recognizing and not acting upon knowledge that will impact on the delivery of corporate objectives in a material manner. Clearly, operating in this manner places a significant strategic level of responsibility on the CAE; however, this has a direct correlation with the need to staff internal audit with competent professionals who can deliver on this world-class agenda. I believe that this would be a very pertinent development given the alignment of assurance to the needs of the stakeholder.

GOVERNANCE REPORTING

The essence of good governance lies in ensuring that the board not only sets the strategic direction for the organization, but that it also receives information that allows it to review progress toward the achievement of corporate objectives and key operational objectives. Alignment of the framework of appropriately focused internal audit reporting through the audit committee would provide independent and trusted assistance in fulfilling this role.

While recognizing the commercial sensitivities of reporting on significant risks and weaknesses, transparent reporting within governance statements is an essential aspect of satisfying stakeholder information needs.

With the knowledge provided by a CAE's report that properly reflected risk at a strategic level, it would be inappropriate for the board to fail to comment on significant weaknesses and remedial action at an appropriate time in the annual reporting cycle.

Additionally, if greater understanding of the role of internal audit were achieved through this link, wider appreciation of the benefit that can be received from internal audit would be realized. A consequence of this may even be that fewer organizations would choose to declare that the need for internal audit had been considered but the organization had chosen not to engage a service at this time, as can currently occur within governance compliance regulations. This would be even more unlikely to occur if a recognition of the availability of an off-the-shelf internal audit service, through outsourcing, was more directly advertised to board directors, and particularly to the nonexecutive directors, by the plethora of outsourced providers that now exists.

In this respect it is certainly good advice that the essential characteristics of a *curriculum vitae* for a nonexecutive member of an audit committee should include "Commonsense, diligence, [and] an attitude of constructive scepticism."[4]

It cannot be a surprise to find that—given the circumstances of each organization, the interests of those responsible for its governance, and the number of professional disciplines and personal visions that proclaim to represent "internal audit"—the delivery of internal audit reflects a spectrum of varied activity. This ranges from the purely financial focus now regarded by most commentators to be traditional, historic by nature, and of limited value, to that which is best described as risk-intelligent and is able to make a positive and demonstrable contribution to the achievement of corporate and operational objectives. In this sense, it has a clear understanding of how it adds real value to the organization.

CASE STUDY: PART THREE

The ARC was concerned regarding progress against the plans for closure of NPSA by the end of the current financial year and that there were therefore emerging governance risks. This concern had arisen mostly as a result of some slippage in the receipt of instructions from the government regarding preferences and future funding.

KPMG was then requested to increase its involvement and to introduce a consultancy element to its plan with a view to providing additional business management skills to support each department to further define, finalize, and risk-assess the closure programs that would enable the board to deliver on its responsibilities, while also delivering a clean governance statement.

MAKING IT HAPPEN

There can be little argument with a statement that if the organization's board does not understand the benefits that can be derived from an effective internal audit service, it runs a risk that things can happen that are beyond its sphere of control. It is also evident that if internal audit does not understand the environment in which the organization operates, it cannot justify a claim to be contributing to the achievement of corporate objectives. Without such understanding it is equally true that recommendations to the organization for improvement are unlikely to be couched in a value-added, strategic, or operational context, and therefore any concept of partnering with senior management or the board would be difficult to demonstrate.

There are therefore a number of steps that can be taken to ensure that internal audit works for you.

- Understand what internal audit can do and promote the role positively throughout the organization.
- Define what independent assurance would be useful regarding the likelihood of achieving corporate objectives.
- Ensure that the internal audit charter supports this perception and that plans are appropriately focused on key residual risks and those areas of highest control risk.
- Invest in internal audit staff either in-house or through outsourcing or co-sourcing to ensure that internal audit has the capability to deliver assurance at the correct level.
- Ensure that internal audit, and therefore the audit committee, are supported by effective risk intelligence that provides a continuous feed of relevant information about potential threats to the achievement of objectives.
- Devise and deliver a formal structure and mechanism for communication regarding assurance that provides for a transparent review of matters that are likely to impact on the achievement of corporate objectives or result in negative opinions in governance statements.
- Periodically obtain independent professional advice on the quality of delivery of internal audit to ensure that it consistently achieves a world-class service that adds value to the organization.

It is the stakeholder agenda that should drive this momentum; the emergence of control and risk issues, necessitating additional cost and investment in recovery operations such as those arising from the BP Deepwater Horizon or Toyota incidents and subsequent stakeholder concern and litigation that have particularly manifested themselves in terms of reputational risk and loss of share value, should in all organizations raise significant assurance questions for the Board. From where can greater assurance be gained over the successful delivery of our operations? The answer must reflect strengthening the call from the board for openness regarding significant risk exposures and weaknesses, transparency in governance statements, enhancement of the role of non-executive directors and rising demand for an effective internal audit service that delivers independent assurance regarding the effectiveness of risk management, governance and control.

It is for the internal audit profession however to rise to this challenge and demonstrate its worth through the delivery of a service that is recognized as world class and which adds value, by making a significant contribution to the achievement of corporate objectives.

Core Principles • Best Practice

MORE INFO

Books:

Chambers, Andrew. *Tolley's Internal Auditor's Handbook*. 2nd ed. Edinburgh, UK: LexisNexis Butterworths, 2009.

Crane, Andrew, and Dirk Matten. *Business Ethics*. 3rd ed. Oxford, UK: Oxford University Press, 2010.

Institute of Internal Auditors (IIA). *International Professional Practices Framework (IPPF)*. Altamonte Springs, FL: IIA Research Foundation, 2009.

Pickett, K. H. Spencer. *The Essential Handbook of Internal Auditing*. Chichester, UK: Wiley, 2005.

Poole-Robb, Stuart, and Alan Bailey. *Risky Business: Corruption, Fraud, Terrorism and Other Threats to Global Business*. Rev. ed. London: Kogan Page, 2003.

Swanson, Dan. *Swanson on Internal Auditing: Raising the Bar*. Ely, UK: IT Governance Publishing, 2010.

Verschoor, Curtis C. *Audit Committee Essentials*. Hoboken, NJ: Wiley, 2008.

Report:

British Petroleum (BP). "Deepwater Horizon accident investigation report." September 8, 2010. Online at: tinyurl.com/36lcn49 [PDF].

Websites:

Birmingham City University Business School: www.bcu.ac.uk/audit
Institute of Internal Auditors (IIA): www.theiia.org
KPMG: www.kpmg.co.uk
Ra Business Services: www.rabizservs.co.uk

Continuous Auditing: Putting Theory into Practice by Norman Marks

EXECUTIVE SUMMARY

- Continuous auditing is a topic that is frequently identified as a method for internal auditors to "raise their game" and improve the value they provide to their stakeholders. For example, in their 2010 *State of the internal audit profession study,* PricewaterhouseCoopers identifies the ability to leverage technology (including the use of continuous auditing techniques) as one of the eight attributes of a maximized internal audit function.
- In a 2010 study *What is driving continuous auditing and continuous monitoring today?,* KPMG reports, "In a volatile economic environment, a number of key drivers are prompting companies to employ continuous auditing and continuous monitoring techniques to do more than manage risk, including help reduce cost, improve performance, and create value."
- This article defines continuous auditing, discusses the ways in which continuous auditing techniques can be used to provide value, and shares guidance on how to design an effective program. It advises that only after the objectives of a continuous auditing initiative have been determined, and the program designed, should auditors evaluate and acquire software.

INTRODUCTION

The Institute of Internal Auditors (IIA) has issued an excellent global technology audit guide (GTAG) on the topic of continuous auditing. The guide, which we will refer to as GTAG-3, covers a lot of ground, including this definition of continuous auditing:[1]

"Continuous Auditing is any method used by auditors to perform audit-related activities on a more continuous or continual basis. It is the continuum of activities ranging from continuous control assessment to continuous risk assessment—all activities on the control-risk continuum. Technology plays a key role in automating the identification of exceptions and/or anomalies, analysis of patterns within the digits of key numeric fields, analysis of trends, detailed transaction analysis against cut-offs and thresholds, testing of controls, and the comparison of the process or system over time and/or against other similar entities."

Continuous auditing enables an internal audit function to:

- provide the board and management with assurance on a more frequent, if not continuous, basis;
- monitor risks and adjust the audit program to ensure that it addresses what matters to the organization today;
- improve the level of activity, in terms of both volume and period of time, that is audited.

It is important to consider the use and value of continuous auditing within the context of how the IIA defines an internal auditing function:

"A department, division, team of consultants, or other practitioner(s) that provides independent, objective assurance and consulting services designed to add value and improve an organization's operations. The internal audit activity helps an organization accomplish its objectives by bringing a systematic, disciplined approach to evaluate and improve the effectiveness of governance, risk management and control processes."

Taking these two definitions together enables the following points to be made. Each of these will be discussed in this article.

1 Continuous auditing is a method used by internal auditors in support of their assurance and consulting services.
2 Continuous auditing includes activities related to one or more of the following:
   a *Continuous risk assessment* (also known as risk monitoring), including the use of analytical techniques to identify trends, etc., to develop and maintain the periodic audit plan;
   b *Continuous testing of controls* to provide assurance that they operate as intended. GTAG-3 refers to this as "continuous controls assessment";
   c *Continuous testing of transactions*[2] to identify anomalies, exceptions, and potential problems.
3 Although continuous auditing typically leverages technology, continuous auditing activities may include manual testing, reviews of reports, etc.

4 Despite its name, continuous auditing is not necessarily performed continuously. The frequency will depend on a number of factors, including:

a The frequency with which transactions occur (for example, journal entries are predominantly a month and quarter-end activity);

b The frequency with which controls are performed;

c The level of business risk being addressed;

d The risk that the control may not be performed as intended.

However, few internal audit departments have made major moves into continuous auditing. One of the reasons is that the value is not clear to every chief audit executive (CAE).[3] We will discuss that first.

THE VALUE OF CONTINUOUS AUDITING

Imagine that you are the CAE of a global company and you are called in to see the CEO. He asks for your assessment of the quality of controls over the hedging of currency risk—which you identified as a high-risk area in your last report to the audit committee.

Is it acceptable to reply to the CEO that you will be able to tell him when you have completed the next audit, scheduled in three months? Is it acceptable to report, instead, on the audit your team completed a year ago?

The answer is clearly "no." When it comes to the more significant risk areas (such as the hedging of currency risk mentioned above), the CAE should try to provide assurance when it is needed by the primary stakeholders.

Value Proposition 1:
Audit at the Speed of Business
This is the first value proposition for continuous auditing: the ability to provide assurance when it is needed. This can be referred to as "audit at the speed of business." The GTAG-3 refers to it as "continuous controls assessment."

What does internal audit provide assurance on? The Institute of Internal Auditors's "International standards for the professional practice of internal auditing" (IIA, 2010) guides us to provide assurance on the "governance, risk management, and control processes for the organization."[4]

Extending that, *continuous auditing enables an internal auditing function to provide assurance, when it is needed, on the more significant areas of the organization's governance, risk management, and related* controls processes. We can refer to this as "continuous risk and control assurance."

The value to the board and executive management of continuous risk and control assurance is generally very high. Although this dimension of continuous auditing can require the most resources to develop and maintain, the value will frequently far exceed the cost.

The next section will discuss how an internal audit department can use continuous auditing techniques for each of the value propositions. The second value relates to fraud.

Value Proposition 2:
Fraud Detection and Control
Internal audit departments have a keen interest in fraud: in the adequacy of controls that prevent or detect fraud, and in investigating potential fraudulent activities. The second value proposition is that *continuous auditing enables the monitoring of risks for indicators of fraud, and of transactions for potential fraudulent activity.*

Continuous testing of transactions to detect potential errors and possible fraudulent activity is generally considered a management activity. However, many internal audit departments have included in their charter the detection of fraudulent activity. Automated techniques can improve the effectiveness and efficiency of a fraud detection program.

Building a business case for continuous fraud detection will depend on the level of risk that fraud represents to the organization, and the quality of existing controls to either prevent or detect significant fraud. The greater the quality of existing controls that can be leveraged, the lower the total cost of a fraud detection program will be.

Value Proposition 3:
Continuous Risk Assessment/Monitoring
The third, but possibly the most important dimension of continuous auditing, is continuous risk assessment or monitoring. The key to an effective internal audit department is to be focused on the risks that are important to the organization *now*. If risk assessment is only performed annually, or even semi-annually, audit engagements may be scoped to address risks that are no longer critical—and the more critical risks may not receive audit attention.

Internal audit departments are moving to more continuous risk assessment, often updating their audit plan on a quarterly basis. Technology can enable many risks to be monitored as frequently as the auditor desires. For example, consider the risk to a global company of sales to customers in Poland. One of the "drivers" of that risk will be the level of sales (or even the pipeline of sales orders) to customers in Poland. As that level rises, so does the risk. Technology can be used to monitor the level of sales or sales orders and send an alert to the audit department if it exceeds a predefined level.

This value proposition can be described as: *continuous auditing can be used to ensure that the internal audit plan remains focused on the more significant risks to the organization as the business changes*. It enables auditing at the speed of business.

Continuous risk monitoring is an essential element in continuous risk and control assurance. Without it, the scope continuous auditing of controls will not be updated as risks change.

SUMMARY

Three value propositions have been identified, each of which will be discussed in more detail below.

- *Continuous risk and control assurance*: Continuous auditing enables an internal auditing function to provide assurance, when it is needed, on the more significant areas of the organization's governance, risk management, and related control processes.
- *Continuous fraud detection*: Continuous auditing enables the monitoring of risks for indicators of fraud, and of transactions for potential fraudulent activity.
- *Continuous risk assessment or monitoring*: Continuous auditing can be used to ensure that the internal audit plan remains focused on the more significant risks to the organization as the business changes.

CONTINUOUS RISK ASSESSMENT OR MONITORING

Although this is the third value proposition, it is a critical element of both continuous risk and control assurance and continuous fraud detection, so it will be covered first. Why is it so critical? Because without continuously updating internal audit's understanding of risks, auditing (whether continuous or not) is likely to remain focused on what used to be important instead of what is important. The same applies to fraud detection, which should also be driven by the types of fraud and fraud schemes that represent a higher level of risk to the organization.

Ideally, internal audit will be able to leverage an effective risk management program (or ERM, for enterprise risk management) that identifies and assesses risks to the strategies and objectives of the organization. The internal auditor should evaluate whether:

- the ERM program can be relied on to identify the more significant risks to the organization;
- the identification of risks is timely, enabling the internal audit department to adjust the audit plan as needed;
- the assessment of risk levels is reliable.

When these conditions exist, the audit department should work with the risk function to ensure that it receives the information it needs, when it needs it, to maintain the risk-based audit plan.

However, many organizations do not have an ERM program that can be relied upon. Presumably , internal audit has raised this as an issue of critical importance with the board and executive management. But internal audit should not use this as an excuse not to try to maintain an audit plan focused on today's risks.

MAKING IT HAPPEN

A Continuous Risk Monitoring Program

One way to build a continuous risk assessment/monitoring program is as follows.

1 Start with the risks you want to monitor. Use the latest risk assessment as a basis.

2 Identify the causes or drivers of the risk. What would cause the risk level (probability or potential impact) to change? For example, if there is a revenue recognition risk related to sales to Thailand, the risk level is likely to rise if the level of sales to Thailand increases.

3 Determine your strategy for monitoring the risk drivers. For example, you can monitor corporate information on orders in the sales pipeline and be alerted when the level (volume or value) is outside a defined range. Why a range? Because if the pipeline is low, the risk level decreases. It is not only increases that should be monitored. The strategy should also include a decision on how often to monitor the risk. If the risk is considered critical and the level is volatile, then monitor more often than if the risk is lower and considered less likely to change.

4 Identify the mechanism(s) that will be used for risk monitoring. Will you rely on existing reports and systems, or will you need to build new capabilities?

Core Principles • Best Practice

5 Define the process for receiving the risk information and responding, generally with updates to the audit plan. How often will you update the plan? Also, a change in a risk level may indicate a need to inquire of management what the causes of the change are—to confirm the risk level and understand whether related controls and/or activity need prompt audit attention. Some changes in risk levels may indicate an increased level of fraud risk, meriting special attention by internal audit or a fraud department.
6 Step back and decide whether the design to date will be sufficient to monitor the risks. Update the plan, or accept the limitations as appropriate.
7 Build and implement the continuous risk assessment program.
8 Consider how to work with management to identify new or emerging risks, and when to add them to the program.
9 Consider metrics with which to monitor whether the continuous risk assessment program is working effectively.
10 Seek to continuously improve. Perform formal reviews on a formal basis to validate performance, including determining whether the program failed to identify risk changes of significance during the period.

CONTINUOUS RISK AND CONTROL ASSURANCE

The idea behind a continuous risk and control assurance (CRCA) program is that internal audit should provide its stakeholders with assurance that the more critical risks to the enterprise are effectively managed—when that assurance is needed.

Building a CRCA program takes time. A typical organization has multiple risks that internal audit will want to address, each of which relies on multiple controls.

Although the decision could be made to provide continuous assurance on only a very few risks and their controls, a larger program that addresses more risks and controls will generally provide a higher return on the investment.

Before considering tools, the CRCA program must be designed. Some internal audit departments are sold tools before they have designed a program, before they have decided how to use the tools—or even whether they are in fact the tools they need. As a result, most of these departments have had limited success.

Design
A CRCA program will include most if not all of the following components, as shown in Figure 1:
• continuous risk monitoring, including the monitoring of key performance indicators (KPI);
• continuous control monitoring;
• continuous transaction or activity monitoring;
• investigation of potential inappropriate activities that have been detected;
• continuous reporting to stakeholders.

Figure 1. A continuous risk and control assurance program

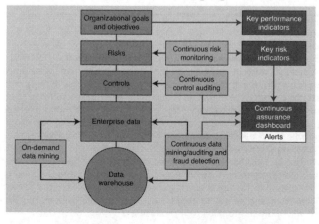

The first step, as discussed above, is to decide which business risks will be included in the CRCA program. These will be subject to continuous risk monitoring (see previous section), which has two aspects:

- Monitoring of key performance indicators. A failure to achieve strategies, goals, or performance targets is a strong indicator that risks were not managed effectively, and that there is a continuing level of risk to achieving goals and objectives.
- Monitoring of risk levels, typically achieved by monitoring the drivers of the risk as discussed earlier. Risk levels are reflected in key risk indicators, or KRI.

Risks are managed through controls. ISO Publication 73 defines a control as a "measure that is modifying risk" and IIA Standard (2010) defines control as "Any action taken by management, the board, and other parties to manage risk and increase the likelihood that established objectives and goals will be achieved."

A higher level of risk is a strong indicator that controls are either not designed or are not working effectively to manage risk within organizational tolerances. The CRCA program should include processes to respond to higher levels of risk, such as reviewing with management the root causes of the higher risk level and whether the system of internal controls remains adequate.

Once the business risks to be addressed are defined, the next step is to identify the controls that are relied on to manage those risks. These are the controls, the *key* controls, that will be tested in the CRCA program. By *key* controls, we mean those controls that have to be in place and operating properly if risks are to be managed. They are not all the controls, just those that if they failed or were not adequately designed would mean that the risks are highly unlikely to be well managed.

Key controls may operate at any level of the organization (corporate, division, location, department, process, etc.) and may be manual or automated. Typically, several controls are required to manage any single risk. If assurance is to be obtained that the risks are well managed, all the key controls have to be addressed in the CRCA program.

If the key controls have not already been identified, consideration should be given to performing an audit. In fact, every time a traditional audit is performed, a deliverable could be the identification of key controls and a strategy for testing them (as described in the rest of this section). This way, the CRCA program is

built with confidence that the key controls are properly identified, and a relationship can be developed with operating management that will serve as a foundation for the program going forward.

TESTING

After identifying the key controls, the next step is to define how they will be tested. Rather than jump straight to detailed testing techniques, it is better to define the strategy for the testing first. In a CRCA program, many controls will be tested and the overall design of testing will be more efficient—especially when considering how to leverage technology and other techniques (such as management reviews or manual testing)—when all the controls are considered together rather than one at a time. Examples of testing strategies include:

- *Rely on management's continuous monitoring program*—for payroll controls, and for the review of financial trends and significant variances from forecast. Obtain reports monthly to review the results and follow up on any issues.
- *Use software to test controls*—to confirm that all journal entries are approved by a manager, and to verify that all changes to the manufacturing computer system were approved by the IT manager.
- *Use manual testing*—to review actions taken with respect to outstanding items on the bank reconciliation, and to confirm that appropriate cutoff procedures are in place for the annual inventory count.
- *Rely on management self-assessments*—to confirm that the code of conduct has been reviewed with all personnel, and that backup generators are in place and tested periodically.
- *Rely on supervision*—by the IT director of controls over the work of the database administrators, and by the manager of the warehouse of the quality inspection of goods received.
- *Use software to test data*—to validate that all payments to suppliers were consistent with purchase orders and records of goods received, and to identify potential duplicate payments.

One important design considerations is the frequency with which assurance should be provided. Just because it is called *continuous* doesn't mean that the testing and the assurance have to be continuous. They key is that the assurance is provided when it is needed, and that the testing is sufficient to support the assurance.

The best assurance for management that risks are being managed effectively is when assurance can be provided on the condition and quality of the controls in place. Although testing transactions provides assurance that risks have been managed in the past, the level of forward-looking assurance is limited.

The value of assurance is that it provides comfort to the board and stakeholders with respect to current and future activity. While the past provides an indication of what will happen in the future, controls assurance is more powerful and valuable. Testing of controls provides direct evidence that they are performing. Testing of transactions provides, at best, limited indirect evidence.

Testing transactions, even when 100% of transactions are examined, only provides assurance relative to those transactions. It does not provide assurance that the controls are adequate and will ensure the integrity of current and future transactions. Consider a hypothetical analysis of home burglaries which shows that while there were several in neighborhood A, there were none in B. Does that prove that everybody in neighborhood B locked their doors and had effective alarm systems? Clearly not. The fact that transactions were accurate does not prove that there were adequate controls to ensure that they were accurate.

Therefore, a risk and controls assurance program aims to provide as much assurance that the controls are adequate as possible. However, there are limitations, especially to the use of technology to enable the continuous auditing of controls:

- Some controls involve the exercise of judgment, such as the review of journal entries. While technology can test that the journal entries were approved by a manager, they cannot test whether the review was perfunctory or whether appropriate judgment was exercised.
- A number of controls involve physical activities, such as the counting of inventory. Technology can test that a count was taken and adjustments approved by a manager, but it cannot test to ensure that all locations were properly examined.

In many cases these limitations can be addressed by including manual testing as part of the CRCA program. For example:

- a manual review of a sample of journal entries can be performed throughout the year;
- auditors can attend the occasional inventory counting procedure.

Where the limitations involved in testing controls cannot be overcome, the auditor may decide that the indirect assurance from testing transactions is sufficient. This may be the case when the risk if the control fails is considered to be low.

In some companies, management has implemented a continuous monitoring program. This involves direct monitoring by management that assures them that the controls are functioning as intended. When such a program is in place, internal audit should seek to place as much reliance as possible on it. Duplication of effort should be avoided. The auditor should:

- Review the scope of management's continuous monitoring program and confirm that it includes the key controls to be covered by the CRCA program.
- Verify that the monitoring by management meets quality and objectivity standards necessary for internal audit reliance. For example, does it simply rely on a manager confirming that he or she has performed the control?
- Determine whether the program produces evidence that can be used by the internal auditor. For example, the program may rely on supervision by a manager that is not documented when it is performed.

For some controls, the auditor may decide to rely on a self-assessment program. This can be valuable, especially where the risk is relatively low, or where direct testing is difficult—such as testing employee awareness of the code of ethics.

The CRCA program design must include consideration of how testing exceptions, or indications that controls may be failing, will be addressed. Most of the time the exceptions will have to be reviewed with management, so that explanations can be obtained and a determination made as to whether the controls have in fact failed—and what actions will be taken in response.

In a few cases, especially where the risk of fraud is considered high, the CRCA program might include "alerts," typically but not necessarily automated, informing internal audit of the control or data exception.

The CRCA program design should include how the results of the testing and monitoring will be summarized for use by internal audit management. What will the summary look like, how often will it be produced (or will it be continuously updated and always available), and how will exceptions be highlighted?

REPORTING

Finally, the design has to address how stakeholders will be informed of the quality of risk management and the related controls.

- How often do executive management and the board require reports?
- Do they prefer to receive reports (such as dashboards) or to be notified when there are exceptions?
- What information will be provided to operating management? How often will it be provided, and in what form?

Once the design is complete, the tests can be developed. With respect to the use of technology, the design will determine what the technology needs to achieve and will define the requirements for the selection of the appropriate set of tools. Since the program needs to address all forms of controls, it is unlikely that a single software tool will meet all needs and a combination of tools will be required. For example, one tool may be used as a repository of risk and control information to capture and report the results of testing. Another may be used for risk monitoring and data analytics. Yet another may be used to monitor IT activity when testing IT general controls.

Figure 1 summarizes all the elements of a fully-featured CRCA program.

- The first two rows address the monitoring of key performance indicators (for business objectives) and risk indicators (for risks to those business objectives).
- Controls auditing is the preferred testing approach, but where that is not possible the testing of data (either in the enterprise systems or in a data warehouse or similar) may be included. This is especially true when the risk of fraud is considered (see below).
- The results of the CRCA program have to be collected for reporting within internal audit and to stakeholders. This is shown on the right side of the diagram.

CONTINUOUS FRAUD DETECTION

Many internal audit functions have taken on the responsibility for detecting fraud. Even where strong controls are in place, it is prudent to monitor transactions and look for the signs of potential fraud.

A CRCA program will typically include fraud risks, monitoring their level, testing the controls, and examining activity for potential issues of concern.

A continuous fraud detection program will follow some of the same principles and steps as a CRCA program, even if the continuous auditing activity is limited to fraud detection rather than a full CRCA program:

- Design the program and define your needs before selecting software or developing detailed testing techniques. ·
- Focus on frauds that represent the higher level of risk to the business. According to the Association of Certified Fraud Examiners's latest global fraud study (ACFE, 2010), the average company experiences fraud amounting to 5% of annual revenue. While this is high, care should be taken not to allocate more resources to fraud detection than the risk merits or the detection costs. This can be done by focusing on those fraud risks and schemes that are more likely to be significant to the business.

MAKING IT HAPPEN

An Effective Fraud Detection Program

The following steps have proven useful in implementing effective fraud detection programs.

1 Identify the fraud risks specific to your organization. Every company is different, and the risks from fraud will vary.
2 Assess each fraud risk for likelihood and potential scale.
3 Select the fraud risks that the program will address.
4 For each risk, identify how the fraud would work: what are the fraud schemes?
5 Determine how an inspection of transactions or other activity (such as trend analysis, comparison of same product margins in different locations, or the detection of transactions approved by the same person who originated the transactions) might detect potential fraud.
6 Design the process for investigating exceptions. Take care to discuss the process with any management personnel who might be involved in reviewing and providing explanations for exceptions.
7 Develop and implement the program.
8 Monitor and adjust the testing procedures as necessary (for example, changing tolerances on any automated tests that are producing false positives).
9 Continue to monitor fraud risks and change the program as needed.
10 Review and continually improve the fraud detection program.

Core Principles • Best Practice

SUMMARY

There are several ways in which continuous auditing techniques can be used to improve the effectiveness of an internal audit program. They include:

- continuous risk and control assurance;
- continuous fraud detection;
- continuous risk assessment.

Before embarking on the continuous auditing journey, the internal audit department should decide what it wants to use continuous auditing for. Will it be for one or more, or for some variant, of the above purposes?

Some departments review the software marketed for continuous auditing or continuous control monitoring and purchase what appears to be the "best." However, they may do this before deciding on the purpose and objectives of their program, which would enable them to define their needs for technology.

Other audit functions understand continuous auditing to be purely an application of technology and do not therefore consider the use of manual testing. Typically, their program becomes one of testing transactions, primarily for potential fraud. It does not provide assurance on the quality of controls, and does not help them to realize their mission of providing assurance and consulting services relating to the effectiveness of governance, risk management, and related control processes.

Finally, some audit departments have left the field entirely. They believe that management should be performing continuous monitoring of controls and that continuous auditing is not necessary. This overlooks the potential for internal audit to review and test management's monitoring program and then rely on it (perhaps supplementing it with its own tests as necessary) to provide their stakeholders with assurance when it is needed by the board and management.

Continuous auditing has great potential. It can move an internal audit from providing assurance based on traditional point-in-time audits to providing assurance when it is needed. But to realize that potential, an internal audit department has to be disciplined.

MORE INFO

Reports:

Association of Certified Fraud Examiners (ACFE). "Report to the nations on occupational fraud and abuse: 2010 global fraud study." 2010. Online at: www.acfe.com/rttn/2010-rttn.asp

Coderre, David. "Global technology audit guide (GTAG) 3: Continuous auditing: Implications for assurance, monitoring, and risk assessment." Institute of Internal Auditors, 2005. Online at: www.theiia.org/guidance/technology/gtag3

Ernst & Young. "Escalating the role of internal audit: Ernst & Young's 2008 global internal audit survey." 2008. Online at: tinyurl.com/6frqjad [PDF].

Institute of Internal Auditors (IIA). "International standards for the professional practice of internal auditing (Standards)." Revised October 2010. Online at: www.theiia.org/guidance/standards-and-guidance/ippf/standards

KPMG. "Continuous auditing/continuous monitoring: Using technology to drive value by managing risk and improving performance." June 2009. Online at: tinyurl.com/5w3huxt [PDF].

NOTES

1 Unfortunately, there is no universally accepted definition of continuous auditing. Many (including KPMG in its 2009 publication, "Continuous auditing/continuous monitoring") have limited continuous auditing to the use of technology to collect and analyze transactions. The present essay uses the IIA definition.

2 Any activity may be tested, including not only transactions but changes to application code, router or automated control configurations, master data, etc. The term "transaction" is used generically to include any activity subject to testing.

3 In its 2008 global internal audit survey (the latest), "Escalating the role of internal audit," Ernst & Young reported that 42% of respondents to its survey had implemented some level of continuous auditing, mainly to "identify deficiencies, monitor risks and identify potential fraud activities." Reasons for not having already implemented continuous auditing included a "lack of skill sets within internal audit, budget constraints and no perceived value in the program."

4 From the definition of "assurance services" in the Glossary to IIA Standards (2010), p.18.

QFINANCE

Starting a Successful Internal Audit Function to Meet Present and Future Demands by Jeffrey Ridley

EXECUTIVE SUMMARY

* Starting an internal audit function requires a clear and inspiring vision to provide the right direction for its success.
* The services provided by the internal audit role must add value and meet the needs of all its customers, at every level in the organization. This demands a wealth of knowledge and experience of governance, risk management and control processes in the function.
* The internal audit charter approved at board level must state the professional standards expected from all staff in the function.
* Internal auditors in the function should be trained to ask the right questions and advise on the impact of present and future change at all levels in the organization, from strategic to operational.
* Quality of performance in the function and its continuous improvement requires a total commitment, measured and reported at board level through key performance indicators, and feedback from its customers.
* The function should contribute to implementation of quality policies in the organization it serves by using its own experience of achieving performance quality.

INTRODUCTION

In 1998 on the occasion of the fifty-year celebration of the establishment of the Institute of Internal Auditors (IIA)'s five chapters in the United Kingdom, I wrote:[1]

"We need to be seen as innovators in the world of regulation, control and auditing. Creativity, innovation and experimentation are now key to our professional success. They must be the vision of all internal auditing functions. This means improving old and developing new products and services for delighted customers, with a focus on their objectives. This means being at the leading edge in all the markets in which we sell our internal auditing services. This means beating our competitors and knowing who these are. This means having the imagination, and foresight into what our organizations will require from us, not just in the year 2000, but also in 2005 and beyond.

In this 50th year celebration of our national institute's past and present teamwork, all IIA-UK [and Ireland] members should continue to set their sights on being inventors of an improved and new internal auditing, to delight all their customers ... and increase its status as an international profession."

Establishing a successful internal audit function requires more than just support and resources approved at board and senior management levels; or an external requirement by government and regulators; or encouragement by external auditors. These are all important drivers and influences for creating the function and setting the boundaries in which it will operate and provide services. But the present and future demands of a successful function require a clear and inspiring vision for the direction of its services, which can only be provided by those who work in the function. It demands their knowledge and experience of risk management, control, and governance processes; their professionalism; their imagination, innovation, and creativity to manage change in what is and will be required from their services. All these attributes are needed if these service providers are to delight all their customers by the quality of their performance. They are needed whether internal auditing is resourced by staff in-house, outsourced, or co-sourced.

CLEAR AND INSPIRING VISION

A vision statement is key to the mission of any organization or function. In 1991 Richard Whitely wrote some inspirational words on vision statements:[2]

* A good vision leads to competitive advantage.
* One way to define vision is ... a vivid picture of an ambitious, desirable state that is connected to the customer and better in some important way than the current state.
* How does this vision represent the interests

of our customers and values that are important to us?

- A vision has two vital functions, and they're more important today than ever before. One is to serve as a source of inspiration. The other is to guide decision making, aligning all the organization's parts so that they work together.
- If your vision is not an impetus to excellence, then it has failed.
- When a company clearly declares what it stands for and its people share this vision, a powerful network is created—people seeking related goals.
- Constantly communicate your vision for your organization to those who work with you and for you. Don't let a day go by without talking about it.

This advice has not dated. It can be seen in many vision statements used by organizations today and will be tomorrow. An inspirational vision for internal auditing in an organization can have a significant impact on those who provide and receive the service. It should be aligned with its organization's vision, creating direction for all its resources, promotion, planning, engagements, and reporting. From the vision should flow the strategic mission of the internal audit role and its business plan, which will set the scene for the resources needed for its achievement. Following the creation of an internal auditing vision statement, all internal auditing staff and senior management should be involved in its development. Seek total organization commitment and board approval for its direction. That direction will set the scene for the services it will provide.

KNOWLEDGE AND EXPERIENCE OF GOVERNANCE, RISK MANAGEMENT AND CONTROL PROCESSES

No internal audit function can be successful unless it is expert in the principles and practices of management, governance, risk management and control in the sector in which it works and across the supply chains developed by its organization. This expertise demands not only knowledge of what these processes require but also an understanding of the principles on which they are based, experience of how they operate at all levels within an organization, and how they are reported to all stakeholders. This expertise has to be at the management level of internal auditing and with all internal auditors.

Successful organizations assess and manage their economic, environmental, and social risks, mitigating these through appropriate strategies

and controls. Successful internal audit functions focus on this corporate social responsibility and its "triple bottom line"[3] in all their engagements—across the entire range of an organization's strategies, policies, processes, and reporting. In many organizations internal auditing is seen as a facilitator in the assessment and management processes addressing these risks. To be successful today, the planning of internal audit engagements and the conducting of assurance and consulting reviews must always be linked to risks and controls in an organization's "triple bottom line."

In 1991, the US Committee of Sponsoring Organizations (COSO) published its integrated control framework exposure draft. This became its risk and control guidance for management and auditors worldwide, published in 1992.[4] Its five integrated elements of "*control environment, risk assessment, control activities, monitoring, and information and communications*" are basic requirements in all risk and control processes. It defines control as a process "designed to provide reasonable assurance regarding the achievement of [effectiveness and efficiency of operations] objectives." Importance of the COSO control elements and key concepts is significant for the mitigation of risks. These have been adopted as best practices by many regulators and organizations. Their importance is even more evident today as organizations embed risk management in their processes, from strategy setting to the achievement of objectives at every level in every operation.

In 2004[5] COSO further developed its framework into an Enterprise Risk Management (ERM) model providing further guidance for the management of risk and control across all levels of an organization. Based on its 1992 control framework, this model demonstrates the importance of embedding each of the 1992 integrated framework elements in the strategic, operations, reporting, and compliance decision-making processes across the whole enterprise. Understanding the description of each of the elements in the ERM model is a good test for management and all auditors in any organization. Such understanding is essential for internal audit success.

The IIA Inc. (2006),[6] in its overview of organizational governance, discusses the internal auditors' role, recommending that "they act as catalysts for change, advising or advocating improvements to enhance the organization's governance structure and practices." Possible steps for the internal auditor to be successful in an organization's governance processes are seen as [*my comments in brackets*]:

1 Review all the relevant internal and external audit policies, codes, and charter provisions, pertaining to organizational governance. [*Look for the key words and phrases about governance.*]

2 Discuss organizational governance with executive management or members of the board. The objective of these discussions is to ensure internal auditors have a clear understanding of the governance structure and processes from the perspective of those responsible for them, as well as the maturity of these processes. [*In these discussions relate direction and control in the organization to the achievement of its vision, mission, and key objectives.*]

3 Discuss options for expanding the role of internal auditors in organizational governance with the board chair, board committee chairs, and executive managers. These discussions could involve explaining the potential actions internal auditors could take and the resources required, as well as the possibility of an assurance gap between the board's assurance requirements and the organization's practices, if internal auditors did not assist in this area. Ensure the internal audit charter is consistent with the expanded role being considered. [*Consider providing education programs on governance for all board, management, and employee training programs.*]

4 Discuss organizational governance topics with other key stakeholders including external auditors and employees of the organization's departments such as legal, public affairs corporate secretary office, compliance, and regulatory affairs. During these discussions, explore their current and future activities as well as how an expanded internal audit role could coordinate with their activities. [*This should also be in every internal audit, not only in the organization but also across all its external relationships.*]

5 Develop a broad framework of the organization's governance structure by identifying potential areas of weakness and concern. [*A real opportunity to be creative in thinking and design.*]

6 Draft a multi-year plan to develop the internal audit role in organization governance areas methodically [*Another opportunity to be creative.*]

7 Perform a pilot audit in one of the areas noted above. Select a single, well-defined, manageable topic and assess the adequacy of the design and execution of the activities related to the topic. Performing a pilot audit will allow the internal auditor a chance to gauge the organization's response to his or her expanded role and learn how to coordinate more effectively with other stakeholders. [*This should only be the start. It should lead the internal auditor along many paths in many different dimensions.*]

Note how these recommendations link in to the guidance for success in this article.

PROFESSIONALISM

Professional attributes and performance requirements for internal auditing are clearly set out in the IIA's International Standards for Professional Practice of Internal Auditing.[7] These *Standards* and their supporting guidelines have been continuously developed internationally since the 1970s. They represent and are recognised as "best practice" internal auditing and will continue to be revised by international teams to reflect both the needs of internal auditors and the organizations in which they provide their services. All internal auditing charters should require the internal audit role to comply with these standards: not all do! Yet every board would expect its external auditors to comply with developed international standards for external auditing. Why should internal auditing be different?

The *Standards* set out requirements and guidance for internal auditing attributes and performance of work. All are based on defined principles of *Integrity*, *Objectivity*, *Confidentiality*, and *Competency* in its *International Code of Ethics*, first published in 1968 and since revised to meet current and future internal auditing needs for all its members and those who have achieved the status of its qualification *Certified Internal Auditor*.[8]

MANAGING CHANGE

All operations in an organization have a past, a present, and a future. This must be recognized in the planning of all internal auditing services and in each of its engagements. What has happened before and what is happening today will influence what will happen in the future. What happens in the future will also be influenced by more change, not only in the organization but also externally, by many of its stakeholders and events beyond its control. Every test and observation in an internal audit engagement needs to be considered in this scenario of past, present, and future change. Future change is change that can be forecast during the engagement, and change that might be hinted at by events leading to "beyond the horizon." Beyond the horizon is not always an easy prediction to make, but it should be attempted by the internal auditor studying events and issues surrounding the operations being reviewed, and in discussion with board members and management at all levels.

QUALITY OF PERFORMANCE

To be successful an internal audit function must have a total commitment to the quality of its performance and continuous improvement.

This is a requirement of the IIA *Standards*. Such commitment will be strongly influenced by its collective knowledge, experience of governance, risk management and control; its professionalism of service; and its ability to question change in the past, present, and future. This can be seen in the cutting-edge internal auditing framework in the figure, developed within the chapters of my book *Cutting Edge Internal Auditing*.[9]

Figure 1. Cutting-edge internal auditing framework

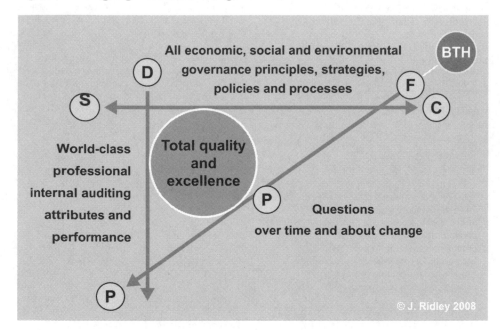

In Figure 1, each of the directional lines demonstrates an importance in the management of internal audit. Each touches and influences the quality of performance in an internal audit function:

- The horizontal line represents the level of knowledge and experience of risk management, control, and governance in the function across the organization's supply chains—supplier through operations to customers, related today to economic, social, and environmental issues and risks. The wider the line the better the service provided by the function and greater the impact on the vertical and diagonal lines and the quality of its performance.

- The vertical line represents the compliance of the function with The IIA International Standards. The deeper the line, the better the compliance and greater the impact on the horizontal and diagonal lines and the quality of its performance.
- The diagonal line represents the function's ability to question change across time past, present, and future, and into beyond the horizon. The wider the line, the greater the involvement of the function in the organization's risk management processes; and the greater the impact on the horizontal and vertical lines and the quality of its performance.

A total commitment to quality by the staff in the function can create opportunities for it to contribute to the organization's quality culture. Gupta and Ray[10] show that "internal auditors can leverage their knowledge of business processes and play an active role in the development and implementation of [the] Total Quality Improvement process." Their research describes the complete range of quality management tools and techniques used by organizations to implement and measure quality improvement programs showing how a knowledge of these and experience in their use can improve an internal audit activity's services and processes. Their research identifies seven steps (Table 4-22, p. 104) to be undertaken to implement Total Quality Improvement in internal auditing:

1 Development of Mission and Vision Statements and establishing internal audit department objectives.
2 Establishment and implementation of performance measures for various stages of the internal auditing process.
3 Identification of customers of internal auditing departments.
4 Development and implementation of internal auditing customer satisfaction surveys and feedback systems.
5 Benchmarking with other internal auditing departments.
6 Introspective self-analysis.
7 TQM training and education of the internal auditing staff.

Note how these steps have been woven into the guidance in this article for establishing a successful internal audit function to meet present and future needs for all its customers.

MAKING IT HAPPEN

Starting a successful internal auditing function requires a chief audit executive who is experienced in the implementation of professional internal auditing processes and has a full understanding of the principles and practices of management, government, risk management and control. That experience and knowledge must be used to educate the board and senior management in the role that internal auditing should assume to add best value to the organization. That role should be written into a charter, approved at board level, showing its purpose, authority, and responsibility. Once established, the internal auditing function should:

* create an inspiring vision linked to its aimed success;
* develop a plan to achieve its vision, focused on adding value;
* employ and train competent qualified professional staff;
* focus all its engagements on changes in the past, present, future and beyond the horizon;
* report its findings on a timely basis to appropriate management and the board;
* continuously measure and improve the quality of its services and delight its customers.

CASE STUDY

Scope and Types of Work in Successful Internal Audit Functions[11]

The scope of internal auditing covers all the activities of an organization, without regard for internal boundaries or geographical restrictions. It encompasses the adequacy and effectiveness of governance, risk management, and internal control processes in identifying and responding to all the risks facing the organization. The following are examples of the different types of work that internal audit may undertake:

* giving assurance to the board that the organization's risks have been properly identified and managed in accordance with the approved risk appetite;
* reviewing the activities undertaken by management to implement the ethical policy across the whole organization;
* giving assurance that business continuity and disaster recovery planning, including for mission-critical information systems, are adequate given the risks facing the organization and the risk appetite;
* giving assurance that the purchase process includes adequate controls to ensure agreed levels of competitiveness, cost savings, and quality performance;

- assisting the management team in evaluating the actual return on investments over a given period of time;
- carrying out an internal audit to verify an organization's compliance with labor laws and regulations;
- giving assurance that measures are properly designed and working effectively to address health, safety, and environmental risks on industrial sites;
- verifying that all purchase and sales contracts comply with the organization's policies;
- giving an opinion on the efficiency and effectiveness of the customer complaints process;
- providing advice to management on the design and implementation of risk management processes.

Consider
- How many of these examples of types of work exist in your internal audit function?
- Have you promoted all of these services in your internal audit charter?

MORE INFO
Websites:
Committee of Sponsoring Organizations of the Treadway Commission (COSO): www.coso.org
European Confederation of Institutes of Internal Auditing (ECIIA): www.eciia.org
Global Reporting Initiative (GRI): www.globalreporting.org
Institute of Internal Auditors (IIA): www.theiia.org
Chartered Institute of Internal Auditors (UK and Ireland): www.iia.org.uk

NOTES

1 Ridley, J. "IIA—UK celebrates 50th." *Internal Auditing* (March 1998): 12.

2 Whiteley, Richard C. *The Customer-Driven Company: Moving from Talk to Action*. London: Basic Books, 1991, pp. 21, 26–28, 32, 37.

3 *Sustainability Reporting Guidelines* 2000–2006.

4 Committee of Sponsoring Organizations. *Internal Control—Integrated Control Framework*. New York: American Institute of Certified Public Accountants, 1992.

5 Committee of Sponsoring Organizations. Enterprise Risk Management—Integrated Framework, New York: American Institute of Certified Public Accountants, 2004.

6 *Organizational Governance: Guidance for Internal Auditors*. Altamonte Springs, FL: Institute of Internal Auditors, 2006.

7 The Institute of Internal Auditors (The IIA), *International Standards for the Professional Practice of Internal Auditing*, Altamonte Springs, FL: 2009.

8 See the IIA website (www.theiia.org) for details of this and other internal auditing qualifications.

9 Ridley, Jeffrey. *Cutting Edge Internal Auditing*. Chichester, UK: Wiley, 2008.

10 Gupta, Parveen P., and Manash R. Ray. *Total Quality Improvement Process and the Internal Audit Function*. Altamonte Springs, FL: IIA Research Foundation, 1995.

11 *Internal Auditing in Europe—Position Paper*. Brussels: European Confederation of Institutes of Internal Auditors, 2005.

Implementing an Effective Internal Controls System by Andrew Chambers

EXECUTIVE SUMMARY

- Effective internal control gives reasonable assurance, though not a guarantee, that all business objectives will be achieved. It extends much beyond the aim of ensuring that financial reports are reliable. It includes the efficient achievement of operational objectives and ensuring that laws, regulations, policies, and contractual obligations are complied with.
- There is growing appreciation that effective internal control does not evolve naturally. It requires concerted effort on an ongoing basis.
- Often initially stimulated by the requirements of the Sarbanes–Oxley Act (2002), many more businesses are now systematically documenting, testing, evaluating, and improving their internal control processes. We show how to do this.
- In a large organization this more rigorous focus on internal control is likely to encourage greater standardization of similar processes in use in different parts of the organization.
- More effective internal control does not necessarily cost more. Aside from reducing costly risks of avoidable losses and business failures, it is often no more costly to organize business activities in ways that optimize control.
- Better internal controls may enable a business to engage safely in more profitable activities that would be too risky for a competitor without those controls.

INTRODUCTION

In some jurisdictions law or regulation may require effective systems of internal control, with serious penalties for irresponsible failure. The Sarbanes–Oxley Act (2002) requires CEOs and CFOs of companies with listings in the United States to certify their assessment of the effectiveness of internal control over reported disclosures (s302) and financial reporting (s404), with penalties of up to US\$1 million and ten years imprisonment for unjustified certification, or up to US\$5 million and 20 years imprisonment for wilful breach of the requirements (s906). The Public Companies Accounting Oversight Board's Auditing Standard No. 5 (2007) requires the company's external auditors themselves to assess the effectiveness of their client's system of internal control over financial reporting, in order to meet the audit requirements of s404 of the Sarbanes–Oxley Act.

Japan and Canada have laws broadly similar to the Sarbanes–Oxley Act. Although not reinforced by the risk of criminal sections, provision C.2.1 of the UK Corporate Governance Code (2010) requires that the board of a company listed on the main market of the London Stock Exchange should satisfy itself that appropriate systems are in place to identify, evaluate, and manage the significant risks faced by the company; and provision C.2.2 requires that the board should, at least annually, conduct a review of the effectiveness of the group's system of internal controls and should report to shareholders that they have done so. The review should cover all material controls, including financial, operational, and compliance controls, and risk management systems. In addition, the UK Financial Services Authority's Disclosure and Transparency Rule DTR 7.2.5 R requires companies to describe the main features of the internal control and risk management systems in relation to the financial reporting process (see Schedule C).

WHAT "EFFECTIVE" MEANS

Although similar requirements exist in many countries, the principal driver for implementing an effective internal controls system should be the enlightened self interest of the company.

Effective internal control is intended to give reasonable assurance of the achievement of corporate objectives at all levels. An internal control framework should be used for the design and evaluation of an internal control system. The COSO framework is the most widely applied of three published frameworks.[1] COSO (the Committee of Sponsoring Organizations of the Treadway Commission) defines internal control as follows:

"Internal control is broadly defined as a process, effected by the entity's board of directors, management and other personnel, designed to provide reasonable assurance regarding the achievement of objectives in the following categories:

1 Effectiveness and efficiency of operations.
2 Reliability of financial reporting.
3 Compliance with applicable laws and regulations."

Other definitions of internal control categorize the objectives of internal control differently, but fundamentally, effective internal control gives reasonable assurance that all of management's objectives will be achieved. For instance, the King Report (2002)² defined internal control as follows:

"The board should make use of generally recognized risk management and internal control models and frameworks in order to maintain a sound system of risk management and internal control to provide a reasonable assurance regarding the achievement of organizational objectives with respect to:

1 Effectiveness and efficiency of operations,
2 Safeguarding of the company's assets (including information),
3 Compliance with applicable laws, regulations and supervisory requirements,
4 Supporting business sustainability under normal as well as adverse operating conditions,
5 Reliability of reporting,
6 Behaving responsibly towards all stakeholders."

Before a conclusion can be reached that internal control is effective, both r sults and processes must be considered. For the results, the test of whether there have been any known instances attributable to significant breakdowns in internal control. Absence of these does not lead automatically to the conclusion that internal control is effective. it is possible that there may have been breakdowns of internal control yet to be discovered; it is also possible that serious weaknesses exist within the system of internal control that have not yet been exposed. So the second test must also be applied, which is to assess the quality of the control processes or "components."

KEY CHARACTERISTICS OF AN EFFECTIVE INTERNAL CONTROL SYSTEM

The COSO internal control framework categorizes into essential components of any effective internal control system.

* The control environment: Values and culture; tone at the top; policies, organizational structure
* Information and communication: Reliability, timeliness, clarity, usefulness.

* Risk assessment: Identification, measurement, and responses to threats.
* Control activities: Procedures followed for a control purpose.
* Monitoring: Review of internal control arrangements.

A common failing in designing and evaluating a system of internal control is to focus almost exclusively on control activities, vitally important though they are, overlooking that the other components are also essential. The Securities and Exchange Commission's rule for management's implementation of s404 of the Sarbanes–Oxley Act requires that a recognized internal control framework is applied. Usually it is the COSO framework that is used, and the framework comprises all of these five as being essential components of an effective system of internal control.

General hallmarks of an effective system of internal control include that controls:

* are designed to meet objectives which are clear;
* have regard to competitive issues;
* enable and ensure that performance is measured,
* aid the identification of risks;
* result in unsatisfactory performance being rectified;
* ensure that activities are completed in a timely way;
* mean the right people do the right jobs;
* are cost effective;
* are phased as early in the process as is practical, so that thereafter there is a ...
* specify and require appropriate authority requirements;
* ensure there is an adequate audit trail;
* are "prohibitive," rather than merely "permissive"
* have no more movements, or steps, than necessary;
* are flexible to allow for adaptation;
* are documented.

Control activities can be categorized ...

Preventive controls ...
bility of an undesirable outcome ...
The more important it is that ...
outcome should not arise, the ...
it becomes to have proper appro...
controls. Examples are when a ...
authority to act without the ...
limitation of authority, or ...
as only those similarly aut...
being permitted to handle ...

Corrective controls: ...
outcomes that have been ...

the design of contract terms to allow recovery of overpayment, or contingency planning for business continuity/recovery after events which the business could not avoid.

Directive controls: *To ensure that a particular outcome is achieved or an undesirable event is avoided.* Examples are a requirement that protective clothing be worn, or that staff be trained with required skills before working unsupervised.

Detective controls: *To identify undesirable outcomes "after the event."* Examples are stock or asset checks which detect unauthorized removals, or post-implementation reviews to learn lessons.

Performance controls: *To orientate and motivate the organization's people to focus on the achievement of targets that are appropriate for the achievement of objectives.* Examples are despatching all orders on the day of receipt of the order, or allowing that less than 2% of production should fail quality control checks.

Investigative controls: To try to understand how the undesirable outcome occurred so as to be able to ensure that it does not happen next time, and to provide a route of recourse to achieve some recovery against loss or damage.[4]

ASSESSING INTERNAL CONTROL EFFECTIVENESS

A widely followed approach to assessing and improving internal control effectiveness has been developed that comprises these steps (see case study 1):

1 Determine the documentation to be used, such as process maps (flowcharts), control registers, and process narratives.
2 Identify the objectives to be achieved.
3 Determine the processes that are key to the achievement of objectives.
4 Learn about each key process, documenting it in narrative, spreadsheet, and/or flowchart form.
5 Within a key process, identify and document the key controls.
6 Judge the potential of each key control to be effective, if followed as intended. Modify the control approach if necessary.
7 Design and document tests to be conducted to assess compliance with each control.
8 Conduct these tests.
9 Interpret the results of these tests. Where necessary, ensure better compliance or modify the control approach if satisfactory compliance is judged impractical.
10 Interpret the control significance of unwanted outcomes that have occurred.

11 Consider the adequacy of the control environment, information and communication, risk assessment, control activities, and monitoring.
12 Conclude on the effectiveness of internal control at the process level.

TESTING INTERNAL CONTROLS

The extent of testing is a compromise between the need for thoroughness and the testing resources available, and will vary according to the criticality of the controls that are being relied upon, the potential for the controls to be circumvented, and the results of initial testing. For controls designed to operate at intervals (such as at week, month, or year ends), initial sample sizes may be as in Table 1. For controls that apply to individual transactions Table 2 may be appropriate, which can also be used for interval controls that are used in multiple locations or on multiple occasions.

Table 1. Sample sizes to be used if the control operates at the frequencies shown

Frequency of control	Sample size
Annually	1
Quarterly	2
Monthly	2
Weekly	5
Daily	20
Many times a day	25

Table 2. Sample sizes for transaction controls

Population size	Sample size
1–3	1
4–11	2
12–50	3
51–100	5
101–200	15
201–300	20
Above 300	25 max

ONGOING MAINTENANCE OF AN INTERNAL CONTROLS SYSTEM

Changing business requirements will result in modified business processes and the risk that controls within those processes may be abandoned or made less effective. Each modified business process that is key to the achievement of a business objective should be reassessed, applying steps 3 to 6 (above), prior to releasing the new or modified business process for operational use.

For established processes, performance criteria should be established to monitor the quality of performance and the extent to which controls fail.

CASE STUDY 1

A multinational company took the requirement to comply with s404 of the Sarbanes–Oxley Act as an opportunity to assess the effectiveness of its internal control generally, not just internal controls over financial reporting.

First, the accounting processes that could lead to financial misstatements were identified. Second, mission-critical operational processes were identified where there were significant risks of not achieving business objectives and/or risks of misstatement. These accounting and operational processes were documented in process maps (flowcharts), using distinctive symbols to denote what were considered to be key s404 controls, other key financial controls , and key operational controls. These controls were described in a spreadsheet-based control register, supplemented where necessary by further process narrative. From this understanding of each process, deficiencies in control procedures were identified and corrected. Using predetermined, documented test scripts, each key control within a process was then tested for compliance prior to drawing a conclusion about internal control effectiveness of the process.

Initially this work was done by the internal audit function, before being transferred to become an ongoing responsibility of management, working to an annual cycle.

CASE STUDY 2

To be useful, process narrative on internal control must be sufficiently specific to indicate whether control is effective. In the three examples below, only the third is adequate. The reader of the first and second examples will be unclear as to whether it is merely the narrative that is inadequate, or that internal control is inadequate.

Control Documentation Poor

A report on duplicate invoices is produced before payments are made. It is looked at and approved by someone who plays no other part in the order-processing and invoicing procedures.

Control Documentation Average

Each day, before the payments processing run, the senior creditors clerk (SCC) investigates a report on possible duplicate invoices. The SCC signs and dates this report when the check has been completed, and sends the report to James Smith for second review and final approval. James signs and dates the report to indicate completion of his review and approval of the SCC's investigation.

Neither James nor the SCC has access to the purchase order or invoice-processing SAP modules or the manual parts of those subsystems.

Control Documentation Good

Daily, before the IT-based processing of payments, the SCC personally prints out a possible duplicate payments report from the payables module in SAP (SAP report code 9VDFZ3). This report may indicate five possible types of duplicate (refer to details in the process narrative).

The SCC investigates the possible duplicate invoices as indicated in the report by checking the accuracy of invoice data captured in the SAP accounts payable module against original invoices, making sure that each invoice is valid by reference to source documentation, such as purchase orders, as necessary.

The SCC has no responsibility for other elements of this system, not having any involvement in, or other access to, the processing of purchase orders or invoices—these access rights are blocked to the SCC by the accounts payable module.

When the SCC has completed the investigation, he signs and dates the possible duplicate payments report to indicate that the investigation has been completed. His manager then reviews the possible duplicate payments report, together with the relevant, supporting evidence and comments from SCC's investigation. If the manager is satisfied by the investigation and supporting evidence, he signs and dates the possible duplicate payments report to indicate approval of the SCC's investigation.

MAKING IT HAPPEN

The approach to follow:

1 Adopt and understand a recognized internal control framework.
2 Engage the board, management, and other personnel in the ownership of internal control.
3 Identify the mission-critical business processes.
4 Consider standardizing processes across the business.
5 Document those processes, highlighting the key controls.
6 Consider the effectiveness of the key controls and improve where necessary.
7 Design tests to confirm satisfactory compliance with key controls, and take remedial action as required.
8 In addition to control activities, consider whether the other essential components of an effective system of internal control are sound—for example, the control environment, information and communication, risk assessment , and monitoring.
9 Draw overall conclusions.
10 Use the results from this process as a continuous improvement tool to improve the internal control system.

MORE INFO

Books:

American Institute of Certified Public Accountants (AICPA). *Internal Control over Financial Reporting: Guidance for Smaller Public Companies.* Institute of Internal Auditors Research Foundation, 2006. Order from: www.theiia.org/bookstore

Chambers, Andrew. *Tolley's Internal Auditor's Handbook.* 2nd ed. London: LexisNexis Butterworths, 2009. See especially chapter 6.

Committee of Sponsoring Organizations of the Treadway Commission (COSO). *Internal Control— Integrated Framework.* 2 vols, 1992. Order from: www.coso.org/IC-IntegratedFramework-summary.htm

COSO. *Guidance on Monitoring Internal Control Systems.* 2009. See exposure/review link at: www.coso.org

Articles:

Sneller, Lineke, and Henk Langendijk. "Sarbanes–Oxley Section 404 costs of compliance: A case study." *Corporate Governance: An International Review* 15:2 (March 2007): 101–111. Online at: dx.doi.org/10.1111/j.1467-8683.2007.00547.x

Wagner, Stephen, and Lee Dittmar. "The unexpected benefits of Sarbanes–Oxley." *Harvard Business Review* (April 2006). Online at: tinyurl.com/4jewuc5

Reports:

Canadian Institute of Chartered Accountants. A number of publications in the series *Control Environment—Guidance on Control.* Online at: www.rmgb.ca/publications/index.aspx

COSO. "Enterprise risk management—Integrated framework." 2004. Summary and print requests online at: www.coso.org/ERM-IntegratedFramework.htm

Financial Reporting Council (FRC), UK. "The Turnbull guidance as an evaluation framework for the purposes of Section 404(a) of the Sarbanes–Oxley Act." 2004. Online at: www.frc.org.uk/documents/pagemanager/frc/draft_guide.pdf

FRC. "Internal control: Revised guidance for directors on the Combined Code." October 2005. Online at: www.ecgi.org/codes/code.php?code_id=178

HM Treasury, UK. "The orange book: Management of risk—Principles and concepts." October 2004. Online at: www.hm-treasury.gov.uk/d/3(4).pdf

Institute of Internal Auditors. "Sarbanes–Oxley Section 404: A guide for management by internal controls practitioners." 2nd ed. January 2008. Online at: www.theiia.org/download.cfm?file=31866

Public Company Accounting Oversight Board (PCAOB). "Auditing standard no. 5: An audit of internal control over financial reporting that is integrated with an audit of financial statements." July 2007. Online at: pcaobus.org/standards/auditing/pages/auditing_standard_5.aspx

Securities and Exchange Commission (SEC). "Commission guidance regarding management's report on internal control over financial reporting under section 13(a) or 15(d) of the Securities Exchange Act of 1934." June 2007. Online at: www.sec.gov/rules/interp/2007/33-8810.pdf. Subject to amendment issued August 2007: www.sec.gov/rules/final/2007/33-8809.pdf

Website:

Institute of Internal Auditors (IIA): www.theiia.org

NOTES

1 Other recognized internal control frameworks are the Canadian "CoCo" framework, and the United Kingdom's Turnbull framework.

2 King Report on Corporate Governance for South Africa (March 2002), "King II," Institute of Directors in Southern Africa. "King III Report and Code" (September 1, 2009) did not include this definition of internal control.

3 For instance, incoming cash should be controlled at the point and time of entry into the business.

4 Institute of Internal Auditors (May 2009): Practice Advisory 2010-2: *Using the Risk Management Process in Internal Audit Planning*, para 4. The meaning PA 2010-2 gives to 'investigative controls' is not identical to the meaning we have given in this chapter.

Effective Financial Reporting and Auditing: Importance and Limitations
by Andrew Higson

EXECUTIVE SUMMARY
* There is a debate about the specification of the objective of financial statements.
* Clear specification of this objective is important for the financial reporting standard-setters (so they can produce consistent and coherent standards), users (so they understand the nature and scope of financial reporting), external auditors (so they can say whether the financial statements are "fit for purpose"), and educationalists (so they can teach the next generation).
* The lack of clarity about the objective of the financial statements appears to have created a financial reporting expectations gap.
* Perceived defects in financial statements have resulted in a call for real-time financial reporting, but this may have the effect of creating more volatility in share price movements.

INTRODUCTION

The major problem with financial reporting is that people with limited financial knowledge can look at a set of accounts and, by attempting to interpret the numbers, feel that they understand what is happening in an organization. While in simpler times this may have been true, the scale and complexity of modern business, together with the limitations of what can be portrayed in financial statements, means that today's statements may have the capability to mislead as much as they can inform their users.

A large telecom business may have over two hundred million transactions a day in its accounting records, and such a scale of activity is almost beyond human comprehension. The complexity, and uncertainty, surrounding some transactions and financial instruments make their inclusion in the financial statements problematic to say the least. In the past accounting was defined as "an art of recording, classifying and summarizing in a significant manner and in terms of money, transactions and events which are, in part at least, of a financial character, and interpreting the results thereof."[1] The need for financial reporting came about with the development of permanently invested capital (today's share capital), which required a return to be made to the shareholders for their investment over a period of time (usually annually). The separation of ownership and management, especially in larger organizations, gave rise to the need for the accountability of the managers (agents) to the owners (principals), the financial statements being a convenient basis for this. In some jurisdictions financial statements also form a basis for the calculation of taxation. This subdivision of an organization's life into artificial accounting periods may not sound exciting, but it is important. It may not cover all aspects of an organization's activities, but originally this was never intended.

DECISION-USEFULNESS

Since the 1960s, the function of accounting has been increasingly regarded as "to provide quantitative information primarily financial in nature about economic entities that is intended to be useful in making economic decisions, in making resolved choices among alternative courses of action,"[2] and accounting was seen as a service activity.

On a simplistic level, the decision-usefulness approach may be intuitively appealing, but it could also be conceptually flawed and an example of circular reasoning: just because some people may take decisions based on the financial statements, does this mean that decision-usefulness should be specified as the objective of financial statements? When one takes a decision, one should be looking to the future—yet the financial statements say very little about an organization's future. One should also consider the future economic climate, an organization's competitors, and expected technological developments; financial statements say very little about these things. Often short-term investors are more concerned about taking their decision in *anticipation* (buy long, sell short) of the publication of the financial statements rather than waiting for them to come out, reading them, and then taking a decision.

An important component in the debate about the objective of financial statements has been the vagueness of the nature, scope and purpose of accounting "theory." One would have expected developments in financial reporting to have been built on theory and thus be conceptually robust. The focus on unspecified users taking unspecified decisions, at unspecified times, with unspecified results hardly seems an appropriate basis for the production of consistent and coherent financial reporting standards, and consequently there is a danger that the financial reporting standard-setters have been building on shifting sands rather than on firm foundations.

THE CALL FOR REAL-TIME REPORTING
Given the prevailing emphasis on decision-usefulness, and the perceived limitations of financial statements in this respect, some analysts and other external parties have been calling for companies to make real-time accounting data available to them. The argument is that immediate access to, and a greater quantity of, data about a company should improve users' decision-making ability and thus improve market efficiency. However, if companies were to adopt real-time reporting (this presumably would be the reporting of results on a minute-by-minute basis rather than just putting the annual accounts on the internet), would the results make sense?

There is a danger that there has been a confusion over the "recording" aspect of accounting and the "reporting" aspect of the financial statements. "Raw" accounting data are simply a means of recording in order to keep track of the transactions undertaken by an organization—which is obviously very important for management to do. The periodic financial statements use these accounting data, and related assumptions and conventions, to allocate profit to the appropriate accounting period and to present the financial figures at a point in time (this is after the necessary cut-off adjustments and checks have been made). Given the scale of modern business, one wonders what users would really make of all the data.

To allow outsiders access to real-time "raw" accounting data does raise the question as to how exactly it would lead to greater market efficiency. Indeed, instantaneous access to real-time accounting data may not necessarily result in greater market efficiency—though greater volatility in share price movements would be a distinctly possible consequence.

THE FINANCIAL REPORTING EXPECTATIONS GAP
It is likely there is a financial reporting expectations gap[3] composed of two elements, one being an expectations gap relating to the financial statements, and the other being the audit expectations gap (Figure 1). There has been much discussion of the audit expectations gap (some users of financial statements think that the external auditors are there to detect fraud, that they produce the financial statements, that they check everything recorded by the client's accounting, etc.). The audit expectations gap has been a driving force behind the expansion of the audit report and has focused the debate about the responsibilities of the external auditors. Compared to the discussion about the audit expectations gap, the possibility of a financial statements expectations gap has almost been ignored.

Figure 1. The financial reporting expectations gap. (*Source*: Higson, 2003, p. 13)

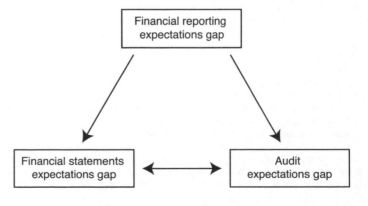

It is suggested that one element is the already discussed focus of the accountancy profession on the decision-usefulness of financial statements. Just because some people do take decisions based on them, it does not mean that they take the right decision. Another problem is the use of financial statements as an assessment of "performance"; this is because the financial statements *per se* say nothing about the economy, efficiency, and effectiveness of the organizations that produce them. There is also the tension between the long-term development of an organization and the short-term results contained in the financial statements. It is easier for users of financial statements to focus on the short-term figures contained in such statements than to try to look long-term. The broadening of the notion of performance could mean that financial statements would then be recognized for what they are—an attempt to allocate profit to the appropriate accounting period and to indicate the financial position at a point in time—and that they would then enable the debate about what constitutes corporate performance to really begin.

IMPLICATIONS FOR THE EXTERNAL AUDITORS

One might assume that the audit report would be saying that the financial statements are "fit for purpose"; however, traditionally the auditors have said nothing about the decision-usefulness of financial statements. Indeed, the Company Law Review Steering Group report[4] stated: "auditors have no liability to existing shareholders who rely on their report for investment decisions (for example to buy or sell shares), or actual creditors of the company who may make similar decisions about maintaining or withdrawing credit, or potential investors whether of equity or debt, or other potential creditors (for example trade creditors), who rely on the audit report for a view of the financial position of the company." It is therefore not surprising that in the United Kingdom, following the Bannerman case[5] in 2003, the auditors added a paragraph to their audit report which included the advice that: "Our work has been undertaken so that we might state to the company's members those matters we are required to state to them in an auditor's report and for no other purpose ... we do not accept or assume responsibility to anyone other than the company and the company's members as a body, for our audit work, for this report, or for the opinions we have formed."

The auditors say nothing about corporate economy, efficiency, and effectiveness in their audit report. The users have to try to make their own assessment of these things based on the limited amount of data in the financial statements available to them.

It can be seen that the auditors tend to think of themselves as doing what is required of them (i.e to follow the auditing standards and ensure that the financial statements have been produced by management in accordance with financial reporting standards), but I wonder how many readers of financial statements will understand this and understand what all these standards mean.

CONCLUSION

The challenges of corporate reporting in the twenty-first century can only be met once there is a real understanding about the nature, scope, and limitations of the financial statements and of the role of the external auditors.

Without a strong theoretical basis, the danger is that the financial reporting standard-setters will merely end up pandering to the perceived needs of the supposed users of financial statements.

The word "performance," in a theatrical sense, could be defined as "an act of make-believe aimed at enchanting an audience." The existence of the financial statements expectations gap may mean that this fate has already befallen the phrase "financial performance" (think about Enron's and WorldCom's financial statements); it is important that it does not befall the phrase "corporate performance."

MAKING IT HAPPEN

An Agenda for Developments in Corporate Reporting

- Give consideration to a tighter and arguably more realistic specification of the objective of the financial statements.
- Increase education about the scope and limitations of financial statements and the external audit.
- Conduct a proper debate about the nature of communicating corporate performance and the assessment of corporate economy, efficiency, and effectiveness.
- Reflect on the usefulness of real-time access to corporate accounting data.

Core Principles • Best Practice

MORE INFO
Books:
Deegan, Craig, and Jeffrey Unerman. *Financial Accounting Theory*. European ed. London: McGraw-Hill, 2006.

Elliott, Barry, and Jamie Elliott. *Financial Accounting and Reporting*. 12th ed. Harlow, UK: FT Prentice Hall, 2007.

Harrison, Walter T., Jr, and Charles T. Horngren. *Financial Accounting*. 6th ed. Upper Saddle River, NJ: Pearson, 2005.

Higson, Andrew. *Corporate Financial Reporting: Theory and Practice*. London: Sage Publications, 2003.

Riahi-Belkaoui, Ahmed. *Accounting Theory*. 5th ed. London: Thomson, 2004.

Website:
Corporate Financial Reporting, the author's website: www.accounting-research.org.uk

NOTES
1 American Institute of Accountants (AIA), Committee on Terminology (1953). *Accounting Terminology Bulletin* No. 1. New York: AIA, 1953, p. 9.

2 Accounting Principles Board (APB). *Statement No. 4: Basic Concepts and Accounting Principles Underlying Financial Statements of Business Enterprises*. New York: AICPA, 1970, para. 40.

3 Higson, 2003.

4 Company Law Review Steering Group. *Modern Company Law for a Competitive Economy: Final Report*. London: DTI, 2001, para. 8.127.

5 Auditing Practices Board Discussion Paper. *The auditor's report: A time for change?* London: Financial Reporting Council, 2007, pp. 11–12.

QFINANCE

Engaging Senior Management in Internal Control by Philip Ratcliffe

EXECUTIVE SUMMARY
- Internal control systems must have the backing of senior management to be effective.
- Internal auditors should make management aware of the importance of sound internal controls, and the serious problems that could arise if they are inadequate.
- The benefits of sound internal controls include efficiency and effectiveness, protection against losses and unpleasant surprises, optimum use of assets, and motivated staff—all in all, they make a major contribution to organizational survival and prosperity.
- Key risks resulting from lack of good internal control are fraud, incorrect accounts, inefficiency and ineffectiveness, damage to the reputation of the organization and its management, and a consequent fall in the value of the company.
- Internal auditors should form their own view of the specific risks facing their organization.
- If the internal control system is inadequate, they should meet with senior management to explain the need for strong, sound controls and their benefits for the organization.

HOW TO GET SENIOR MANAGEMENT TO TAKE INTERNAL CONTROL SERIOUSLY

Top managers in any organization have many calls on their time and attention. Vying for their attention will be customers, suppliers, employees, consultants, and many others. Internal controls can easily be squeezed out of their agenda. The problem this can create is that if senior management does not take control seriously, the "tone from the top" will be wrong—and if the people in charge don't care, then why should anyone else in the organization? Rightly or wrongly, this is the message that will be perceived across the organization, and internal control will suffer.

So, as a corporate auditor, how can you push internal control up the priority list? Showing clearly to management the benefits of strong internal control on the one hand, and the consequences of failure of internal control on the other, is one path to this goal.

Benefits of Control

A key message to communicate to management is that effective, active controls give positive benefits as well as avoiding negative outcomes. Having controls that are effective will ensure that the directions of the board and senior management are implemented as intended; that operations and activities are carried out efficiently and meet their objectives; and that the assets used in an organization are not only properly accounted for, but also that they are used effectively and efficiently for the benefit of the organization. Procedures which follow sound control principles enable people to carry out their work in an environment that is orderly and satisfying to work in. Good internal control will also protect an organization and its staff against the temptations of dishonesty, fraud, and theft.

Organizations that have sound internal controls will know where they are, and where they are going, because management information controls will tell the organization's management what they need to know when they need to know it. If the first imperative of most organizations is survival, then good internal control can play a major role in achieving that objective. Additionally, and very importantly, there can also be an efficiency dividend for an organization if good, cost-effective internal control systems are in place; for example, when processes are streamlined and well controlled, fewer people may be needed to do the work.

The Impact of Control Failure Inside the Business

All too often, internal control only becomes a concern to top management after it breaks down. Out of the blue comes the sudden discovery of a massive fraud or a major hole in the accounts, or a business segment that was thought to be profitable is dramatically discovered not to be. There is a myriad of such possibilities. Management discovers, painfully, that when there is such a breakdown of control, almost everything else has to be thrown out of the window while the breakdown is investigated. It has to engage with internal auditors, external auditors, consultants, and specialists to uncover the root causes of the problem, as there is no cure without first making a diagnosis. The managers immediately responsible for the failure must be identified, and a conclusion reached on their degree of culpability. And if someone has to be fired, who is going to take on their responsibilities?

Then, senior managers have to make up their minds what to do about the underlying problem. What changes have to be made to ensure that it can never happen again? Should they commission reviews in other similar parts of the organization to gain assurance that the problem isn't endemic elsewhere? Are major investments in systems or capital items needed to fix things? Should procedures be revised? Do staff need retraining or reorganizing? If so, who is going to implement the changes, and where is the money going to come from?

Control Breakdown Can Have External Implications

Another vital aspect is the impact of a breakdown on external relations. Do investors and the stock markets have to be informed? Is a profits warning necessary? How will stakeholders react? What will the (inevitably negative) impact be on the share price, and therefore the value, of the organization? Often such an announcement will create a loss of shareholder value that is many times the original operating loss. At times like these, an executive director may be lucky to keep his job; at the very least, there is a major risk of loss of personal and corporate reputation.

The Opportunity Cost Is Great

On top of this, in a serious case the opportunity cost of the time that management will lose in attending to the consequences of an internal control breakdown can be massive. Strategic issues, tactical issues, business development—all these and many more normal concerns of senior management will have to take a back seat until the problem is resolved. Add to this the loss of reputation and of confidence, inside and outside the organization, because news will inevitably

leak out however carefully those involved try to prevent it.

The case here has been made in the context of a commercial organization, but similar considerations apply to all other types of organization, whether governmental, private, or in the not-for-profit sector.

GETTING MANAGEMENT BACKING: WHERE TO START

If the benefits of sound controls are so tangible, and the aftermath of a failure of internal control is so dreadful, how does the corporate auditor make a start on obtaining top management's backing for a regime of sound internal control? Corporate governance regulations in many countries, and best practice, now require organizations formally to analyze and record the risks they face. The purpose of this requirement is, first, to ensure that organizations actually understand their risk profile, as only then can they seriously and properly consider whether they have the right mitigation arrangements in place. Often a management team, in making explicit the risks they face, will discover that initially they do not have a common view as to what the risks are. Only when they have a unified vision can they expect to come up with a coherent and balanced response. Only then can they hope to design and develop a comprehensive internal control system that meets the needs of the organization. The corporate auditor can assist by becoming involved in the risk identification process, by emphasizing to senior management the immediate impact of failure to mitigate the risks (for example, by pointing out that the accounts will be incorrect), and the secondary, but possibly even more drastic, consequences (for example, that a profits warning will have to be issued and the share price will nosedive.)

It is not least by confronting management with the consequences of control failure that it can be helped to take internal control seriously. The internal auditor can help to create an understanding and appreciation of

CASE STUDY

When a new chief executive officer joined his company, the chief audit executive arranged an early meeting with him. The CAE discussed the internal controls in the organization, demonstrated his knowledge of their strengths and weaknesses, and explained his view of the importance of controls and the vital role to be played by the CEO in setting an example—the tone from the top. As a result, the CEO agreed to have regular meetings to discuss internal controls and to review the assurance provided by internal audit and any resultant need for action, undertakings he subsequently fulfilled. Expectation that these meetings would take place helped to ensure that management throughout the organization gave high priority to internal control and to responding to internal audit findings.

MAKING IT HAPPEN

- Collect evidence about the state of internal controls and any opportunities that exist for improving them.
- Present the benefits of better controls in terms with which management can identify.
- Review the organization's code of conduct or similar document; if none exists, it is worth raising the issue.
- Seek a meeting with the head of the organization and influential members of the board. Have a clear but short agenda. Aim for some specific goals from your meeting. Go prepared with a succinct presentation and some practical recommendations.
- Use the opportunity to argue for the importance of tone from the top where internal control is concerned; if the top people in the company take internal control seriously, so will everybody else. Ask whether they like unwelcome surprises, and what they are prepared to do to avoid them.
- Point up the risks facing the organization, and show how a well-designed control structure can help to avoid or mitigate the worst consequences.
- Don't expect everything to be achieved with just one meeting. Be prepared to keep going back with the same messages until they are not only accepted, but also acted on.

the consequences of control failure by making presentations and having one-to-one meetings with influential people, such as the chairman/president, chief executive, chief financial officer, audit committee chair, other board members, and senior managers. The objective is to create an awareness of internal control in the organization and, through that awareness, to change the attitude to it.

While some risks may be external to the organization and not susceptible to internal control, many can be mitigated by internal controls. In some cultures, management is reluctant to accept the need for internal controls, believing that staff should be trusted. Internal auditors should point out to such management that trust is not a substitute for internal control. A proper system of internal controls should be considered a force for moral good, in that it effectively removes temptation from employees by ensuring that undesirable behaviors will be promptly detected and corrected; if employees

understand this, they will be less likely to attempt to defraud their employer.

CONCLUSION

Management's role in ensuring effective internal control is vital. Management sets the tone from the top. Unless management engages and commits, the rest of the organization will not take internal control seriously. The internal auditor can help management to appreciate the importance of internal control by demonstrating its value—not least, the efficiency dividend to an organization if good, cost-effective internal control systems are in place—and by making management aware of the consequences of failures of internal control. The internal auditor can further assist management by highlighting the need to set tone from the top, to allocate sufficient resources for internal control, and to ensure that internal control processes are suitably designed for the needs of the business.

MORE INFO

Book:

Sawyer, Lawrence B., Mortimer A. Dittenhofer, James H. Scheiner, et al. Sawyer's Internal Auditing: The Practice of Modern Internal Auditing. Altamonte Springs, FL: Institute of Internal Auditors, 2003.

Reports:

American Institute of Certified Public Accountants. "Internal control—Integrated framework." May 1994. Order online at: www.theiia.org/bookstore

Financial Reporting Council. "The combined code on corporate governance." June 2008. Online at: www.frc.org.uk/corporate/combinedcode.cfm

Role of Internal Auditing at Board Committee Level by Sridhar Ramamoorti

EXECUTIVE SUMMARY

- Boards of directors and their committees, despite receiving extremely summarized and condensed information, now have a well-established responsibility for managing the overall organizational risk.
- The effective management of risk is a prerequisite for ensuring good corporate governance.
- Because governance seems to be so intertwined with risk, one strategy might be to leverage the internal audit function to work with different board committees and provide risk-relevant information.
- The independent audit committee fulfills a vital role in corporate governance. The audit committee can be a critical component in ensuring quality reporting and controls, as well as the proper identification and management of risk.
- A summary of internal audit-audit committee interactions is provided through the perspective of *20 Questions Directors Should Ask of Internal Audit*
- The internal audit function has long been serving as the "eyes and ears" as well as the "arms and legs" of the audit committee of the board.
- Internal audit role plays a critical role in keeping the audit committee abreast of the latest developments and goings-on of the company, and without such assistance, the audit committee cannot realistically fulfill its risk oversight responsibilities.

INTRODUCTION

In the aftermath of the Wall Street financial crisis, one of the major areas that has been identified as needing improvement is corporate governance. Boards of directors and their committees, despite receiving extremely summarized and condensed information, now have a well-established responsibility for managing the overall organizational risk (Kolb and Schwartz, 2010). A critically important element that was lacking before and during the financial crisis was relevant risk intelligence—most boards were caught off-guard and were truly surprised by the turn of events. Recent guidance from the Information Systems Audit and Control Association (ISACA, 2010) highlights the importance of risk monitoring by noting that "better monitoring means fewer surprises."

The effective management of risk is a prerequisite for ensuring good corporate governance. Organizations exist to achieve their goals and objectives; however, because these goals and objectives have to be achieved in the context or environment of risk, they are not always assured (McNamee and Selim, 1998). Although the practice of risk management, on an enterprise-wide basis, is fundamentally the responsibility of executive management, the internal auditing function is typically charged with examining and reporting on risk exposures, as well as on the quality of the organization's risk management efforts. The board has oversight responsibility with respect to management and, by extension, has responsibility for both effective risk management and governance.

It is evident that organizations worldwide need to strengthen their governance mechanisms. Nevertheless, placing the governance burden in its entirety on the board of directors is an unrealistic position to advocate, given the infrequency of meetings and their limited knowledge of business operations on a day-to-day basis. Because governance seems to be so intertwined with risk, one strategy might be to leverage the internal audit function to work with different board committees and provide risk-relevant information. In this article we will focus on the internal audit function supporting the audit committee with respect to enterprise risk management.

INTERNAL AUDIT–AUDIT COMMITTEE INTERACTIONS

Treating the internal audit function as one of the cornerstones of corporate governance, Swanson (2010) says that "internal auditing can provide strategic, operational and tactical value to an organization's operations." He proceeds to emphasize that audit committee members should not only empower the internal audit function by providing it with resources and encouraging it to take on a leadership role, but that they should also actively oversee its performance. To help formulate the right perspective and ensure that these interactions are ideal, he usefully refers to a publication by the Canadian Institute of Chartered Accountants, *20 Questions Directors Should Ask of Internal Audit* (Fraser and Lindsay, 2008). It is worthwhile to excerpt these 20 questions across six categories, *viz.*

1 *Internal audit's role and mandate*
   a Should we have an internal audit function?
   b What should our internal audit function do?
   c What should be the mandate of the internal audit function?

2 *Internal audit relationships*
   a What is the relationship between internal auditing and the audit committee?
   b To whom does internal auditing report administratively?

3 *Internal audit resources*
   a How is the internal audit function staffed?
   b How does internal auditing get and maintain the expertise it needs to conduct its assignments?
   c Are the activities of internal auditing appropriately coordinated with those of the external auditors?

4 *Internal audit process*
   a How is the internal audit plan developed?
   b What does the internal audit plan not cover?
   c How are internal audit findings reported?
   d How are corporate mangers required to respond to internal audit findings and recommendations?
   e What services does internal audit provide in connection with fraud?
   f How do you assess the effectiveness of your internal audit function?

5 *Closing questions*
   a Does internal auditing have sufficient resources?
   b Does the internal audit function get appropriate support from the CEO and senior management team?
   c **Are you satisfied that this organization has adequate internal controls over its major risks?**
   d Are there any other matters that you wish to bring to the audit committee's attention?
   e Are there other ways in which internal auditing and the audit committees could support each other?

6 *Audit committee overall assessment*
   a Are we (the audit committee) satisfied with our internal audit function?

(Item 5(c) above has been bolded to indicate that in a very significant way enterprise risk management does pertain to the audit committee, and this is the focus of the next section of this article).

ENTERPRISE RISK MANAGEMENT

Risk is best considered at the portfolio, aggregate, or organization- or enterprise-wide level. Enterprise risk management (ERM) is a process-driven methodology combined with tools that enable senior management to visualize, assess, and manage significant risks that may adversely impact the attainment of key organizational objectives (see COSO, 2004). ERM risks can be categorized as follows.

- *Strategic:* affects the achievement of strategic goals and objectives.
- *Compliance:* affects compliance with federal, state, and local laws, rules and regulations.
- *Reputational:* affects public perception and reputation, including employee morale.
- *Financial:* affects assets, technology, financial reporting, and auditing.
- *Operational:* affects ongoing management processes and procedures.

As noted above, it makes sense for the internal audit function be viewed as the ideal group within an organization to work on ERM issues that are pertinent to each of the committees of the board. The International Professional Practices Framework (IPPF) issued by the Institute of Internal Auditors (IIA, 2011a) supports such an arrangement.

The IPPF Standard 2120 (see below) can be interpreted as follows.

- Implementation of this standard helps assess whether risk management processes are effective and encapsulates the internal auditor's assessment of:
  - whether organizational objectives support and align with the organization's mission; whether significant risks are identified and assessed;
  - whether appropriate risk responses are selected that align risks with the organization's risk appetite; and
  - whether relevant risk information is captured and communicated in a timely manner across the organization, enabling staff, management, and the board to carry out their responsibilities.
- The internal audit activity may gather the information to support this assessment during multiple assurance and/or consulting engagements. The results of these engagements, when viewed together, provide an understanding of the organization's risk

management processes and their effectiveness.
- Risk management processes are monitored through ongoing management activities, separate evaluations, or both (see also COSO, 2009).

All that is needed is a requirement that the internal audit function considers direct reporting to different board committees—the governance, nominating, compensation, and audit committees—in their review of risk management efforts undertaken, their effectiveness, and any significant residual exposures.

APPLICABLE PROFESSIONAL STANDARDS

2120 Risk Management
The internal audit activity must evaluate the effectiveness and contribute to the improvement of risk management processes.

2120.A1 The internal audit activity must evaluate risk exposures relating to the organization's governance, operations, and information systems regarding the:
- Reliability and integrity of financial and operational information;
- Effectiveness and efficiency of operations and programs;
- Safeguarding of assets;
- and Compliance with laws, regulations, policies, procedures, and contracts.

2120.A2 The internal audit activity must evaluate the potential for the occurrence of fraud and how the organization manages fraud risk.

2120.C1 During consulting engagements, internal auditors must address risk consistent with the engagement's objectives and be alert to the existence of other significant risks.

2120.C2 Internal auditors must incorporate knowledge of risks gained from consulting engagements into their evaluation of the organization's risk management processes.

2120.C3 When assisting management in establishing or improving risk management processes, internal auditors must refrain from assuming any management responsibility by actually managing risks.
Source: IIA, 2011b.

BOARD COMMUNICATIONS

Board Communications
Although internal audit work plans and programs may be conducted at a detailed level, most board members are unlikely to appreciate the results and findings of assurance engagements at that level of granularity. They would like for internal audit to aggregate their findings and recommendations and present

them in a "big picture" fashion. In other words, the chief audit executive (CAE) must consciously work at making board briefings relevant to their corporate governance mandate. Key audit risks may be highlighted in this connection, keeping in mind the level of communications that are appropriate when dealing with board committees (Orsini, 2004).

Some of these risks, as highlighted by Orsini (2004), are outlined below.
- *Risk of missing the big picture:* Organization-wide governance and enterprise-wide risk management necessarily involve looking at risk at an aggregate, macro-level, so that the organizational (risk) profile assessed and opined upon is comprehensive and strategic.
- *Risk of missing the dynamics of change:* The auditors use a maturity-capability model and factor in the current stage of development in the executive management agenda. For instance, it would be helpful for them to use a control baselining methodology in order to track effectively any changes in people, processes, and technology, as well as the overall risk profile (see COSO, 2009).
- *Risk of subjective second-guessing of management:* Audit assessments are based on formal analyses and typically eschew opinions, hearsay, rumor, etc., that are "notoriously unreliable." However, where there exists an "execution capability" concern based on track record, it may be appropriate to drive outcomes and accountability by making critical assessments of management integrity and leadership.
- *Risk of providing insightful but not actionable intelligence:* Audit assessments of (governance) risk exposures should not merely be insightful, but meaningful, practical, and actionable. Thus, if the organization lacks the means to respond effectively or in a timely fashion because it lacks the tools, or because the solutions are simply too costly or would take too long to implement, it is imprudent for the internal auditor to raise the issue (as an extension of the idea of second-guessing management).

ASSISTING THE AUDIT COMMITTEE: A BROAD MANDATE AND MYRIAD OPPORTUNITIES FOR INTERNAL AUDIT

The report of the National Association of Corporate Directors' Blue Ribbon Commission on Audit Committees (NACD, 2000) provided the following rationale for why corporations need audit committees:

"The independent audit committee fulfills a vital role in corporate governance. The audit committee can be a critical component in ensuring quality reporting and controls, as well as the proper identification and management of risk."

Internal auditing can not only play a critical role in helping establish and define appropriate risk oversight expectations, but also identify the source(s) of information and associated monitoring processes to meet these expectations. Clearly, the audit committee of the board must be the conduit for such information.

Bromark and Hoffman (1992) note that the role of the audit committee is expanding because of the need to meet the challenges of constantly changing business conditions. They highlight the following primary responsibilities of the audit committee:

- assisting the board to fulfill its oversight responsibilities as they relate to the financial reporting process and the internal structure;
- maintaining, by way of regularly scheduled meetings, direct lines of communication between the board, financial management, the independent accountant, and internal audit.

Additional responsibilities quoted in Braiotta *et al.* (2010) include the following:

- reviewing corporate policies related to compliance with laws and regulations, ethics, conflict of interests, and the investigation of misconduct and fraud;
- conducting periodic reviews of current pending litigation of regulatory proceedings bearing on corporate governance in which the corporation is a party;
- coordinating annual reviews of compliance with corporate governance policies through internal audit or the company's independent accountants;

- performing or supervising special investigations;
- reviewing executive expenses;
- reviewing policies on sensitive payments;
- reviewing past or proposed transactions between the corporation and members of management; · reviewing the corporation's benefits programs;
- assessing the performance of financial management.

The internal audit function has long been serving as the "eyes and ears" as well as the "arms and legs" of the audit committee of the board. In the context of the above detailed list of responsibilities of the audit committee, it is evident that the internal audit role plays a critical role in keeping the audit committee abreast of the latest developments and goings on of the company.

CONCLUSION

Audit committees have typically been viewed as the group within the board structure with responsibility for risk oversight. As such, they end up relying to a large extent on the internal audit function to assure them about management's effectiveness in assessing, measuring, and responding to the array of risks that affect the organization. Although internal audit must undertake certain types of assurance engagements in this connection, establish safeguards to preserve independence and objectivity in other circumstances, and eschew taking on those activities that would compromise its independence and objectivity, it is clear that it does have a substantive role to play with respect to ERM. Without such involvement, it would simply not be possible for the audit committee to discharge its own ERM oversight function effectively.

MORE INFO

Books:

Braiotta, Louis, Jr, R. Trent Gazzaway, Robert Colson, and Sridhar Ramamoorti. *The Audit Committee Handbook*. 5th ed. Hoboken, NJ: Wiley, 2010.

Information Systems Audit and Control Association (ISACA). *Monitoring Internal Control Systems and IT: A Primer for Business Executives, Managers and Auditors on How to Embrace and Advance Best Practices*. Rolling Meadows, IL: ISACA, 2010.

Institute of Internal Auditors (IIA). *International Professional Practices Framework*. Altamonte Springs, FL: IIA Research Foundation, 2011a.

Kolb, Robert W., and Donald Schwartz (eds). *Corporate Boards: Managers of Risk, Sources of Risk*. Chichester, UK: Wiley, 2010.

McNamee, David, and Georges M. Selim. *Risk Management: Changing the Internal Auditor's Paradigm*. Altamonte Springs, FL: Institute of Internal Auditors Research Foundation, 1998.

National Association of Corporate Directors (NACD). *Report of the NACD Blue Ribbon Commission on Audit Committees*. Washington, DC: NACD, 2000.

Swanson, Dan. *Swanson on Internal Auditing: Raising the Bar*. Ely, UK: IT Governance Publishing, 2010.

Articles:

Bromark, Ray, and Ralph Hoffman. "An audit committee for dynamic times." *Directors and Boards* 16:3 (Spring 1992). Online at: tinyurl.com/65txg4o

Orsini, Basil. "Auditing governance: The Canadian government offers an audit tool for addressing the risks in implementing management reform." *Internal Auditor* (June 2004). Online at: tinyurl.com/6xaagbv

Reports:

Committee of Sponsoring Organizations of the Treadway Commission (COSO). "Enterprise risk management—Integrated framework." September 2004.

Committee of Sponsoring Organizations of the Treadway Commission (COSO). "Guidance on monitoring internal control systems." February 2009.

Fraser, John, and Hugh Lindsay. "20 questions directors should ask about internal audit." 2nd ed. Canadian Institute of Chartered Accountants, 2008. Online at: www.theiia.org/download.cfm?file=2927 [PDF].

Standards:

IIA. "International standards for the professional practice of internal auditing (Standards)." Rev. ed. Altamonte Springs, FL: IIA, 2011b. Online at: www.theiia.org/guidance/standards-and-guidance/ippf/standards

Internal Auditors and Enterprise Risk Management by Ian Fraser

EXECUTIVE SUMMARY
* Organizations should implement effective risk management as a component of good corporate governance.
* Internal audit has a natural affinity with risk due to its centrality to audit and auditor expertise in monitoring and systems review.
* The key issue for determination is the parameters of the internal audit responsibility in the risk management area. Is internal audit best focused on a monitoring and review role, or might this extend to risk identification and the establishment of risk management systems?
* There is no one "best-fit" solution, and much will depend on organizational size, safeguards to protect objectivity, and the range and scope of available internal auditor expertise.

INTRODUCTION

Traditionally, internal auditors have been "policemen," and their efforts have been concentrated on the more detailed, and arguably less appealing, aspects of financial auditing within organizations. Often, therefore, internal auditors have been regarded in the past as the poor relations of their external auditor cousins. This no longer applies, however, as the purpose of many internal audit functions has evolved over time.

From a concern with (arguably) low-level financial audit, internal auditors have progressed to systems audit and an involvement with economy, efficiency, and effectiveness (the 3Es), to their contemporary focus on enterprise risk management. I generalize here, of course; not every internal audit function in every organization has been involved with each of these areas. In the public sector, for example, there has tended to be more involvement with the 3Es. This chapter is concerned with the internal audit role in connection with how enterprises manage risk.

INVOLVEMENT OF INTERNAL AUDIT WITH RISK

To an extent, the traditional role of internal auditors in connection with financial auditing gave them an initial knowledge base with which to get involved with risk management. Financial auditing has a concern with the risk of financial misstatement, whereas (although this burden falls primarily on the external auditors) audit risk is primarily concerned with the risk of issuing a wrong opinion on the financial statements. The recent external audit phenomenon of business risk auditing has pinpointed that effective financial audit (whatever the ostensible audit methodology employed) has to engage with business risks. The rationale for the latter assertion is, of course, that entity business risks, of whatever nature, ultimately affect the risk of misstatement in the financial statements. There is, therefore, a clear link between business risk and audit risk.

Thus, in one sense, it is natural for auditors (whether internal or external) to be concerned with the management of risks within organizations. External auditors tend to be involved with organizations on an occasional, rather than an ongoing, basis, and so it is difficult for them to have anything other than a relatively superficial appreciation of the business risks. Indeed, this is a valid criticism that has been made of "business risk auditing" as an external audit methodology. Arguably, therefore, there is a ready-made role for internal auditors in connection with risk.

Undoubtedly, however, the UK Turnbull Report (henceforth "Turnbull") on corporate governance was an important catalyst in the process of involving internal auditors with risk management. The Turnbull emphasis on the adoption by corporations of risk-based approaches to the establishment of internal control systems, and on the subsequent monitoring of these systems' effectiveness, created a role for high-level monitoring agencies within organizations. Internal audit functions were the clear beneficiaries of this, and Turnbull provided an opportunity for internal auditors to align their work to real business issues and to make an impact at board level. There was a clear opportunity for internal auditors to enhance their (in many cases) erstwhile humble status and to expand their jurisdiction as a professional interest group.

THE INTERNAL AUDIT RISK ROLE— WHAT SHOULD IT BE?

While it is now probably fairly uncontroversial to argue that internal auditors certainly have a role to play in relation to risk management, the parameters of the role are far less easily defined. Are internal auditors executive managers specializing in risk management, or, alternatively, are they concerned primarily with the monitoring of organizational risk management systems? There has certainly been a tendency, post-Turnbull, for internal audit functions to gravitate toward the former role. The intention of Turnbull, however, was primarily that the internal audit role should largely be focused on the *evaluation* of risk management and the monitoring of internal control effectiveness. While the post-Turnbull era has seen some companies assign ownership of risk management to internal audit, there is recognition of the pitfalls involved in this. With most internal auditors still receiving what is primarily a financial training, there may be a danger of nonfinancial risks receiving inadequate consideration.

There is also a real danger of internal audit departments losing their independent status within organizations if they evolve into risk management functions. There is evidence that when risk management initially became a priority for organizations, many internal audit heads were assigned responsibility for risk management audit. This, however, has not always been the case as distinct functions for internal audit and risk management have been established in some organizations.

In brief, the internal audit role might be summarized as: "The provision of objective assurance to corporate boards and senior management on risk management effectiveness; specifically, to ensure that key risks are managed appropriately and that internal control systems are operating effectively."

This is a general definition, though, and might be interpreted in various ways as far as the fine detail of responsibilities is concerned.

PROFESSIONAL GUIDANCE AND POTENTIAL DIFFICULTIES

The available professional guidance goes into more detail by emphasizing the distinction between the risk *management* and *monitoring* roles. The Institute of Internal Auditors (IIA), for example, suggests (in its position statement *The Role of Internal Audit in Enterprise-Risk Management*, available on the IIA website) that internal auditors should be responsible for:

- "Providing assurance on the design and effectiveness of risk management processes, providing assurance that risks are correctly evaluated, evaluating risk management processes, evaluating the reporting on the status of key risks and controls, and reviewing the management of key risks, including the effectiveness of the controls and other responses to them."

But not for:

- "Setting the risk appetite, (the willingness of an organization to accept a defined level of risk), imposing risk management processes, providing assurance to the board and management, making decisions on risk responses, implementing risk responses on management's behalf, accountability for risk management."

The IIA suggests that internal functions may be responsible for the following functions as long as safeguards are put in place to protect internal independence:

- "Championing the establishment of Enterprise Risk Management (ERM) within organizations, developing a risk management strategy for board approval, facilitating the identification and evaluation of risks, coaching management on responding to risks, coordinating ERM activities, consolidating the reporting on risks, maintaining and developing ERM frameworks."

It's when we come to this last category, however, that delineation of responsibilities may be unclear. This may be especially the case with the distinction between monitoring and advice by internal auditors on the one hand, and the exercise of a management role on the other. There has arguably been a tendency for some internal auditors to assume more executive-type roles in the ERM area as a way of enhancing their professional jurisdiction. The Institute of Chartered Accountants in England and Wales (ICAEW) takes a broadly similar line to the IIA by emphasizing the internal audit role in assessing the various processes by which risks are *identified,managed, controlled*, and *reported*.

Overall there is certainly not one "easy-fit" solution. Various legitimate approaches to delineating responsibilities might be taken. For example, internal audit would normally be responsible for such functions as the evaluation and monitoring of risk management processes and controls. It would not normally be regarded as appropriate for internal audit to assume ownership of organizational risks or to set the risk appetite.

CASE STUDY

Tonko—Shaping the Internal Audit Role through Experience

- Tonko is a large conglomerate group, with around 50,000 employees. It operates in several international geographies over several industrial sectors. Tonko is based in the United Kingdom and has had a strong internal audit function operating from the home country for around 25 years.
- The corporate governance and risk agendas of the 1990s saw the profile of risk management being enhanced significantly within the group, with responsibility for the area being given initially to the group's internal audit function. This appeared to be the natural home for risk management because of the prominence given to internal audit by Turnbull and by other authoritative corporate governance pronouncements. This worked well.
- Internal audit established business risk management systems and reporting mechanisms that flowed up from business units to divisions and ultimately fed into the group risk strategy. Internal audit carried out the usual monitoring role on these, making sure, first, that risks (and changes in these) were being reported on, and, second, that action was taken as appropriate.
- Internal audit also ran risk workshops at various levels to facilitate the identification of risks. Line management subsequently took action to control and mitigate the risks identified.
- Internal audit was involved in a two-way facilitation process. It was first ensured that business unit and divisional risk concepts and appetites were aligned with those of the group. At the same time internal audit made sure that lower-level concerns fed into the overall group risk evaluations and group risk register where appropriate.
- While this system worked quite well and could have continued indefinitely, some confusion was expressed about the internal audit role. It was unclear whether the internal auditors were acting as facilitators/risk identifiers or as monitors/assessors. There was also some loss of focus on basic controls in the work of internal audit.
- As a result a separate group of risk specialists was established with the remit of working with group business units and divisions in identifying risks and prioritizing them. Internal audit retained responsibility for the review and monitoring of risk management systems and for making sure that there was alignment of concepts and priorities at all group levels.
- It is not suggested that the Tonko experience is a template that should be followed by all organizations. Smaller entities, in particular, sometimes find that the combined approach works best. The size, and available skill set, of the internal audit function will be important determinants of the process.

CONCLUSION

Effective risk management is a necessity for all organizations and is an important component of good corporate governance. Internal audit needs to be involved in the process—at a minimum it has an important role to play in the monitoring of risk management systems. In many cases there may be sound arguments for extending this to functions such as developing reporting frameworks for risk management and facilitating the identification of risks. The size of the organization, independence safeguards, and the range of internal audit expertise are all important issues requiring consideration when determining the boundaries of external audit responsibilities.

MAKING IT HAPPEN

- Whatever the responsibilities of the internal audit (or, if it exists, risk management) function, the board has to get involved by setting the "risk appetite" of the organization and by assigning broad functional responsibilities.
- It is important that in a large or diversified organization individual divisions and business units feel involved in the process.
- It will generally be appropriate for internal audit, at a minimum, to be responsible for evaluating and monitoring risk management processes and for providing assurance on the adequacy of risk evaluation and reporting.

- *If* the independence and objectivity of internal audit are protected, and *if* the internal audit function has access to the appropriate range of expertise, *then:*
- The internal audit role might be extended to the facilitation of risk identification and the development of risk reporting frameworks.

MORE INFO

Books:

Fraser, Ian A. M., and William M. Henry. *The Future of Corporate Governance: Insights from the UK*. Edinburgh, UK: Institute of Chartered Accountants of Scotland, 2003.

Pickett, K. H. Spencer. *Auditing the Risk Management Process*. Hoboken, NJ: Wiley, 2005.

Pickett, K. H. Spencer. *Audit Planning: A Risk-Based Approach*. Hoboken, NJ: Wiley, 2006.

Report:

CIMA/IFAC. "Enterprise governance: Getting the balance right." February 2004. Online at: tinyurl.com/48z6fyx [PDF].

Websites:

Committee of Sponsoring Organizations of the Treadway Commission—provides guidance on organizational governance, business ethics, internal control, enterprise risk management, fraud, and financial reporting: www.coso.org

Personal website by David M. Griffiths introducing risk-based internal auditing: www.internalaudit.biz

Institute of Internal Auditors (IIA), for internal auditing standards and other professional pronouncements: www.theiia.org

The Effect of SOX on Internal Control, Risk Management, and Corporate Governance Best Practice by David A. Doney

EXECUTIVE SUMMARY
- The effect of the Sarbanes–Oxley Act of 2002 (SOX) has been dramatic and global. SOX enhanced the regulatory framework for investor protection and confidence.
- SOX has required or encouraged a variety of best practices related to management accountability, auditor independence, audit committees, internal control reporting, risk management, and improvement of financial processes.
- One of the important contributions of the regulatory guidance is the "top-down risk-based assessment," a robust framework for identifying and assessing financial reporting risks.
- Compliance approaches, benefits, and costs continue to evolve as practice and regulatory guidance change.

INTRODUCTION

The Sarbanes–Oxley Act of 2002 was passed in the context of a series of high-profile corporate scandals, a brief recession, and the events of 9/11. These factors were cited by President George W. Bush as a threat to investor confidence and the US economy overall. He also declared: "This law says to every dishonest corporate leader: you will be exposed and punished; the era of low standards and false profits is over; no boardroom in America is above or beyond the law."[1]

US Senator Paul Sarbanes stated that during the development of the law, a series of Senate hearings with experts from business, government, and academia resulted in a "remarkable consensus on the nature of the problems."[2] These included inadequate oversight of the accounting profession, conflicts of interest involving auditors and stock analysts, weak corporate governance procedures, inadequate disclosure rules, and insufficient funding for the Securities and Exchange Commission (SEC).

The SOX law, corresponding guidance from regulators, and evolving approaches to implementation have resulted in a variety of internal control, risk management, and corporate governance best practices.

HOLD MANAGEMENT ACCOUNTABLE

The law requires that the CEO and CFO sign certifications quarterly and annually attesting that they have reviewed the financial statements and (to their knowledge) believe them to be fair, accurate, and complete. Penalties for fraudulent certification are severe. This requirement has encouraged such best practices as:

- Disclosure committees: A cross-functional group of top-level managers that meets to discuss pending public disclosures, including quarterly and annual financial reporting.
- Representation letters: To support the certification by the CEO and CFO and ensure that material information is made known to them, a variety of senior finance and operations managers sign representation letters regarding financial reporting matters relevant to their areas of responsibility.
- Improvement of finance organization: Many companies expanded the number and quality of financial personnel, particularly with respect to US Generally Accepted Accounting Principles and SEC reporting requirements.

MAINTAIN AUDITOR INDEPENDENCE

Auditors are the primary watchdogs of the corporation. Prior to SOX, auditors performed significant consulting work for publicly traded companies ("issuers") that they audited. Further, auditors often moved into senior financial management positions in the client company. These factors created at least a perceived conflict of interest.

SOX prohibits auditors from providing many types of consulting services to issuers they audit. The law also prohibits auditors from auditing an issuer if the issuer's CEO or top financial management worked for the audit firm during the past year.

EMPOWER THE REGULATORS

Prior to SOX, the audit industry was self-regulated. SOX also established the Public

Company Accounting Oversight Board (PCAOB), a nonprofit, nongovernmental entity, to oversee the audit firms. The PCAOB sets standards and publicly discloses the results of its auditor reviews and any disciplinary action taken.

Critics also argued that the SEC, the regulator tasked with investor protection and corporate disclosure standards, was significantly underfunded and understaffed. The SEC budget was nearly doubled in the wake of SOX and remains at that level today.

ENGAGE AUDIT COMMITTEES

Prior to SOX, former SEC Chairman Arthur Levitt stated that "qualified, committed, independent and tough-minded audit committees represent the most reliable guardians of the public interest."[3] The many scandals that resulted in SOX indicated that audit committees were not performing their financial oversight responsibilities effectively.

SOX mandated that the audit committee, rather than management, be accountable for the relationship with the auditor, including selection, compensation, retention, and review of independence. Issuers are now required to disclose whether or not the audit committee has a financial expert, which has encouraged additional financial expertise on audit committees. Auditors are now required to provide more robust disclosures to the audit committee regarding alternative accounting policies and their discussions with management. Audit committees must also ensure the availability of an anonymous reporting channel for accounting or auditing matters (i.e. a "whistleblower hotline"). The law also expanded protection for whistleblowers and penalties for retaliation against them.

EVALUATE KEY FINANCIAL CONTROLS

The infamous SOX "Section 404" guidance requires both management and the external auditor to provide a report that includes an opinion regarding internal control over financial reporting (ICFR). This is additional to the traditional auditor's opinion on the accuracy of financial statements. It requires management to document and comprehensively test financial controls necessary to address "material misstatement risks."

Any controls that are assessed as not effectively designed (i.e. not capable of addressing the related risk, even if executed) or not operating effectively (i.e. not executed consistently) result in "deficiencies." More serious deficiencies are categorized as "significant deficiencies" or

"material weaknesses" and must be reported to the external auditor and audit committee. Material weaknesses require public disclosure during the quarter in which they are identified and, if not remediated as of year-end, an unfavorable opinion on ICFR in the issuer's annual report.

The requirement to perform a comprehensive control assessment has resulted in several improvements in the art and science of financial management. For example, controls related to the "tone at the top," incentives, and conflicts of interest were often not formally assessed prior to SOX. Focus on effective controls has significantly improved. Further, the quality of the SOX assessment (for example, project management, technology use, risk assessment, and quality of presentation materials) is a good proxy for "tone at the top" in the organization and the process management skills of the finance team.

In the aftermath of SOX the focus of internal auditing efforts also shifted significantly to financial controls, as opposed to operational processes. Many issuers expanded the staffing and capabilities of their internal auditing teams to absorb incremental SOX responsibilities. The New York Stock Exchange (NYSE) listing standards now require that all listed companies have an internal audit function. Tracking deficiencies to resolution also establishes good discipline for internal audit follow-up of all issue types, as required by internal auditing standards.

IMPROVE RISK MANAGEMENT

Pressure is increasing on businesses to improve risk management practices. This comes from a variety of sources, including regulators, credit rating agencies, and activist shareholders. Further, the subprime mortgage crisis which became apparent in 2007 has (arguably) exposed systemic risk management concerns.

The 2007 guidance from the SEC and PCAOB regarding SOX Section 404 established a comprehensive framework for conducting a "top-down" financial reporting risk assessment. For example, management is required to identify material misstatement risks and related controls, which then must be tested. (See the Case Study for details.)

Techniques used in top-down risk assessment are applicable to other risk categories. Under the COSO Enterprise Risk Management (ERM) framework, risks fall into strategic, operational, legal/regulatory, and financial reporting categories. SOX compliance implies substantial coverage of financial reporting risks. The SOX

Best Practice • Core Principles

compliance process also provides a framework that relates processes, risks, and controls, and the network of managers involved, which can be used to help establish an ERM program.

Many companies also use SOX-compliance database software, which may also be useful for retaining risk information to support an ERM program and as an internal audit workflow tool. For example, as internal audits are completed, the amount of risk and control information expands in such a database, across all risk types.

In response to increased expectations around risk, many audit committees have expanded their scope to include overall risk management. With SOX efforts addressing financial reporting risks, they can focus more attention on strategic and operational risks. Some issuers have also created board risk committees to address non-financial reporting matters.

IMPROVE FINANCIAL PROCESSES

The significant cost of the ICFR assessment required under SOX Section 404 represents a "tax" on inefficiency, providing additional incentives for process improvement. Redundant systems, processes, or locations generally require some type of incremental assessment, increasing the scope and cost of compliance. The Financial Executives International (FEI) survey of SOX 404 compliance costs in 2007[4] indicated that, for companies with average revenue of US$4.7 billion, the costs in *decentralized* companies averaged US$1.9 million, 46% higher than the

US$1.3 million in *centralized* companies. The difference is likely to be a fraction of the savings available from addressing the underlying process inefficiency.

In addition, manual control procedures involve substantially higher testing costs. For example, a manual control that operates daily may require a sample size of 30 to be evaluated by an expert. However, the same control if automated requires a sample size of just one and does not have to be evaluated each year if certain criteria are met. Leading companies track the number of manual versus automated controls and seek automation opportunities. Reducing the number of manual journal entries is another means of improving the reliability of financial statements and reducing closing-cycle time, while reducing both compliance and personnel costs.

Section 404 is one of the more contentious elements of SOX, due to the significant cost of compliance. According to a survey by FEI that included issuers with an average revenue of US$4.7 billion, compliance costs were US$1.7 million during 2007, or 0.36% of revenue. The total cost includes internal and external labor and auditor attestation fees.[5]

Compliance costs have continued to decline since 2004, when Section 404 became applicable for most issuers. The 2007 SEC and PCAOB guidance has provided management with additional flexibility in addressing risk and determining the timing, nature, and extent of testing procedures, further reducing costs.

CASE STUDY
SIRVA, Inc.—Implementing a Top-Down Risk Assessment

SIRVA, Inc., is a decentralized global moving and relocation services company with revenues of US$4 billion in 2007. Under new internal audit leadership in 2007, the company implemented a top-down risk assessment, new SOX compliance software, and brought the effort substantially in-house. This resulted in *annual* savings of over US$3 million and brought costs into line with benchmark companies.

First, management completed a risk-ranking of each balance sheet account (and certain sub-accounts) to assess the risk of material misstatement. The ranking was also used to identify key process/location combinations ("processes"). For example, revenue and receivables might be significant (i.e. in-scope) for one location but not another.

Second, processes were risk-ranked. Higher-risk processes or topics included entity-level controls, period-end reporting, revenue, and key accounting estimates and judgments. Other transactional processes such as accounts payable, payroll, tax, and treasury were lower risk and received less assessment effort. Nearly 200 material misstatement risks (MMR) were documented by systematically considering key accounting policies and financial statement assertions for each process or account. Risks represented "what could go wrong" in relation to the account or assertion.

Third, the number of key controls tested was reduced from the prior year by 50% (from nearly 1,000 to 500) by including only those entity-level and transaction-level controls needed to address the MMR. In other words, specific risks determined which controls mattered, as opposed to merely large dollar balances, locations, or systems. Management assigned each control a risk-ranking of

QFINANCE

Core Principles • Best Practice

high, medium, or low. This ranking was based on a combination of account-specific and control-specific factors in the SOX guidance. Sample sizes used in testing were based on the ranking and the frequency of control operation.

Fourth, SOX compliance software was implemented to document the risks, controls, and tests. Comprehensive status and quality reporting was developed and discussed in weekly meetings with the global audit team and management.

Finally, multiple domestic general ledger systems were consolidated into one system. Further, two major operating platforms were consolidated into one, removing an entire financial process.

CONCLUSION

SOX has resulted in dramatic changes in internal control, risk management, and corporate governance. Management and audit committees are more focused on financial reporting. The internal control and risk management best practices discussed above continue to evolve in practice. Companies continue to focus and reduce costs in their SOX 404 efforts through top-down risk assessment and compliance software, which have broader applications to other risk management efforts.

MAKING IT HAPPEN

SOX regulations and implementation have provided a series of best practices to help companies improve risk, control, and governance, even if technically they are not required to comply.

* Identify and remove conflicts of interest that affect your business. These can involve auditors, management, the board, vendors, outside consultants, etc.
* Ensure that your external auditors and internal auditors are independent by having their continuing employment, performance rating, and compensation determined by the audit committee or board.
* Help to ensure that financial disclosures are transparent and fairly describe the organization's performance by using a disclosure committee and management representation letters.
* Insist on a robust top-down risk assessment of financial reporting processes. The extent of testing to perform (the primary cost-driver) can then be determined appropriately.
* Capture risk and control information in compliance database software. User-friendly software that can be customized and administered by non-IT personnel is available at very reasonable prices.
* Establish risk committees at the senior management and board level. These committees can direct risk management efforts and help the audit committee to focus on financial reporting matters.
* Develop reporting of operating metrics that are predictive of financial results and share it with the audit committee and board.
* Communicate periodically to the audit committee any significant deficiencies identified (financial or otherwise) and management's progress towards remediating them.
* Use the financial reporting effort and framework to initiate or improve an ERM program.

MORE INFO

Book:

Farrell, Greg. *America Robbed Blind. How Corporate Crooks Fleeced American Shareholders (and How Congress Failed to Stop Them)*. Buda, TX: Wizard Academy Press, 2005.

Websites:

Committee of Sponsoring Organizations of the Treadway Commission (COSO): www.coso.org. For *Enterprise Risk Management—Integrated Framework (2004)*: www.coso.org/-erm.htm

Institute of International Auditors (IIA): www.theiia.org. For *The International Standards for the Professional Practice of Internal Auditing*: www.theiia.org/guidance/standards-and-guidance

Public Company Accounting Oversight Board (PCAOB): www.pcaob.org

QFINANCE

PCAOB Auditing Standard No. 5, "An audit of internal control over financial reporting that is integrated with an audit of financial statements and related independence rule and conforming amendments" (2007): pcaobus.org/standards/auditing/pages/auditing_standard_5.aspx

Sarbanes–Oxley. The text of the Act can be found at: fl1.findlaw.com/news.findlaw.com/hdocs/docs/gwbush/sarbanesoxley072302.pdf

Securities and Exchange Commission (SEC; US): www.sec.gov

"Commission guidance regarding management's report on internal control over financial reporting under Section 13(a) or 15(d) of the Securities Exchange Act of 1934." Interpretive guidance release 33-8810, etc. (2007): www.sec.gov/rules/interp/2007/33-8810.pdf

Best Practice • Core Principles

NOTES

1 Office of the Press Secretary, The White House. "President Bush signs corporate corruption bill" (Sarbanes–Oxley Act 2002): www.whitehouse.gov/news/releases/2002/07/20020730.html

2 Lucas, Nance. "An interview with United States Senator Paul S. Sarbanes." *Journal of Leadership & Organizational Studies* 11:1 (January 2004): 3–8.

3 Levitt, Arthur. "The numbers game." Speech dated September 28, 1998. Online at: www.sec.gov/news/speech/speecharchive/1998/spch220.txt

4 Financial Executives International (FEI). News release "FEI survey: Average 2007 SOX compliance cost $1.7 million." Online at: fei.mediaroom.com/index.php?s=43&item=204

5 *Ibid.* A complete cross-referenced index of SEC filers, audit firms, offices, CPAs, services, fees, compliance/enforcement actions, and other critical disclosure information can be found at: www.sarbanes-oxley.com

QFINANCE

The Internal Audit Role—Is There an Expectation Gap in Your Organization?
by Jeffrey Ridley

EXECUTIVE SUMMARY

- Every internal audit role should be established with a charter approved and reviewed annually at board level.
- The internal audit charter should describe the internal audit role in the organization it serves, including its purpose, authority, responsibility, and relationships with external organizations.
- The internal audit charter should be promoted across the organization at all levels and as appropriate across its supply chains and to its stakeholders.
- Internal audit should have measures in place to demonstrate its level of performance to the organization.
- Expectation gaps at organization and individual customer levels should be identified, and all performance measures continuously monitored if the full added value of the internal audit role is to be achieved.
- New dimensions of the internal audit role in an organization should be continuously explored to ensure that it is at the cutting edge of its professional attributes and in its performance.

INTRODUCTION

Establishing the internal audit role in any organization requires formality to ensure that it is understood not only by the board and management but also by its customers across the organization and, where necessary, those external to the organization. The internal audit assurance and consulting role should be explained clearly in a charter to minimize any expectation gaps at board and organization levels. When the role is being established, it is important that internal audit management should have an input into the formal process through discussion with the board and senior management.

The Institute of Internal Auditors (IIA), as the global professional body representing internal auditing in every country, has always recommended and now requires in its *Standards*[1] the purpose, authority and responsibility of an internal audit activity to be formally approved and kept under review at the highest level in an organization." In some sectors this may also be a requirement of one or more of an organization's stakeholders, such as government or a sector's regulator.

PURPOSE, AUTHORITY, AND RESPONSIBILITY OF THE INTERNAL AUDIT ROLE
Purpose
The purpose of professional internal audit is described in the IIA's 2009 definition as:

"Internal auditing is an **independent objective assurance and consulting activity** designed **to add value and improve** an organization's operations. It helps an organization accomplish its objectives by bringing **a systematic, disciplined approach to evaluate and improve** the effectiveness of **risk management, control, and governance processes**."

Key to this definition of internal auditing are the words in bold:
- Independence of the internal audit and its objectivity are critical for all dimensions of the role practiced by the internal auditor.
- The value it adds to improve an organization's operations should be measured and reported continuously.
- All its services require systematic and disciplined processes.
- It requires a wide and deep knowledge and understanding of risk management, control and governance within the organizations it serves, across their supply chains, and with all their stakeholders.

Writers on internal auditing have been promoting its independent assurance and consulting roles since the first statement of responsibilities of the internal auditor was published by the IIA in 1947. Consultancy and training were never mentioned as such in the IIA's statements but were implied by its scope of responsibilities. The best evidence for this is in the "objective and scope of internal auditing" in its 1957 statement:

"The overall objective of internal auditing is to assist all members of management in the effective discharge of their responsibilities, by furnishing them with objective analyses, appraisals, recommendations and pertinent comments concerning the activities reviewed. The internal auditor therefore should be concerned with any phase of business activity wherein he can be of service to management. The attainment of this over-all objective of service to management should involve such activities as:

- Reviewing and appraising the soundness, adequacy and application of accounting, financial and operating controls.
- Ascertaining the extent of compliance with established policies, plans and procedures.
- Ascertaining the extent to which company assets are accounted for, and safeguarded from losses of all kinds.
- Ascertaining the reliability of accounting and other data developed within the organization.
- Appraising the quality of performance in carrying out assigned responsibilities."

The 1971 revision to this statement changed the fourth activity from "accounting and other data" to "management data," and added a sixth activity— "Recommending operating improvements." This widened the scope of internal audit into all operations. In 1981, the statement was further changed to state that internal auditing is a service to the "organization," not just to "management." This brought the board and all operating levels in the organization into the internal auditing market place.

Lawrence Sawyer[2] supported the role of internal auditors as consultants (and trainers) in his 1979 writings. He draws vivid pictures of "problem-solving internal auditors" providing reviews, appraisals, communications and advice on management: "the [internal] auditor has a duty to know the functions of management as thoroughly as the manager does." He discusses various consulting opportunities for internal auditors in the services they can provide, and he also gives recognition to internal auditors as teachers: "the internal auditor's role as a teacher is little known, insufficiently practiced, and generally not believed or accepted."

As the IIA scope statement was being revised, practicing internal auditors were broadening their services by increasing the number of dimensions in the role they provided in their organizations. Dr James Wilson and Dr Donna Wood[3] researched the behavioral dynamics of internal auditing, recognizing seven dimensions and conflicts in the internal auditor's role at that time (1985):

1 Accountant
2 Policeman
3 Watchdog
4 Teacher
5 Consultant
6 Communicator
7 Future Manager

These dimensions and conflicts still exist in internal auditing. They should all be addressed at board level and, as appropriate, be clearly seen in its charter. They are currently seen in the IIA's definition of internal auditing and in its *Standards*.[4] The two roles in the definition— assurance and consultancy—are defined thus:

- **Assurance services** are an objective examination of evidence for the purpose of providing an independent assessment on governance, risk management, and control processes for the organization.
- **Consulting services** are advisory and related client services, the nature and scope of which are agreed with the client, are intended to add value and improve an organization's governance, risk management and control processes without the internal auditor assuming management responsibility.

The other dimensions can all be seen in these roles in practice and in the *Standards* and supporting guidelines.

Authority
The authority of internal audit should always lie at board level, evidenced by its reporting lines to the board and senior management and reviews of its performance at these levels. That authority may include reporting lines to the chair of an audit committee and presence at its meetings. It should also include open access to all an organization's employees, operations, systems, records, and property.

Responsibility
The responsibility of internal audit should clearly state the scope of its work in the organization and its reporting requirements to the board, senior management, and customers. In some organizations this may also include reference to the internal audit role in the organization's training programs, code of conduct, procedure for dealing with whistleblowing, and fraud prevention, detection, and investigation processes.

PROMOTING THE INTERNAL AUDIT ROLE
The internal audit charter approved by the board is only the beginning of the promotion of the

internal audit role throughout an organization. It has to be visible to all its customers in the services it provides and in its planning and engagement processes. Internal auditing has developed many ways to do this through the publishing of internal brochures, intranet websites, and even organization websites. Examples of each can be found in many internal auditing text books.

Cindy Cosmas (1996)[5] studied how internal auditing in North America marketed itself within the organizations to which it provided services. She concluded that it required some initial planning and formality, but that it brought significant benefits:

"A marketing program, or plan, is essential for every internal auditing department. A well-devised plan will direct internal auditors in their quest to provide valuable services to their organization."

Cosmas goes on to say that such a plan should consist of specific objectives, a well-developed customer base, effective promotional tools, a plan of action, and a way to monitor success: in other words, a business strategy. It is not about internal auditing living on an island in an organization, separated from its customers! She discusses internal auditing marketing its creativity in her chapter on internal audit participation in management teams: "Utilizing creative instincts is one of the internal auditor's most powerful marketing tools." She recognized at the time the growing participation by internal auditors in team projects across organizations, working closely with operating staff and management. Seeing internal auditing creativity as an important part of the marketing, she writes:

"As a marketing tool, audit participation on project teams has been beneficial overall in winning management's praise and support. Internal auditing brings a unique perspective to project teams through their background and training."

MEASURING THE INTERNAL AUDIT EXPECTATION GAP

Cindy Cosmas also saw the marketing of internal auditing services as one of its key indicators for success and an important performance measure for assessing its continuous improvement: "The primary purpose of a performance measurement system is to support continuous improvement," and "To improve a process we must know how our customer intends to use the process outcome." Knowing what the internal auditing customer wants is fundamental to a good marketing plan. Knowing whether the customer understands the internal audit services approved by its charter is also very important.

A current performance measurement tool with many internal audit activities is the use of a questionnaire during its engagements to seek feedback from its customers on the service it provides. Such a questionnaire is an effective way to seek views on how the customer understands the internal audit's role in the organization and whether it is perceived to be as written in its charter. Another practice is to use discussion and training groups within the organization to spread the purpose, authority, and responsibility of the internal audit role.

One example of an expectation gap in the internal auditing role is in the prevention, detection, and investigation of fraud. This is too often not always clear and can cause different perceptions across an organization at all levels. Chambers (2005)[6] recognizes this:

"There is undoubtedly an expectation gap for internal auditors in the area of fraud…Other parties expect…internal auditors to be effective at detecting significant fraud…[and] preventing significant fraud…Much effort is needed by the chief audit executive to explain internal audit's interface with fraud."

Today's New Image for Internal Auditing
In my book *Cutting Edge Internal Auditing* I cite an article published in 2005[7] in which I wrote:

"By the late 90s some different aspects of the internal auditor's role were identified in new IIA research—assurers of control, risk facilitators, in-house consultants, business analyst, fraud detectors, innovators, quality advocates, advisers on governance. Later research in the UK[8] in 2002 supported these aspects; showing internal audit in the UK is currently adding value in the following six elements of the governance process, ranked in order of perception by those it serves:

- Assurance that the internal control framework is operating effectively.
- Assurance that major business risks are being managed appropriately.
- Detection and prevention of fraud and irregularities.
- Improving business performance by sharing knowledge of best practices.
- Identification of new business risks.
- Use of knowledge and experience to tackle urgent issues.

The first three are the traditional approaches to internal audit work. Most board members and management recognise these. The last three require a participative teamwork approach and for some internal audit functions are still relatively new services: in some internal audit

Best Practice • Core Principles

activities they have been provided for many years. Today's professional internal auditors should be well trained and competent to add all of these values in their organizations. A measure of their professionalism is whether they can and do. Board and audit committee members should expect and ensure that all are well provided."

Since 2005 these new services have changed the internal audit role in many organizations and continue to do so, encouraged at board level and by management. They have also been pioneered by many internal auditors as they develop their professional attributes and practices to increase their value.

Consider
1 Are these nine points all reflected in your internal audit role and charter?
2 Are there any expectation gaps in your organization concerning these nine points?

CASE STUDY
Nine Important Points to Avoid Internal Audit Expectation Gaps[9]

More and more organizations are beginning to benefit from professional internal audit practice. This can be seen from the growing number of internal auditors in Europe that can be found in all sectors, public and private. This growth has been accelerated by legislation and regulation that requires organizations to demonstrate the effectiveness of their governance, risk management, and internal control processes because it is clear that an internal audit activity is uniquely positioned to support management. In the detailed paper,[9] we set out what we consider to be best practice in internal auditing and how organizations should use internal auditing to help achieve good governance and risk management practice. The most important points are:

1 Professional internal auditors will apply and uphold the IIA's Code of Ethics in all circumstances.
2 The audit committee will ensure that the mandate and responsibility of the internal audit activity is formalized in a charter that it approves.
3 The audit committee will ensure that the internal audit activity has a direct reporting line to the chief executive of the organization and an open and direct communication line to the board and itself, in order that it maintains its independence.
4 The chief audit executive will support the board and executive management in fulfilling its responsibilities for the systems of governance, risk management, and internal control.
5 The audit committee will ensure that the internal audit activity is adequately resourced and competently staffed by investing in their qualification and their continuing professional development. The promotion of qualifications, endorsed by the profession of internal auditing, will be central in this approach.
6 The chief audit executive will develop and maintain a quality assurance programme that covers all aspects of the internal audit activity, monitoring its effectiveness by using both internal assessments and assessments by appropriate external review bodies.
7 The chief audit executive will plan the internal audit work on the basis of the risks facing the organization, will make relevant and timely reports to other participants in the governance process, and will follow-up internal audit recommendations to enable the drive for continuous improvement in the organization to be successful.
8 The internal audit activity will promote internal controls that effectively mitigate risks in all activities of the organization.
9 The audit committee and the chief audit executive will work to improve the cooperation between all those active in the field of governance, in particular, optimizing cooperation with statutory auditors to ensure the comprehensive audit of all activity.

Best Practice • Core Principles

MAKING IT HAPPEN

The internal audit role has a variety of independent professional dimensions, created and approved at board level to meet management governance, risk management, and control needs at all levels in an organization, and across its supply chains. To minimize any expectation gaps in the services it provides it is important that:

- the purpose, authority, and responsibility of the role are clearly established in a charter;
- that charter is promoted at all levels across the organizations it serves;
- customer perceptions and expectations of the internal audit role are measured continuously;
- expectation gaps are identified and monitored;
- dimensions of the internal audit role are, and remain, at its professional cutting edge.

MORE INFO

Websites:

Chartered Institute of Internal Auditors (UK and Ireland): www.iia.org.uk
European Confederation of Institutes of Internal Auditing (ECIIA): www.eciia.org
Institute of Internal Auditors (IIA): www.theiia.org

NOTES

1 Institute of Internal Auditors (IIA). *International Standards for the Professional Practice of Internal Auditing*. Altamonte Springs, FL: IIA, 2009.

2 Sawyer, Lawrence B. *The Manager and the Modern Internal Auditor*. New York: Amacom, 1979.

3 Wilson, James A., and Donna J. Wood. *Managing the Behavioral Dynamics of Internal Auditing*. Altamonte Springs, FL: IIA, 1985.

4 Anderson, Urton, and Andrew J. Dahle. *Implementing the Professional Practices Framework*. 2nd ed. Altamonte Springs, FL: IIA, 2006.

5 Cosmas, Cindy E. *Audit Customer Satisfaction: Marketing Added Value*. Altamonte Springs, FL: IIA, 1996.

6 Chambers, Andrew. *Tolley's Internal Auditor's Handbook*. 2nd ed. Edinburgh, UK: LexisNexis Butterworths, 2009.

7 "Is internal auditing's new image recognized by your organization?" In Ridley, Jeffrey. *Cutting Edge Internal Auditing*. Chichester, UK: Wiley, 2008; ch. 4.

8 *The Value Agenda*. London: Deloitte & Touche and IIA, 2002.

9 *Internal Auditing in Europe—Position Paper*. Brussels: European Confederation of Institutes of Internal Auditors, 2005.

QFINANCE

Managing the Relationships between Audit Committees and the CAE
by Richard E. Cascarino

Best Practice • Core Principles

EXECUTIVE SUMMARY
- Audit committees are a fundamental part of the proper governance of any organization, together with executive management and internal as well as external audit.
- An audit committee can only be as effective as is permitted by the information it receives.
- The relationship between the committee and the chief audit executive (CAE) is critical to the successful functioning of the audit committee.
- The relationship will be effective in an environment of mutual trust and common understanding.
- Of all the committees involved in the management and control of an organization, perhaps the audit committee has the most significant impact on the life of the CAE.
- Although, in general, all audit committees fulfill a similar function within the organization, the nature of the organization itself can prescribe a particular emphasis in the working of the audit committee. This, in turn, affects the nature of the relationship between the CAE and the committee as a whole.

THE ROLE OF THE AUDIT COMMITTEE

The audit committee is intended, overall, to assist an organization to achieve an effective internal control structure derived directly from the tone at the top. The authority of an audit committee is drawn from the board of directors, the rules and regulations of the organization, and any relevant governance legislation of the country or countries within which the organization operates.

This role, of necessity, involves ensuring that the risk management process remains both comprehensive and ongoing instead of the annual process that is implemented in many organizations. Corporate policies regarding legal compliance, compliance with corporate codes of conduct, and conflicts of interest must be maintained and policed. In addition, the audit committee has a duty to review both current and pending legislation as it relates to corporate governance within the country or countries wherein it operates. Communication is the key to good governance and includes ensuring that the financial statements presented to the shareholders are both understandable and reliable, and facilitating internal communication with senior management and internal audit. Communication with internal audit should go beyond the scheduled committee meetings, and the CAE should be encouraged to communicate with the chair of the audit committee directly. The audit committee, as a whole, should meet privately with the CAE at least annually to seek assurances about the independence of the internal audit function.

To ensure effective use of internal auditing, the audit committee would normally review internal audit plans as well as reports and significant findings. It would seek to ensure that internal auditing is carried out by professionals with a comprehensive understanding of the business systems and processes as well as of the corporate culture within the organization.

The audit committee relies on the internal audit function to provide objective opinions, information, and, when necessary, education to the audit committee, while the audit committee in turn will provide oversight and validation to the internal audit function. In today's environment this could include the outsourcing or co-sourcing of all or part of the internal audit function; however, the audit committee should ensure that the role of the CAE remains within the organization itself.

INTERNAL AUDIT REPORTING STRUCTURE

In order to ensure transparency and to prevent undue influence internally, the Institute of Internal Auditors (IIA) recommends that the CAE maintain a dual reporting relationship. Typically, this would involve the CAE reporting to executive management at as high a level as possible for administrative purposes to ensure alignment with corporate direction, support at a managerial level, and the normal administrative support required for a staff function. The second relationship, with the audit committee, is for operational and

QFINANCE

functional purposes, to ensure that independence and objectivity is maintained. The audit function's independence and reporting structure are normally laid out in the internal audit charter, which specifies the dual reporting structure as well as the internal auditors' right of access to personnel and records without hindrance or impediment, a critical part of their independence. The charter would normally be signed by both the chief executive and the chair of the audit committee.

The audit committee should provide oversight, strategic direction, accountability, and enforcement where required. Part of such oversight includes ensuring that the internal audit function is properly positioned, resourced, and supported. This involves reviewing and approving:

- the internal audit activity's charter, and mission statement where appropriate, to ensure they meet the needs of the organization;
- the annual work plan to ensure that all significant risk areas are being addressed and that no restrictions are placed on the scope of internal audit activities;
- the resources, skill levels, and budget to ensure that the work plan is achievable within the appropriate time;
- internal audit activities, performance, and recommendations.

At the same time, the audit committee is responsible for providing input into the appointment, dismissal, evaluation, compensation, and succession planning of the CAE. This is a critical activity of the audit committee since the CAE will, of neccessity, have a high degree of interaction with the audit committee. The committee will typically seek to ensure that candidates for a CAE position have distinguished themselves professionally. They would normally have an advanced degree, the appropriate professional designation, and several years experience in an audit supervisory role. Typical professional designations could include the Certified Internal Auditor (CIA), Certified Government Auditing Professional (CGAP), Certified Financial Services Auditor (CFSA), or Certified Information Systems Auditor (CISA) among others.

The committee is also responsible for ensuring that a continuous quality assurance and improvement program exists within internal audit and that full disclosure of the results be made to the audit committee.

THE RELATIONSHIP WITH INTERNAL AUDIT

The audit committee chair can foster a healthy relationship with the internal auditors, and particularly the chief internal auditor, by keeping communication channels open, getting to know the CAE as a person, frequently touching base between meetings, and taking an interest in and caring about the internal audit function. It is also a good idea for the audit committee chair to meet with the entire senior internal audit staff from time to time to get to know some of the individuals who report to the CAE, and to thank them for their efforts.

It is critical that the internal audit function be positioned well within the organization so that the internal auditors are not limited in what they can review, and that they, and the recommendations they propose, are respected by line management. It should always be remembered that the accountability for, and ownership of, good internal controls are the responsibility of management—not of the internal auditors and not of the audit committee. The internal auditors, nonetheless, must recognize that theirs is a unique yet critical role.

The CAE needs to be up to date on best practices and trends in governance, as well as on "emerging issues," and the audit committee will seek reassurance in this area. The audit committee also needs assurance that the internal auditors understand the corporate strategy and have the professional judgment to identify all forms of risk at an early enough opportunity to allow management to take appropriate action. In order for the audit committee to be appropriately assured in these areas, performance assessment of both the CAE and internal audit will be required.

MUTUAL TRUST

Most critical to the relationship between the audit committee and the internal audit activity is trust. The audit committee chair needs to be sure that the CAE understands and shares the committee's concerns and priorities. In addition, the CAE must be willing to communicate results and opinions without fear or favor and regardless of who is involved. Due to its unique position and the sensitivity of information passing through its hands, the audit committee needs assurance that the internal audit activity maintains the highest level of integrity and values.

The committee needs to be able to trust that, when confronted with management resistance or a failure of management integrity, the CAE will make the right decision and take appropriate action. By the same token, the CAE must be able to rely on the support and backing of the chair of the audit committee, and the committee as a whole. This ensures that the "internal audit activity [is] free from interference in determining the scope of internal auditing, performing work, and communicating results" (IIA Standards).

Two Cases in Point

In one government department, accusations of corruption were made against the chief executive. The CAE who reported to the chief executive took the accusations directly to the audit committee chair. Although the responsible Minister was notified, it was the audit committee, acting independently, that commissioned an external forensic investigation into the allegations. The external route was chosen so that, regardless of the outcome, the CAE would be able to continue to function effectively within the department. In the event, the allegations proved unjustified, but it was the trust between the CAE and the audit committee chair which made it possible for such allegations to be brought forward without fear of reprisal. In a contrasting case involving a pension fund, allegations of abuse of power by the chief executive were brought to the attention of the CAE. These were taken to the chair of the audit committee, who immediately called the chief executive to discuss them privately. There was no follow-up. The trust between the audit committee and the CAE was destroyed, ultimately resulting in the resignation of the CAE.

ASSESSING PERFORMANCE AND PLANNING AHEAD

The *International Standards for the Professional Practice of Internal Auditing*[1] promulgated by the Institute of Internal Auditors requires that an external assessment, performed by appropriately qualified reviewers and carried out to professional standards, be conducted every five years. This is designed to give the audit committee assurance that the work of the internal audit function is being conducted to internationally accepted standards.

In addition, the CAE is required to ensure quality on an ongoing basis. The CAE may utilize benchmarking to develop an internal auditor balanced scorecard for the audit committee to use for assessing the performance of the internal audit function. An objective evaluation would, nevertheless, include such areas as audit scope and coverage (including financial,

compliance, operational, IT, and fraud auditing), audit capabilities, independence, objectivity, supervision, and internal audit assignment quality control. In addition to ensuring the quality of the work of the internal audit function, the audit committee chair will also seek assurance on the performance of the audit committee itself. The CAE can assist in benchmarking the committee's performance in terms of committee structure and composition, the role of audit committee members, and leadership of the committee against standards such as The Board Institute's Audit Committee Index[2] on behalf of the chair of the audit committee. The European Corporate Governance Institute (ECGI) has produced an excellent paper on such benchmarking.[3] This presents an opportunity for the audit committee to review and discuss all areas of its performance, as well as to bring to the table items that committee members feel should be covered in the future, and training opportunities that would enhance performance.

It is critical that proactive succession planning for the internal audit function and the CAE be an important area of focus and support by the audit committee. Many organizations use internal audit as a training ground for future executive managers and rotate candidates through the internal auditing function. While this is beneficial to the organization in terms of managers who understand internal control, it can be devastating to the effectiveness of the internal audit function if carried out to excess. One internal audit function lost seven out of eight senior auditors in a six-month period as they were head-hunted by operational areas of the organization. Succession planning is intended to ensure that, while some of the current team may get appropriate and substantive positions in the organization as rotations end, the effectiveness of the internal audit function is not impacted. Professional, career-oriented internal auditors form the backbone of the function and they must see career opportunities with internal audit itself. In addition, succession planning is critical to the organization's ability to attract the right talent into the internal audit activity.

CONCLUSION

The mere existence of the audit committee does not necessarily translate into an effective monitoring body over corporate governance. By the same token, the existence of an internal audit function, in-sourced or out-sourced, does not guarantee the effectiveness of the system of internal controls. It is the combination of the

Best Practice • Core Principles

QFINANCE

Core Principles • Best Practice

two, both acting in a professional manner for the benefit of the organization as a whole, which contributes significantly to the achievement of sound corporate governance.

Audit Committee Characteristics
- independence
- financial knowledge and experience
- frequency of meetings
- involvement in CAE appointment and dismissal

- reviewing internal audit program and processes
- ensuring internal audit quality

Internal Audit Function Characteristics
- independence and objectivity
- availability of adequate resources
- internal audit staff expertise
- use of external subject matter experts where appropriate

MAKING IT HAPPEN
In Order to Manage the Relationship the CAE Must:
- Keep the audit committee informed on risks faced by the organization. Monitor the risk environment for new/changed risks which need to be brought to the audit committee's attention.
- Check that the audit committee's charter, activities, and processes are appropriate. Periodically review the audit committee's practices against international standards and "best practices" on behalf of the chair of the audit committee.
- Educate the audit committee on the internal audit team's charter, role, and activities. The CAE should seek to obtain management and audit committee buy-in on internal auditing's goals, objectives, risk assessments, and audit plan by demonstrating their appropriateness and relevance.
- Ensure that the internal audit function is responsive to the needs of the audit committee and the board. Meet frequently with the audit committee chair to ensure that the committee's needs are fully understood and met.
- Ensure open and effective communication with the audit committee and its chair. Effective communication is one of the best tools for understanding organizational priorities and reinforcing the benefits and value of internal auditing.
- Provide training, when appropriate, to audit committee members on the topics of risk and internal control. Not all committee members will initially be up to speed on the changing needs and legislation.
- Confirm the quality of the services provided. Internal auditing should provide quality performance indicators to show that it complies with the IIA's *International Standards for the Professional Practice of Internal Auditing* and the IIA's *Code of Ethics* and that it adds value on an ongoing basis.
- Provide feedback on the internal audit function's achievement of its operational plans and objectives.

MORE INFO
Books:

Braiotta, Louis, Jr, R. Trent Gazzaway, Robert Colson, and Sridhar Ramamoorti. *The Audit Committee Handbook*. 5th ed. Hoboken, NJ: Wiley, 2010.
Burke, Frank M., and Dan M. Guy. *Audit Committees: A Guide for Directors, Management, and Consultants*. 3rd ed. New York: Aspen Publishers, 2004.
Cascarino, Richard E., and Sandy van Esch. *Internal Auditing: An Integrated Approach*. 2nd ed. Lansdowne, South Africa: Juta Academic Publishers, 2006.
Moeller, Robert. *Brink's Modern Internal Auditing*. 7th ed. Hoboken, NJ: Wiley, 2009.
Ruppel, Warren. *Not-for-Profit Audit Committee Best Practices*. Hoboken, NJ: Wiley, 2005.

QFINANCE

Articles:

Collier, Paul Arnold. "Audit committees in major UK companies." *Managerial Auditing Journal* 8:3 (1993): 25–30.

Goodwin, Jenny. "The relationship between the audit committee and the internal audit function: Evidence from Australia and New Zealand." *International Journal of Auditing* 7:3 (November 2003): 263–278. Online at: dx.doi.org/10.1046/j.1099-1123.2003.00074.x

Reports:

Australian National Audit Office. "Public sector audit committees." February 2005. Online at: tinyurl.com/6fo5xwz

Blue Ribbon Committee on Improving the Effectiveness of Corporate Audit Committees. "Report and recommendations of the blue ribbon committee on improving the effectiveness of corporate audit committees." New York Stock Exchange and National Association of Securities Dealers, 1999.

European Corporate Governance Institute (ECGI). "Institutional position paper: a benchmark for audit committees." November 2002. Online at: www.ecgi.org/codes/documents/auditcom_final_paper.pdf

Institute of Internal Auditors. "Chief audit executive (CAE) reporting lines." Practice Advisory 1110-2. December 2002.

Institute of Internal Auditors. "Relationship with the audit committee." Practice Advisory 2060-2. December 2002.

Institute of Internal Auditors. "A global summary of the Common Body of Knowledge 2006." Online at: www.theiia.org/research/common-body-of-knowledge/

Websites:

Audit Committee Effectiveness Center: www.aicpa.org/forthepublic/auditcommitteeeffectiveness/pages/acec.aspx

Securities and Exchange Commission: www.sec.gov

Best Practice • Core Principles

NOTES

1 Available from the Institute of Internal Auditors: www.theiia.org

2 See www.theboardinstitute.com/web/products.asp?f=prod_acix

3 Online at: www.ecgi.org/codes/documents/auditcom_final_paper.pdf

Optimizing Internal Audit
by Andrew Chambers

EXECUTIVE SUMMARY

To optimize an internal audit function it is necessary to:

- conform with the International Professional Practices Framework of the global Institute of Internal Auditors;
- define the role, responsibilities, and authority of the internal audit function within a formal charter approved by the board;
- report to the board;
- embrace both assurance and consulting roles within the internal audit mission;
- function independently;
- ensure that no business areas are "off-limits" to internal audit;
- plan future audit engagements based on the chief audit executive's risk assessment;
- be committed to continuous improvement of the internal audit function.

INTRODUCTION

Internal auditing is defined by The Institute of Internal Auditors (IIA) as follows:

"Internal auditing is an independent, objective assurance and consulting activity designed to add value and improve an organization's operations. It helps an organization accomplish its objectives by bringing a systematic, disciplined approach to evaluate and improve the effectiveness of risk management, control, and governance processes."[1]

It is widely accepted that whether or not the staff of an internal audit function are affiliated to The IIA, if the internal auditing corresponds to the above definition, best-value internal auditing will only result when generally accepted internal auditing standards are applied. Internal auditing should be a valued part of the total assurance process. To be so it requires independence from the activities it audits and it needs to report independently to all those who rely on the assurance that internal audit provides.

Today, internal audit is a service for management and also for those, such as boards and audit committees, charged with governance. Particular internal audit functions may also have certain obligations to report to outside parties, such as regulators. It is important that the roles, responsibilities, and authority of internal audit are clearly set out and supported within the organization.

ESSENTIAL PREREQUISITES FOR INTERNAL AUDITING

Clear ground rules must be kept to if internal audit is to add best value to both its assurance and consulting roles. In any entity, these should be set out in the internal audit charter, which must be approved by the board or by the board's audit committee on behalf of the board. The most senior level that relies on the assurance given by internal audit needs to be confident that internal audit is not subordinating its judgment on professional matters to that of anyone else. Usually, at its most senior level internal audit reports to the audit committee of the board. Compromised professional judgment may occur with respect to:

- determining the planned programme of audits;
- accessing information and personnel necessary to properly conduct an audit;
- deciding the content of internal audit reports.

While it may appear that the chief audit executive is reporting directly to the audit committee, as indeed should be so, that reporting is of little value if it is in effect censored by senior management before it reaches the audit committee.

Internal audit is both an audit *for* management and also an audit *of* management *for* the board through the board's audit committee. If internal audit is compromised professionally, then it is essential that those who rely on the assurance that internal audit gives are fully cognizant of this. An audit committee needs to have time alone with the chief audit executive, with other executives not being in attendance; this can take place in a 15-minute session at the start of each audit committee meeting. Audit committees should also be involved in advance in decisions relating to the appointment, reappointment, dismissal, and remuneration of heads of internal audit.

Organizationally it is preferable that the internal audit function does not belong to the finance/accounting function of the organization as this makes it harder for internal audit to audit financial and accounting matters with sufficient independence and objectivity. It also makes it more difficult for internal audit to be welcomed as having a valuable contribution to make when it audits the operational areas of the business. Ideally, internal audit should report directly to the chief executive or, alternatively, to someone, or to a committee, outside of the main functional areas of the business.

"The chief audit executive must report to a level within the organization that allows the internal audit activity to fulfill its responsibilities. The chief audit executive must confirm to the board, at least annually, the organizational independence of the internal audit activity."[2]

THE SCOPE OF INTERNAL AUDIT

Contemporary internal auditing provides assurance to management and to the board, and also offers consulting services. The nature of both these services should be set out in the internal audit charter. The two services overlap: an assurance audit is likely to lead to advice on making improvements; consulting work may reveal issues that have to be taken up by internal audit in the context of its assurance role. Of the two, assurance is the core role, but some would argue that not to offer consulting services would now be inconsistent with professional internal auditing standards and would miss an opportunity to add value.

There should be no no-go areas for internal audit assurance as this limits the assurance that internal audit is able to provide; where there are no-go areas (i.e. restrictions of scope) the implications need to be clearly understood by

CASE STUDY 1

Management and internal audit of a multinational company knew about an overstatement of oil reserves for some two years before the board and the board's audit committee learnt about it. Executive directors are said to have met before board meetings to agree a common line to be taken at the board. Reports from the chief audit executive passed across the desk of the chief financial officer before going to the audit committee. The chief executive, director of exploration, and chief financial officer left the company; when the company next appointed a new chief audit executive, the company sought an external candidate for the first time.

CASE STUDY 2

The independent chairman of the board of a bank fired the bank's chief executive. The inside story was that the in-house chief audit executive used his direct access to the chair of the audit committee to contact that chair, by phone, between audit committee meetings, to discuss his concerns about apparent misconduct by the chief executive.

The chair of the audit committee, which comprised exclusively independent directors, convened a special meeting of the committee to follow this up. No executives other than the chief audit executive, who was invited to attend part of the meeting, knew that it was taking place. At the meeting the audit committee asked internal audit to investigate the matter further and report the findings directly to the committee. The chief audit executive timed the audit fieldwork to coincide with the annual vacation of the chief executive. The internal auditors gathered evidence which showed that the chief executive was using company resources for his personal benefit. Hence, when the chief executive returned from vacation, the chairman of the board dismissed him.

Had the chairman of the board not been independent, it would have been harder for the audit committee to deal with this matter effectively. His independence meant that the chairman the audit committee was able to keep him "in the loop" throughout, without risk that the confidentiality of the enquiry would be jeopardized.

Had internal audit been outsourced to an external service provider, it might have been less likely to learn about the alleged misconduct by the chief executive. However, internal audit is often identified as a point where concerned employees may blow the whistle, and this can be so whether or not internal audit is in-house.

those who rely on the assurance that internal audit gives.

Unlimited scope for internal audit includes the authority to audit across the operational areas of the business, not just within accounting and finance, and at all levels. An emerging issue is whether internal audit is able to provide assurance to boards themselves that the policies of boards are being implemented by management and that there are no banana skins round the corner, unknown to the board, on which the company may slip in the future.

Consulting services by internal auditors may include the provision of counsel and advice, of facilitation (such as facilitating control self-assessment workshops of managers and staff), or of training services. Internal auditors avoid assuming any management responsibilities as part of their consulting services, neither would they take on responsibility for designing processes except in an advisory capacity. One reason is that internal auditors need to be independent of management processes in order to be able to audit those processes objectively.

Internal auditors will undertake consulting work only when both internal audit and the client consider this to be justified. On the other hand, the management of a business activity should not be allowed to prevent an assurance audit from taking place.

"The chief audit executive should consider accepting proposed consulting engagements based on the engagement's potential to improve management of risks, add value, and improve the organization's operations. Accepted engagements must be included in the plan."[3]

More and more heads of internal audit are being asked not just to report the results of individual audits but also to provide overall assurance opinions, annually or more frequently, to top management and to boards or their audit committees. This makes it more important that internal audit optimizes the utilization of its scarce internal audit resources—in order to maximize the reliability of the overall opinion that internal audit gives.

Internal audit should plan its program of audits annually, based on a risk assessment which makes use of inputs from management and from the board or the board's audit committee. Internal audit should map its plan of audits to management's own risk map or risk register. But a proportion of internal audit time should be set aside to "look round the corners" that top management are not looking around in case there are major unnoticed or concealed risks. Not all critical risks may be on top management's radar screen, and so value is added when internal audit spends a proportion of its available time auditing in areas of the business that are not perceived to carry significant risks.

While the future plan of audits will be determined annually, the internal audit function should have a longer perspective on audit coverage that takes into account audit work done over previous years and earmarked to be done over the next three years or so. The chief audit executive should consider the extent to which work done in earlier years can be utilized in coming to the overall assurance opinion.

PROFESSIONAL BODIES AND SUPPORT

The internal auditing profession is organized globally, as is appropriate for a function that so often operates transnationally. The IIA, established in the United States in 1941 and headquartered in Florida, now has many members outside of North America, belonging to 250 chapters and affiliated institutes in 165 countries. Membership has grown from 100,000

CASE STUDY 3

Following a fatal, high-profile explosion at one of its oil refineries and a number of other environmental failures, the board of a multinational oil company commissioned an enquiry by an outside panel. It must have appeared to the board that the board's policy that the company should be a green and safe oil multinational was not being implemented by management. The board agreed to the panel's recommendation that the panel should appoint an external expert to provide independent assurance to the board on health and safety matters for at least five years.

Two questions arise from this. First, whether (and if not, why not) the board had been receiving sufficient internal assurance that the policies of the board were being implemented by management; and second, the extent to which internal audit could be relied on to provide the board with that assurance. The panel's solution addressed the board's needs for assurance only in the area of health and safety, and was after the failures had occurred.

in 2004 to over 160,000 in 2008, of whom about 75,000 are fully professionally qualified certified internal auditors (CIAs). The IIA also offers the following specialist qualifications:

- Certification in Control Self-Assessment (CCSA);
- Certified Government Auditing Professional (CGAP);
- Certified Financial Services Auditor (CFSA).

Exams for The IIA's professional certifications can be sat at 90 sites throughout the world and in 18 languages. They can be taken at times of the candidate's choosing, rather than at two set dates during the calendar year. If a candidate fails an exam, he or she may retake the exam when at least 90 days have elapsed.

All members of The IIA commit to observe a common *Code of Ethics*, which includes an obligation to apply the *Standards* of The IIA.[4] There are approved translations of the *Standards* in 32 languages. The global Association of Chartered Certified Accountants (ACCA) has recently endorsed The IIA's *Standards* as applicable to ACCA members working as internal auditors, and the 2009 version of the United Kingdom's HM Treasury *Government*

Internal Audit Standards is modeled on the IIA's *Standards*. The International Professional Practices Framework of The IIA, which includes the *Standards* as well as the *Code of Ethics*, practice adviseries and practice guides, was very significantly revised, with effect from January 1, 2009. Thereafter, the intention is to issue any necessary revisions with effect from January 1 of each year.

QUALITY ASSURANCE ASSESSMENTS AND INTERNAL AUDIT MATURITY FRAMEWORKS

An effective opportunity to ensure optimum quality internal auditing is to be found in the quality assurance requirements of the *Standards* of The IIA. These require that there should be annual internal assessments of each internal audit function, and independent, external quality assessments at least once every five years. The benchmark to be used is the *Standards* of The IIA. These Standards represent the approach to internal auditing that should be followed if an organization is to obtain optimum value from its investment in internal audit. Internal audit maturity frameworks are now being applied to assess the quality of internal audit functions.[5]

MAKING IT HAPPEN

Key guidance to get best value from your internal audit function:

1 Develop a charter for your internal audit function, approved by the board or by your audit committee of the board.
2 Staff your internal audit function with professionally qualified people and those in the process of becoming qualified.
3 Require adherence to relevant internal auditing standards.
4 Ensure a scope for internal audit that includes assurance and consulting work.
5 Don't ever ask your internal audit function to subordinate its judgment on professional matters to anyone else.
6 Benchmark your internal audit function against others.
7 Take seriously the need for both internal and external quality assurance assessments of your internal audit function.
8 Support your internal auditors and ensure that they are properly resourced.

MORE INFO

Websites:

AuditNet, a US information and resources site developed for the benefit of the internal audit profession by Jim Kaplan. There are a number of discrete areas on AuditNet. The IIA now hosts this site, which has links to and from its own: www.auditnet.org

The Institute of Internal Auditors: www.theiia.org

The IIA's Florida-based website is a fund of information. It carries the internal auditing *Standards* and *Code of Ethics* as well as, for members, the rest of the International Professional Practices Framework. Also on this site is the IIA's excellent bookstore on internal auditing.

The IIA Inc.'s Research Foundation has sponsored the development of an Internal Auditing Capability Maturity Model (IA-CMM), published late 2008. Lead researcher and author is Elizabeth (Libby) MacRae.

The IIA runs the Global Audit Information Network (GAIN), a very effective and economic online benchmarking service for internal audit functions. More information at: www.theiia.org/guidance/benchmarking/gain

United Kingdom HM Treasury website: www.hm-treasury.gov.uk. This has a wealth of guidance on internal auditing including:

"The Orange Book"—Management of Risk: Principles and Concepts: www.hm-treasury.gov.uk/media/C/6/1104_orange_book.pdf

Internal Audit Quality Assessment Framework, including the Treasury's own internal audit maturity model: www.hm-treasury.gov.uk/psr_governance_risk_iaqaf.htm

Government Internal Audit Standards: www.hm-treasury.gov.uk/psr_governance_gia_guidance.htm

NOTES

1 Institute of Internal Auditors (IIA). *International Standards for the Professional Practice of Internal Auditing* ("*Standards*"). Altamonte Springs, FL: IIA, 2010. Can be downloaded from www.theiia.org, along with the *Code of Ethics*, Practice adviseries and Position papers. See "Websites" in "More Info."

2 IIA (2009). Standard 1110: Organizational Independence.

3 IIA. Standard 2010.C1.

4 See note 1.

5 For example, the UK HM Treasury's *Internal Audit Quality Assessment Framework*, which includes its internal audit maturity model (see "Websites" in "More Info"); or the IIA Inc. Research Foundation's Internal Auditing Capability Maturity Model (IA-CMM), authored by Elizabeth MacRae, 2009, www.theiia.org/bookstore/product/internal-audit-capability-model-iacm-for-the-public-sector-1422.cfm

Total Quality Management and Internal Auditing by Jeffrey Ridley

EXECUTIVE SUMMARY
- The concept of total quality management (TQM) requires a total commitment by everyone in an organization to a vision of quality and continuous improvement, controlled and measured in all its practices, products, and services it provides to its customers.
- The concept of TQM requires the same commitment, controls, and measures by the suppliers of products and services to the organization.
- This vision of total quality by suppliers and to customers applies to both internal and external suppliers and customers.
- TQM is an important contributor to good corporate governance practices.
- The profession of internal auditing requires, in its code of ethics, all internal auditors to achieve high standards of quality and to implement continuous improvement in all the practices, products, and services they provide to their customers.
- Internal auditing can and should contribute to an organization's TQM policies and programs in the best practices of its independent and objective assurance, consultancy, and teaching roles.

INTRODUCTION

The 1980s and 1990s saw a worldwide increase in the teaching and implementation of quality schemes. Most of these programs focused on economics and customer satisfaction, with controlled processes, key performance indicators, and feedback mechanisms. All involved a need for continuous improvement. All required total commitment. Many evolved from existing quality control and assurance functions, and many were new, established because of regulatory, competitive, or cost pressures.

During this period "quality objectives" in business and public-sector organizations moved into all levels of direction and management decision-making. Strategic plans embraced the need for quality and customer satisfaction, *if not delight*. Directors of quality appeared on many boards. The results could be seen in a growth of quality cultures and quality system standards, fuelled by many governments and consultants. Competitive national and international quality awards were created to stimulate the development of these cultures. These awards still attract many organizations to quality self-assessment programs and external quality audits across all sectors.

TQM becomes embedded in an organization when quality programs are created by a "total commitment" to quality in all strategies, structures, and systems. Quality gurus across the world have created exciting quality principles,

motivating many organizations to adopt TQM practices. These often bring significant benefits, not just for the organization, but also for its customers, suppliers, employees, and all other stakeholders. Best-practice internal auditing achieves high levels of quality in all its services and reviews quality achievements by the organization in all its planning and engagements.

CLEAR AND INSPIRING TOTAL QUALITY PRINCIPLES AND STANDARDS

The following five key quality principles underlie all TQM practices. They exist in all cutting-edge internal auditing practices. One of the most important principles is the achievement of quality and customer satisfaction with that quality across all supply chains, internal and external to the organization; this is essential for all of the principles.

1 Customer focus
- All customers are different, but their satisfaction is paramount.
- Focus on both internal and external customers, primary and secondary.
- View all customers as partners in your supply chains.
- Understand all your customers' needs.
- Aim for customer delight at all times, not just satisfaction.
- Ignore customer complaints at your peril.

QFINANCE

2 Management leadership
- Organize for quality.
- Establish a clear and motivating vision that is understood by everyone.
- Identify your key success factors and build these into a clear mission statement.
- Provide the right structures, methods, and resources for quality achievement.
- Communicate well at all levels, both in clarity and timeliness.
- Give high visibility to your quality policy.

3 Teamwork
- Recognize and encourage the power of teams.
- Develop teams across the whole supply chain, internal and external.
- Interlock all teams at operational, functional, and cross-functional levels.
- Reinforce and reward teams for success.
- Teach teams to focus on your vision and mission statements.
- Delegate responsibility for action to teams.

4 Measurement
- If it cannot be measured, it cannot be improved.
- Measure by statistics—do not inspect.
- Establish measures with high visibility in all processes, across all supply chains.
- Relate all measures to your vision and mission statements.
- Focus measures on customers, both internal and external.
- Take prompt corrective action on all measurements.

5 Total commitment to continuous improvement
- Look for problems, develop solutions, and train.
- Create a learning organization with a constant commitment to improve.
- Encourage a constant and continuous search for excellence.
- Be creative—look for paradigm shifts.
- Benchmark, internally and externally.
- Verify the success of change.

Oakland (1989) describes quality chain theory (now referred to by many as supply chain theory) as a continuous chain of meeting customer requirements across processes, both external and internal to the organization:

"Throughout and beyond all organizations, whether they are manufacturing concerns, banks, retail stores, universities, or hotels, there is a series of quality chains which may be broken at any point by any one person or piece of equipment not meeting the requirements of the customer, internal or external."

An understanding of my following definition of quality in the supply chain is fundamental to the achievement of quality: "**TQM** is all the internal and external **chains of supplier, process and customer**, directed by **quality strategies** and **policies, managed** through **total commitment** to **quality principles** and **measured** by the achievement of quality **key performance indicators** and **continuous improvement** to **satisfy customer needs**."

Note the emphasis on the words in **bold**.

Oakland (2001) defines quality as "simply meeting the customer requirements." But it is more than this, as explained in his book. It is about customer "satisfaction in ownership." It is about a consistency in meeting customer requirements that moves quality "to a different plane of satisfaction—delighting the customer and maintaining customer loyalty." In his thoughts on the pursuit of quality today in the global market place, he emphasizes how important this approach is:

"The complexity of today's supply chains requires a rigorous approach to quality management that integrates quality assurance, quality control and quality improvement. Quality is not just an issue for the quality department or quality management. It has a major strategic significance in delivering superior business results and enhancing shareholder value."

There can be very few internal auditors, if any, who would disagree with this statement in their pursuit of added value in the services they provide. Today, quality is still a driver of continuous improvement in products and services in many, if not all, organizations, of whatever size. The pursuit of quality is often driven by competition, but also by its association with trust and the need for long-term success—attributes that are necessary for all professional internal auditing. The framework in Figure 1 shows how TQM is embedded in an organization, from quality policy to a commitment to world-class status, across all supply chains, inside and across an organization, from suppliers (internal and external) to customers (internal and external).

Figure 1. TQM framework: total commitment across the supply chain. (*Source*: Ridley, 2008)

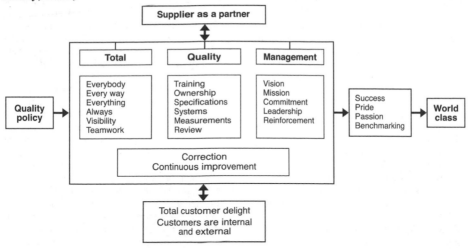

Use this framework to assess your own organization's commitment to quality. It can be applied in all organizations, however small or large, and to units within organizations, including internal auditing.

ISO 9000 and TQM

There have been many debates over the years as to whether a quality system registered to ISO 9000 is TQM. Those who agree that it is usually base their opinion on the detailed requirements of ISO 9000 and supporting 1994 guidelines (9004-1). These guidelines did not form part of the registration process. However, they were advisory for the development of a quality system and clearly written in a TQM context, requiring quality systems to meet and satisfy the needs and expectations of both customer and organization:

• The customer's needs and expectations: For the customer, there is a need for confidence in the ability of the organization to deliver the desired quality, as well as in the consistent maintenance of that quality.

• The organization's needs and interests: For the organization, there is a business need to attain and to maintain the desired quality at an optimum cost; the fulfilment of this aspect is related to the planned and efficient utilization of the technological, human, and material resources available to the organization.

Those who did not agree at the time usually based

their opinion on the detailed documentation required for registration of a quality system and the compliance nature of quality auditing. Many also believed that there was not sufficient focus on customer satisfaction and continuous improvement in ISO 9000 at that time, even though both were referred to in the guidelines. This debate was reflected in the revisions to ISO 9000:1994, which consolidated the family of ISO 9000 standards into four primary standards (9000, 9001, 9004, and 10011 ("Guidelines for auditing quality systems")). The introduction to the final draft of ISO 9000:2000 gave "customer needs" as the main force driving the revision. It also introduced revised guidelines ISO 9004:2000, developed to be consistent with the new ISO 9001:2000. Today, a further revised ISO 9001:2008 more clearly addresses the quality management system requirements for an organization to demonstrate its capability to meet customer requirements, and a revised ISO 9004:2009 provides a wider focus on quality management, based on eight quality management principles: customer focus, leadership, involvement of people, process approach, system approach to management, continual improvement, factual approach to decision making, and mutually beneficial supplier relationships. The ISO 9000 series of standards, with its quality principles, guidelines, and required auditing of quality management systems, is now fully supportive of TQM.

TOTAL QUALITY IN GOVERNANCE, RISK MANAGEMENT, AND CONTROL PROCESSES

The achievement of economic success for an organization will always depend on the quality of its products and services and how well it is governed by direction and control. Bain and Band (1996) recognized that economic success is part of good governance:

"Companies and other enterprises with a professional and positive attitude to governance are stronger and have a greater record of achievement. In fact, some company directors... suggest that there is an important direct relationship between a country's corporate governance system and its economic success."

Sir Adrian Cadbury, in his foreword to Davies (1999), also links governance to effectiveness:

"The essential point is that good governance is an aid to effectiveness. It is not there to shackle enterprise, but to harness it in the achievement of its goals."

OECD (2004), in its principles of corporate governance, recognizes the importance of high standards of quality in all management practices in an organization, including flows of information, accounting, auditing, and all communications:

"V. *Disclosure and Transparency* B. Information should be prepared and disclosed in accordance with high quality standards of accounting and financial and non-financial disclosure."

The Committee of Sponsoring Organizations of the Treadway Commission (COSO) is dedicated to improving the quality of financial reporting through business ethics, effective internal controls, and corporate governance. In its latest report, *Guidance on Monitoring Internal Control Systems* (2009), it *'...presents the fundamental principles of effective monitoring and develops the linkage to the COSO integrated framework'* (the control environment, risk assessment, control activities, monitoring, information, and communication): reinforcing the importance of quality in the monitoring of all aspects of internal control:

"Over the past decade, organizations have invested heavily in improving the quality of their internal control systems. They have made the investment for a number of reasons, notably: (1) good internal control is good business—it helps organizations ensure that operating, financial and compliance objectives are met, and (2) many organizations are required to report on the quality of internal control over financial reporting, compelling them to develop specific support for their certifications and assertions."

Monitoring the quality of internal control systems as part of good governance should always include benchmarking to the TQM principles and standards mentioned earlier.

TQM IN INTERNAL AUDITING

Quality assurance in internal auditing performance has always been part of professional guidance by the Institute of Internal Auditors (IIA). In 1978, its standards for the then professional practice of internal auditing recognized the importance of this, recommending four steps to achieving quality in internal auditing work: *due professional care, supervision, internal reviews,* and *external reviews.* These will always be a fundamental part of any quality assurance framework in internal auditing, reinforced by the mandatory quality assurance and continuous improvement requirements in the IIA's current "international professional practices framework" (2011) for professional internal auditing.

The IIA and the Chartered Institute of Internal Auditors, United Kingdom and Ireland (IIA UK and Ireland) published statements on internal auditing and TQM in the early 1990s—quality assurance in internal auditing is not new. In 1993 the IIA interviewed a number of North American organizations that were using TQM to improve internal auditing processes as well as a means of contributing to the improvement of control environments, risk assessment, control activities, and monitoring. Internal auditing benefits from involvement in TQM were seen at that time to come from improved training, teamwork, measurement techniques, and benchmarking.

The IIA UK and Ireland started its professional briefing notes series in 1992 with a definition of TQM and an exploration of the following options for internal auditors to explore:

- Internal auditing appraisal of departmental TQM activities.
- The relationship between internal auditing and quality auditing.
- The extent to which heads of internal audit might seek to gain ISO 9000 registration for their audit departments.

In the 1990s some internal auditing functions had registered to the international quality management standard ISO 9000. This required all their processes to comply with the standard's quality requirements. The IIA UK and Ireland (1993) published an example of such a registration. This internal auditing interest in ISO 9000 continues today, with many internal auditing functions choosing this road to meet high quality standards in the practices and services they provide in their organizations. The IIA Research Foundation (1996) published an analysis of internal auditing registrations to ISO 9000, identifying the following reasons for registration:

Procedural
- need to update procedures;
- need to improve procedures;
- need to motivate internal auditing staff to comply with procedures;
- need for more uniform procedures.

Strategic
- requirement by an organization to pursue ISO 9000;
- requirement by an organization to demonstrate quality in services provided.

Organizational
- need to change the structure of global/national service;
- need to improve supervision;
- to improve team-building.

Marketing
- part of a program to market-test the internal auditing service in competition with other bids;
- part of a program to market internal auditing services within the organization.

The same research showed that benefits gained from registration were as listed below. These were mainly in the quality vision and mission, which required management leadership, teamwork, and good communication to mould existing internal auditing practices into compliance with ISO 9000 quality requirements. The changes also required training and writing, or rewriting, of audit procedures.

Quality policy: Like the IIA standards, ISO 9000 requires a declaration of purpose in respect of quality. For ISO 9000, this takes the form of publication of a quality policy. Each of the internal auditing functions had incorporated such a statement in its charter.

Standard of conduct: The IIA standards require internal auditors to take due professional care in their audit work. Compliance with ISO 9000 quality requirements promoted diligence in audit work and established an environment which embraced many of the principles in the IIA code of ethics.

Documentation: The IIA standards require written policies and procedures for all audit work. Such evidence was reinforced by the ISO 9000 quality requirements for controlled documentation and records.

Quality assurance: The IIA standards require evidence of supervision and quality assurance in all audit work. The ISO 9000 quality assurance and quality audit requirements provided a framework for the supervision and management of all internal auditing practices.

Mandatory quality assurance requirements are essential for all professions. In its latest statement on quality assurance and improvement programs for internal auditing, the IIA UK and Ireland (2007) states:

"Just like any other professionals, internal auditors are responsible for delivering to their customers and stakeholders a reliable service that meets their existing professional standards. To achieve this day-in and day-out, heads of internal audit should develop and maintain a Quality Assurance and Improvement Programme."

IIA UK and Ireland (2007) introduces and discusses its own quality management principles for internal auditing: customer (increasingly stakeholder) focus;
- leadership;
- people;
- processes and systems;
- fact-based decision-making;
- continuous or continual learning;
- partnerships, particularly with suppliers.

Compare these with the TQM principles and standards mentioned earlier.

CONTRIBUTION OF INTERNAL AUDITING TO TQM

Gupta and Ray (1995), in their research into total quality and internal auditing, also saw internal auditors as "quality champions":

"Internal auditors, by virtue of their role, are in a unique position to lead and pro-actively support the quality movement in their organizations. The internal auditing function does not need to be a bystander and wait to get on the quality bandwagon only when someone else in the organization sounds the quality horn. If the internal auditing function so desires there is ample opportunity to lead and support the total quality movement in an organization."

Such a championing role should never be far from any internal audit engagement—be it assurance, consulting, or teaching.

Whatever the role internal auditing follows to implement TQM principles in its own function, it is clear that the challenge of quality cannot be left out of audit planning and risk assessment in those systems and functions which it reviews in others. All internal audit engagements should:

- provide advice on all quality programs in their organization;
- link all quality policy requirements to risk management;
- benchmark TQM principles to all governance practices.

MAKING IT HAPPEN

- Starting a TQM program requires an inspiring vision that will motivate everyone to a commitment to "total quality" in all processes and services which they provide.
- Define and agree what you mean by "quality" in relation to yourselves, your customers, and all your stakeholders.
- Publish a quality policy that requires continuous assurance of its implementation and effectiveness.
- Establish quality systems for all your processes.
- Respond *immediately* to customer and stakeholder complaints.
- Agree your key quality performance indicators and measure against these on a regular basis; publish the results to all your staff, customers, and stakeholders.
- Implement internal quality auditing and independent external quality assessment.
- Reward success in implementing or raising quality.
- Correct all failures so that they do not happen again.
- Aim to be *right first time*.
- Continuously improve—quality is a journey, not a destination.

CASE STUDY

Internal Auditing in 1975, Today and Tomorrow[1]

In 1975, at my inaugural address as president of the then United Kingdom Chapter of the Institute of Internal Auditors, Inc., I said the following:

"We live in times of high economic risk and important social and business decisions. Every day we are reminded at work, in newspapers and by television of the opportunities that can be taken to develop ourselves and the profession we have chosen. The apparent insoluble problems of the present economic situation; the controversial discussions caused by exposure drafts and new accounting practices; involvement in the European Community; a new awareness of social responsibilities; higher health and safety standards; the now clearly recognised need for more efficient manpower planning and training; the urgency of energy saving; the complexity of advanced computer technology are all changes that management cannot ignore, and neither can we as internal auditors. To be successful we must be sensitive to the problems of each day. All can have an impact on our professional activities far beyond the changes we may foresee at the present time."

I have repeated this many times since as a commentary on the environment in which internal auditing operates across all sectors, both nationally and internationally. It is still a challenging statement, requiring a high level of quality in all internal auditing activities. Consider the quality needs of your customers for each of these challenges and how they are being managed. Measure the quality of your own internal auditing and how it meets these challenges. That is what TQM is all about.

MORE INFO

Books:

Bain, Neville, and David Band. *Winning Ways through Corporate Governance*. London, UK: Macmillan Business, 1996.

Davies, Adrian. *A Strategic Approach to Corporate Governance*. Aldershot, UK: Gower, 1999.

Oakland, John S. *Total Organizational Excellence: Achieving World-Class Performance*. Oxford, UK: Butterworth-Heinemann, 2001.

Oakland, John S. *Total Quality Management*. Oxford, UK: Butterworth-Heinemann, 1989.

Ridley, Jeffrey. *Cutting Edge Internal Auditing*. Chichester, UK: Wiley, 2008.

Reports:

Chartered Institute of Internal Auditors (UK and Ireland). "Total quality management: The implications for internal audit departments, PBN 1." IIA UK and Ireland, 1992.

Chartered Institute of Internal Auditors (UK and Ireland). "A quality system manual for internal auditing." IIA UK and Ireland, 1993.

Chartered Institute of Internal Auditors (UK and Ireland). "Quality assurance and improvement programme." IIA UK and Ireland, 2007. [Available to members only].

Committee of Sponsoring Organizations of the Treadway Commission (COSO). "Internal control—Integrated framework." AICPA, 1992.

COSO. "Guidance on monitoring internal control systems." 3 vols. AICPA, 2009.

Gupta, Parveen P., and Manash R. Ray. "Total quality improvement process and the internal auditing function." IIA Research Foundation, 1995.

Institute of Internal Auditors (IIA). "Internal auditing in a total quality environment: A reference manual." 1993.

Institute of Internal Auditors (IIA). "International Professional Practices Framework (IPPF)." 2011.

IIA UK and Ireland, *see* Chartered Institute of Internal Auditors (UK and Ireland).

International Organization for Standardization (ISO). "ISO 9000 series." Geneva: ISO, 2010.

Oakland, John S., and Mike Turner. "Global sourcing and outsourcing and the pursuit of quality: Dream or nightmare? Three ways for companies to improve." Oakland Consulting, 2008. Online at: www.oaklandconsulting.com

Organisation for Economic Co-operation and Development (OECD). "Principles of corporate governance." 2004.

Ridley, Jeffrey, and Krystyna Stephens. "International quality standards: Implications for internal auditing." IIA Research Foundation, 1996.

Websites:

Institute of Internal Auditors (IIA): www.theiia.org

Chartered Institute of Internal Auditors (UK and Ireland): www.iia.org.uk

Committee of Sponsoring Organizations of the Treadway Commission (COSO): www.coso.org

International Organization for Standardization (ISO): www.iso.org

Best Practice
In Practice

What Is the Range of the Internal Auditor's Work? by Andrew Cox

EXECUTIVE SUMMARY

The range and type of the internal auditor's work depend on a number of factors:

- The mandate for internal audit contained in the internal audit charter.
- What the audit committee and management want internal audit to do.
- To whom the chief audit executive (head of internal audit) reports.
- The capability and skills of the internal auditors.
- Any legislative or regulatory requirements of internal audit.

But it's a bit like Forrest Gump when he said "Life is like a box of chocolates—you never know what you're gonna get." Internal auditing is a bit like that box of chocolates as the range and quality of the services are variable—and, indeed, often you really don't know what you're going to get.

INTRODUCTION

Internal auditing is an evolving profession. It has been around for a very long time, probably since the pharaohs in Egypt. But it wasn't until 1947—when the foremost professional body for internal auditing, the Institute of Internal Auditors (IIA), was formed—that internal auditing was set on its path to emerging as a profession.

Subsequently, professional standards and a code of ethics for internal auditing have been established, and in 1974 professional certification for internal auditing was created, with the designation Certified Internal Auditor. Over that time, the scope of internal auditing has changed significantly.

THE EVOLUTION OF INTERNAL AUDITING

The evolution of how internal audit determined what it would audit can be tracked in Table 1.

Table 1. The evolution of internal auditing—up to the 1990s

Then (up to the 1990s)	Advantages	Disadvantages
Areas for internal audit identified on a functional basis from historic information.	Often cyclical (every year).	Done in isolation of the business.
	Well known to internal auditors.	Time-consuming.
Set of one-dimensional risk factors applied (high, moderate, low).	Safe approach.	Focus on functional areas.
		May not be timely, relevant, or responsive.
Input into a model and prioritization based on risk rankings.		
		Correlation between risk rankings and internal audit plan often weak.
3- or 5-year strategic internal audit plan based on risk rankings.		Assumed a static organization.
Annual internal audit plan based on available resources.		
Presented to the audit committee (but not always).		

Nowadays, Table 2 could be the best representation.

Table 2. The evolution of internal auditing—1990s–2008

Now (1990s–2008)	Advantages	Disadvantages
Areas for internal audit identified on a functional, cross-organizational, and strategic basis—may use the organization's risk register.	Well known to internal auditors.	Can be challenging.
	Done in consultation with the business.	Time-consuming.
Discussed with senior management—additional internal audit areas may be added.	Broader scope that considers business risks.	May not be timely, relevant, or responsive.
Set of risk factors applied, input into a model, and prioritized based on risk rankings.	Facilitates integration of internal audit, risk management, and strategic planning.	
3-year strategic internal audit plan based on risk rankings.	Requires strong understanding of the business.	
Annual internal audit plan based on available resources.		
Presented to the audit committee.		

In the future Table 3 would be more accurate.

Table 3. The evolution of internal auditing—2008 onward

Future (2008 onward)	Advantages	Disadvantages
Areas for internal audit identified on a functional, cross-organizational, and strategic basis using the organization's risk register and other relevant information.	Done in consultation with the business.	Requires strong commitment from senior management.
	Timely, relevant, and responsive.	Requires discipline to ensure that the internal audit consultation process is effective.
Develop base audit plan.	Broader scope taking into account business risks.	
Discuss with senior management, including facilitated workshops—additional audit areas may be added.	Facilitates integration of internal audit, risk management, and strategic planning.	May not be well known to internal auditors.
Develop annual or longer-term assurance plan.		
Develop flexible, rolling internal audit consulting plan to provide timely, relevant, and responsive services. Present to audit committee.		

The point is this: The range of an internal auditor's work will generally be related to where the he or she is currently placed in regard to these three evolutionary phases of the internal audit continuum. As we move into the more difficult methods of operating an internal audit function, the complexity of internal audit work increases, and the capability and skills of the internal auditor need to be greater. Many internal auditors are still in the early evolutionary phases of internal auditing, because the future is seen as too difficult and daunting.

WHAT DO THE STANDARDS SAY?

The internal auditing standards we will consider here are those issued by the Institute of Internal Auditors (IIA, 2007). The internationally accepted definition of internal auditing issued by the IIA is:

"Internal auditing is an independent, objective assurance and consulting activity designed to add value and improve an organization's operations. It helps an organization accomplish its objectives by bringing a systematic, disciplined approach to evaluate and improve the effectiveness of risk management, control, and governance processes."

This was a step up from the previous definition, which concentrated on assurance. This definition expanded the role of internal audit to encompass consulting services. To understand the difference between assurance services and consulting services, we need a couple of definitions:

Assurance: An objective examination of the evidence for the purpose of providing an independent assessment of risk management, control, or governance processes for an organization. Examples may include financial, performance, compliance, system security, and due diligence engagements.

Consulting: Advisory and related client service activities, the nature and scope of which are agreed with the client, and which are intended to add value and improve an organization's governance, risk management, and control processes without the internal auditor assuming management responsibility. Examples include counsel, advice, facilitation, and training.

It should be noted that the definitions of internal auditing and the standards focus on risk management, control, and governance:

Risk management: Internal audit should assist the organization by identifying and evaluating significant exposures to risk and contributing to the improvement of risk management and control systems.

Control: Internal audit should assist the organization in maintaining effective controls by evaluating their effectiveness and efficiency and by promoting continuous improvement.

Governance: Internal audit should assess and make appropriate recommendations for improving the governance process in its accomplishment of the following objectives:

- Promoting appropriate ethics and values within the organization.
- Ensuring effective organizational performance management and accountability.
- Effectively communicating risk and control information to appropriate areas of the organization.
- Effectively coordinating the activities and communicating information among the board, external and internal auditors, and management.

WHAT TYPE OF WORK?

So, what should be the range and type of work carried out by internal audit for an organization? The IIA believes that the work and methods of internal audit should encompass:

- Conducting enterprise risk assessment.
- Utilizing risk and control self-assessment.
- Using internal control processes based on COSO (Committee of Sponsoring Organizations) guidelines.
- Partnering with management.
- Integrating corporate governance into practice.
- Increasing staff performance.
- Communicating more effectively.
- Developing staff, both personally and professionally.
- Using technology to increase staff efficiency.
- Establishing an assurance function.
- Providing consulting services.
- Conducting audits in emerging areas.
- Utilizing performance measures.

This leads to the types of internal audit provided by the internal audit function, which may include some or all of the following:

Compliance audit: The review of both financial and operating controls and transactions to see how they conform with established laws, standards, regulations, and procedures.

Financial audit: The examination of the financial records and reports of a company to verify that the figures in the financial reports are relevant, accurate, and complete. The general focus is on making sure that all assets and liabilities are properly recorded on the balance sheet, and that the statement of income and expenses is correct.

Information technology (IT) audit: A review of the controls within an entity's technology infrastructure. These reviews are typically performed in conjunction with a financial statement audit, internal audit review, or other form of attestation engagement.

On-demand audit: A request for an internal audit initiated by the board, audit committee, or management in response to their particular concerns, and which has not been scheduled in the internal audit plan of work. It may also be known as a management-initiated review.

Operational audit: Sometimes called program or performance audits, these examine the use of resources to evaluate whether those resources are being used in the most efficient and effective way to fulfill an organization's objectives. An operational audit may include elements of a compliance audit, a financial audit, and an information systems audit. This term is mainly used in the private sector.

Performance audit: The independent and systematic examination of the management of an organization, program, or function for the purpose of identifying whether the management is being carried out in an efficient and effective manner, and whether management practices promote improvement. This term is mainly used in the public sector, and a performance audit may be the same as or similar to an operational audit.

Quality audit: The systematic examination and evaluation of all activities related to the quality of a product or service, to determine the suitability and effectiveness of the activities to meet quality goals.

Value for money (VFM) audit: An examination of how resources are allocated and utilized. The audit is concerned with interrelated concepts of efficiency, effectiveness, economy, and organizational outcomes. VFM audits are more common in the public sector than the private sector since the profit criterion is lacking in the public sector, and they may be the same as or similar to a performance audit.

WHAT INFLUENCES THE TYPE OF WORK?

The range and type of the internal auditor's work depend on a number of factors:

The mandate for internal audit contained in the internal audit charter: This is what the audit committee and the organization want internal audit to do. Although ideally this should include both assurance services and consulting services, it is true to say that some audit committees and management believe that internal audit should not stray from its roots of providing assurance, so in some organizations the internal audit charter has focused only on the provision of assurance services. This attitude peaked following the corporate collapses of the 1990s. However, more enlightened audit committees and management of today seek a more comprehensive internal auditing service for the organization. This has the potential to add a lot of value, rather than just reporting what is wrong in compliance and financial areas.

To whom the chief audit executive reports to: The chief audit executive should report to the audit committee functionally and for operations, and to the chief executive officer for administration. Where a chief audit executive

CASE STUDY

Designing a Comprehensive Internal Audit Plan

A large public sector organization with a significant commitment to internal auditing provided sufficient funds to resource an internal audit function of 25,000 audit hours each year. The audit committee wanted an annual internal audit plan of work that provided assurance and examined how well the organization was operating, but which was also responsive to the changing needs and risks of the organization. The risk-based annual internal audit plan of work to achieve this designed by the chief audit executive is summarized in Table 4.

Rather than have a static annual internal audit plan, the plan shown in the table was designed to cover an 18-month period with a refresher every six months so that workflows could be smoothed and work allocated to internal auditors continuously. The plan encompassed the following areas:

- **Cyclical 12 months scheduled**: For high-risk areas worthy of annual internal audit attention.
- **Rolling 6 months scheduled**: Higher-risk areas scheduled for periodic or one-off internal audits.
- **Rolling 3 months reserve**: Areas held in reserve in case of postponement or cancellation of other internal audits.
- **Rolling 3 months unassigned**: Reserved for on-demand internal audits initiated by management for emerging business issues and risks.

Table 4. The chief audit executive's risk-based annual internal audit plan

Audit type	Cyclical 12 months scheduled hours	Rolling 6 months scheduled hours	Rolling 3 months reserve hours	Rolling 3 months unassigned hours	Annual total hours
Compliance					6,000
Assurance	6,000	0	0	0	
Consulting	0	0	0	0	
Financial					5,000
Assurance	750	2,500	1,000	500	
Consulting	250	0	0	0	
IT					6,000
Assurance	3,000	0	0	0	
Consulting	3,000	0	0	0	
Performance					5,000
Assurance	0	0	0	0	
Consulting	500	2,500	1,000	1,000	
Internal audit planning	500	0	0	0	500
Audit monitor and follow-up	500	0	0	0	500
Audit committee	500	0	0	0	500
External audit coordination	1,500	0	0	0	1,500
					25,000

may have other reporting arrangements—for example to a chief executive officer for operations and administration, or worse, to a chief financial officer—there is a risk that internal audit may lose a measure of its independence. This has a potential to impact negatively on the range and type of work to be performed by internal audit.

The capability and skills of the internal auditors: As the work of internal audit moves toward more difficult methods of operating, the complexity of internal audit work increases. his means that the capability and skills of the internal auditor need to be greater, and many internal auditors see this as a quantum leap so great that they prefer to remain comfortable where they are.

Any legislative or regulatory requirements of internal audit: The work of internal audit will nearly always have a role to provide assurance of legislative and regulatory compliance; this is an important role that should never be forgotten.

CONCLUSION

The range and type of the internal auditor's work depend on a number of factors:
- The mandate for internal audit contained in the internal audit charter.
- What the audit committee wants internal audit to do, and how enlightened it is.
- What management wants internal audit to do.
- To whom the chief audit executive (head of internal audit) reports.
- The capability and skills of the internal auditors.
- Any legislative or regulatory requirements of internal audit.

MAKING IT HAPPEN

Chief audit executives should look to his or her audit committee and management for guidance on the range and type of work to be performed by the internal audit function. However, the chief audit executive, as an internal audit professional, should be using his or her knowledge and experience to identify and influence the formulation of a risk-based internal audit plan of work that best provides for the needs of the organization. This is likely to be a blended plan of internal audit work that encompasses both assurance services and consulting services:

Assurance Services
- Part of the overall internal audit plan of work.
- Annual or longer-term focus.
- Risk-based.
- May include cyclical internal audits of higher-risk areas.
- Need to consider legislative and regulatory requirements.
- Need to consider external audit to avoid duplication of audit effort.
- Estimated hours for audit topics assessed from previous internal audits (structured gut feel).
- Focus on compliance, financial issues and risks, financial controls, and IT reviews.

Consulting Services
- Part of the overall internal audit plan of work.
- Flexible, rolling focus—rather than fixed in time.
- Risk-based and customer-focused.
- If limited previous data are available, estimate hours needed for internal audit topics on the basis of the best available information and past experience (unstructured gut feel).
- Focus on current and emerging business issues and risks, and system under development reviews.

MORE INFO

Books:

Picket, K. H. Spencer. *Audit Planning: A Risk-Based Approach*. Hoboken, NJ: Wiley, 2006.

Reding, Kurt F., Paul J. Sobel, Urton L. Anderson, Michael J. Head, *et al*. *Internal Auditing: Assurance and Consulting Services*. 2nd ed. Altamonte Springs, FL: IIA Research Foundation, 2009.

Sawyer, Lawrence B., Mortimer A. Dittenhofer, and James H. Scheiner. *Sawyer's Internal Auditing: The Practice of Modern Internal Auditing*. 5th ed. Altamonte Springs, FL: Institute of Internal Auditors, 2003.

Reports:

Australian National Audit Office. "Public sector audit committees: Having the right people is the key." Better Practice Guide. February 2005. Online at: tinyurl.com/6eezvzf [zipped PDFs].

Australian National Audit Office. "Public sector internal audit: An investment in assurance and business improvement." Better Practice Guide. September 2007. Online at: www.anao.gov.au/uploads/documents/Public_Sector_Internal_Audit.pdf

Standards:

Institute of Internal Auditors. "International standards for the professional practice of internal auditing." October 2010. Online at: www.theiia.org/guidance/standards-and-guidance/ippf/standards

Website:

Institute of Internal Auditors (IIA): www.theiia.org

Aligning the Internal Audit Function with Strategic Objectives by Ilias G. Basioudis

EXECUTIVE SUMMARY

- Due to high-profile scandals at the beginning of the century, regulators and the accounting profession worldwide have put forward a series of initiatives to repair the damage and restore faith in corporate governance.
- Globally, more companies are adopting corporate governance best practice.
- An independent internal audit function is widely recognized as an integral part of a company's strategic objectives, corporate governance, and risk management.
- The internal audit standards issued by the Institute of Internal Auditors serve as authoritative guidance for members of the internal audit profession.
- Internal audit's role is to evaluate the appropriateness and effectiveness of companies' systems and processes, and to identify and manage risks present in the normal course of conducting business activities.

INTRODUCTION

Given today's complex and rapidly changing management climate, companies must implement continuous improvements to achieve efficiency, and assure investors and other concerned parties of solid corporate governance.

The recent scandals at Enron, WorldCom, Parmalat, and others have raised the profile of corporate governance across the globe. Trust in the process of financial accounting, corporate governance, and auditing has been undermined by these high-profile corporate scandals. In response, regulators and the accounting profession worldwide have put forward a series of initiatives to repair the damage and restore faith in corporate governance. Furthermore, companies must continuously implement improvements to achieve effective and efficient management in order to assure the investors, other stakeholders, and concerned parties in general of its good and sound corporate governance. Globally, more companies, governments, states, and regulators are adopting corporate governance best practice, and placing more emphasis on improving corporate governance in companies, which in turn improves the confidence of investors and stakeholders in companies.

Worldwide legislative initiatives, of which the Sarbanes–Oxley Act (US) and Directive No. 8 (EU) are the most famous, make senior management responsible for establishing, evaluating, and assessing over time the effectiveness of risk management processes, systems of internal control, and corporate governance processes. In tandem, companies play a critical role in the national economy, or economies, in which they have activities. A country's competitiveness, wealth, efficiency, and high level of economic growth may depend on the competitive nature of its companies. There is no doubt that a transparent and reasonable corporate governance structure has a positive impact on a company.

The audit committee is a subcommittee of the board of directors, and is widely recognized as an integral part of a company's corporate governance, and, together with the internal audit function, they contribute towards the company implementing continuous improvements. In fact, one line of thought claims that the audit committee, especially in large organizations, could not possibly be effective without an efficient, effective, and independent-minded internal audit function.

As a result, the internal audit function has the potential to be one of the most influential and value-adding services available to a company's senior management and board of directors. Furthermore, with the growing focus on corporate governance issues, organizations are increasingly exploring the potential benefits to be gained from establishing an effective and efficient internal audit function. Company boards must identify the opportunities, risks, and exposures that can determine success or failure. The establishment of an internal audit function can become an integral part of overall strategy, and assist in achieving corporate objectives.

THE PURPOSE AND ROLE OF INTERNAL AUDITING

According to The Institute of Internal Auditors' (IIA) definition of internal auditing, the internal audit function should provide independent, thorough, timely, and objective results of quantitative and qualitative testing to senior management, and, in essence, help evaluate organizational risk management. Internal auditing assists public and private organizations to meet overall corporate objectives by establishing a systematic and disciplined approach to assessing, evaluating, and improving the quality and effectiveness of risk management processes, systems of internal control, and corporate governance processes. This systematic approach and analysis is implemented across all parts of an organization, and the internal auditor reports directly and independently to the most senior level of management. The role of the internal auditor, therefore, is to provide an overall assurance to management that all key risks within an organization are managed effectively, so that the organization can achieve its strategic objectives.

An internal audit function should be independent and unbiased, and hold a neutral position within an organization. The audit function looks beyond the narrow focus of financial statements and financial risks (although these risks are included in the remit of the internal auditor's job), and it may, for example, involve auditing reputational, operational, environmental, or strategic risks. Reputational risks could involve labor practices in host countries; operational risks include poor health and safety procedures; environmental risks might involve pollution generated by a factory; while a strategic risk might involve the board stretching company resources by producing too many products.

An internal audit function should have the ability itself to define the scope of internal audits (after consultation with the internal audit's primary stakeholders), the authority to obtain information and resources, and have an appropriate reporting structure to senior management. The internal audit team members do not test their own work, or the work of persons that they report to. Any actual or potential conflicts of interest that hinder an honest, independent, and unbiased assessment must be disclosed.

INTERNAL AUDIT STANDARDS

In order to operate an internal audit function that is objective, independent, effective, and useful to an organization, it is essential that the internal audit function complies with the International Standards for the Professional Practice of Internal Auditing, developed by the Institute of Internal Auditors. The International Standards are authoritative guidance for the internal audit profession, and are principles-focused. Implementation standards refer to either assurance or consulting activities, and are embedded in the attribute and performance standards. Attribute standards refer to the composition of the audit department in terms of staff expertise and ongoing training, as well as independence and objectivity. Attribute standards also refer to the internal audit department's purpose, authority, and responsibility.

Performance standards refer to how the internal audit function should operate, and how the planning, scope, and reporting activities should be conducted and by whom. The performance standards reflect the purpose of the internal audit function in that they define the activities to be completed, which help make sure that the internal audit function is operating as designed for the benefit of the organization.

Another authoritative guidance issued by the IIA is the Code of Ethics. This is a statement of principles and expectations governing the behavior of individuals and organizations in the conduct of internal auditing, and provides a description of minimum requirements for conduct, and describes behavioral expectations rather than specific activities. The Code of Ethics refers to the integrity, objectivity, confidentiality, and competence of internal auditors.

DESIGNING A STRATEGICALLY FOCUSED INTERNAL AUDIT FUNCTION

How well an organization is able to recognize, understand, and manage its risks plays a critical part in the success, or failure, of the organization, and, consequently, the value it is able to deliver to customers, shareholders, and other stakeholders.

The internal audit function contributes to better overall governance when it operates within a strategic framework established by the audit committee and senior management. Once this strategic framework is in place, the corporation will be well positioned to define the mission, organizational structure, resource model, working practices, and communications protocols for the internal audit function.

Hence, when designing and implementing an effective internal audit function, the corporation's strategic objectives must be followed closely, and not vice versa. In other words, the internal audit's primary stakeholders must determine how the function will deliver the desired value, and what the specified outcomes expected of the new function are to be.

Common internal audit outcomes include:

- assessment of internal control effectiveness and efficiency;
- risk management and control assurance;
- regulatory and corporate compliance assurance;
- legislature readiness assessment and ongoing testing, such as Sarbanes-Oxley Act (US) and Directive No. 8 (EU);
- fostering awareness of risk and control across the organization;
- ability to respond to urgent events.

Once the function is established and the specific outcomes have been identified and defined, the internal audit's stakeholder expectations should be reassessed on a regular basis, and the mission for the internal audit function must be clearly articulated, so that the performance of the function can be evaluated on a regular basis. In addition, a formal mission statement for the internal audit function should be laid out by the head of the audit function, with the cooperation of senior management and the audit committee. The mission statement must also be aligned clearly and directly with stakeholder expectations and the internal audit's specified outcomes, as otherwise it would be of little value and possibly detrimental to achieving corporate strategic performance. Furthermore, the mission statement must be shared and communicated, to achieve full understanding and buy-in among key stakeholders and staff.

Once the mission statement is agreed, a formal strategic plan must be approved. This plan formally defines the value proposition of the new function, the customers it serves, and the value it will create now and into the future. The strategic plan serves as an operational manual of the new function, and as guidance on the key objectives and outcomes of the function, and how they will be achieved. The strategic plan sets a standard against which future decisions and results can be measured. Ideally, the plan should be reviewed at least annually, with changes considered and approved by all primary stakeholders as appropriate. For large companies, a full audit cycle of three years generally may seem appropriate; that is, the whole organization should be audited in an appropriate manner within three years. However, high risk areas should be audited at least annually.

Next, it is critical for the internal audit to develop a systematic process to analyze risk, and ensure that the audit plan is sufficiently broad in scope and executed in a timely manner. Internal auditors should segment the corporation into well-defined, reasonably sized, auditable units (often collectively called the "audit universe"), and then identify, determine, and prioritize/rank the inherent risks in each unit. Even a small business unit is likely to have a range of risks, some of which are higher priority than others. Inherent risks are those present in the normal course of conducting business activities. These include external risks such as changes to global, national, and economic climates, as well as technological, legal, social, and political changes. Inherent risks also include internal factors that warrant special attention, including changes in operating systems, new product launches, entry to new markets, management and organizational changes, and the expansion of foreign operations. Therefore, the risk assessment should evaluate current and prospective risks, particularly where new risks are emerging due to a change in the corporation's strategy or product mix.

The senior management and the audit committee must ensure the risk assessment executed by the audit function is not limited by reference to its own skill sets. In other words, a misalignment must be avoided between the technical competencies necessary to execute the audit plan and the skill sets resident in the internal audit function. An effective way to prioritize processes for audit purposes is to look at a matrix of probability of occurrence versus severity of loss for each of the processes, and develop a risk-based audit plan according to this classification.

Furthermore, other departments and functions within an organization gather intelligence and other important information, and senior management and the audit committee must ensure that the internal auditors are aware of these, and use them accordingly in determining and prioritizing risks. However, it is not necessary that the internal audit's independent view on risks coincide with other functions' perspectives in the organization, and this needs to be recognized and accepted. Senior management and the audit committee should also evaluate whether any "strong" executives or directors outside of the internal audit function, or "strong" business areas within the organization, have played a major role in shaping the internal audit's plan, and, if so, in what way. After the risk assessment is performed and the risk-based audit plan is drawn up, it is then important that timely and comprehensive coverage by the internal audit function is secured in order that the reliability and effectiveness of the internal controls in mitigating the significance and/or likelihood of a risk occurrence are considered. Another step to be taken after the assessment of risks and the audit plan are completed is the creation of current and longer-term budgets for the internal audit function. Budgets must provide sufficient resources for internal auditors to deliver the developed risk-based audit plan, as well as the flexibility to respond to changing business needs.

Budgets should be aligned with corporate strategies, and look to internal audit benchmarks developed by the IIA or other third parties to establish a budgetary baseline as compared to similar internal audit functions within the same industry. The budget should be projected on a three-to-five-year horizon.

The fieldwork should begin as soon as possible, even prior to having all staffing and infrastructure in place. Key stakeholders in an organization want to see demonstrable progress promptly, so it is important to begin conducting the audits without delay, in order for the internal audit function to create immediate value. In a start-up internal audit department, the first three months are important in completing the audits of three to five known high-risk areas, such as general computer systems and controls, inventory management, and other business areas with known internal control problems and challenges.

At times, corporations are impatient for results and, thus, they may choose to outsource all, or nearly all, of the internal audit to a third-party specialist firm. This is in contrast to the IIA's recommendation, which states that internal audit activity should never be fully outsourced, but should be managed from within the organization. Outsourcing can have several advantages, including employing professionals who are more independent as they are not beholden to management for their compensation; access to resources necessary to complete specific high-risk audits; access to an array of technical, up-to-date expertise; and, possibly, knowledge transfer to the organization's employees as the function converts into a full in-house or co-sourced resource model.

On the other hand, full or near-full outsourcing brings with it specific governance challenges for senior management and the audit committee. These problems may include the following: limited communication and level of interaction between the organization and the third-party audit professionals; increased difficulty for the third-party auditors to gain sufficient standing in the corporation; outsourcing is significantly more expensive on a per-hour basis than undertaking

the function in-house; and, the corporation has limited ability to influence audit team appointments when the internal audit function is fully outsourced. If some level of dependence on third-party firms for specialist audit skills is necessary for a corporation, then selective use of co-sourcing arrangements should be in place.

By revisiting stakeholder-specified outcomes and the internal audit function's mission statement developed earlier in the start-up process, a balanced staffing model must be adapted to each corporation's needs. Best practice requires corporations to staff their internal audit functions with long-tenured audit career professionals, as well as rotating talented executives from across the organization for two-or three-year rotations in internal audit. Furthermore, the necessary internal audit infrastructure and methodologies should be developed at the same time. These will greatly improve the efficiency, quality, and consistency of the internal audit process, and will provide assurance towards compliance with both the organization's methodologies, policies, and desired outcomes, and the standards developed by the IIA. Corporations should establish routine, robust, and frank lines of communication with their key internal audit professionals. It is imperative that an internal audit function communicates effectively and freely with all its internal stakeholders (and, primarily, with senior management and the audit committee). On a regular, if not daily, basis, the internal audit should seek opportunities for dialogue and communication with the corporation's senior management and the audit committee, creating a strong, clear connection between the internal audit mission and the corporation's strategic issues and risks.

In addition, the external auditors also have a role to play in an organization's corporate governance, and, as such, the audit committee should seek to establish and maintain good links and cooperation between internal and external audits.

Finally, it is important that the internal audit demonstrates results, and its reports are actionable and implemented. The reports should be generated and circulated in a timely fashion after the audit is complete, and senior management and the audit committee should ensure that an effective and timely follow-up to the reports has been implemented.

CONCLUSION

Organizations serve their stakeholders. Senior management's role is to ensure that the organization's resources are managed and applied effectively to meet objectives and responsibilities. A crucial part of this process of governance is the design of appropriate systems and processes in order for them to be able to identify and manage risks effectively and efficiently. Internal audit's role is to evaluate the appropriateness and effectiveness of those systems and processes, whether they are related to finance, IT, brand reputation, health and safety, legal and regulatory compliance, human resources, and/or major projects.

Internal auditors perform their role by working with boards of directors, audit committees, and senior managers to help them understand the consequences of risks and ineffective processes to manage them. They encourage and support managers to have appropriate systems in place. Internal auditors then report to senior management and the audit committee on how effectively these systems of control are operating. In such a way, the corporation succeeds in aligning the internal audit function with its strategic objectives.

MAKING IT HAPPEN

- Define stakeholder expectations.
- Articulate the mission, structure, resource model, working practices, and communication protocols for the internal audit function.
- Develop a formal strategic plan and assess company risks.
- Establish short- and long-term budgets for the internal audit function.
- Launch fieldwork quickly and, concurrently, assess any further needed skill sets.
- Develop internally or acquire (by outsourcing) enabling internal audit infrastructure, methodologies, and technologies.
- Determine clear lines of communication between the internal audit function and all company stakeholders (primarily, however, with senior management and the audit committee).
- Measure the results of the internal audit function.

MORE INFO

Books:
Pickett, K. H. Spencer. *The Essential Handbook of Internal Auditing*. Chichester, UK: Wiley, 2005.
Pickett, K. H. Spencer. *Audit Planning: A Risk-Based Approach*. Hoboken, NJ: Wiley, 2006.

Standard:
"Auditing standard no. 5: An audit of internal control over financial reporting that is integrated with an audit of financial statements." Public Company Accounting Oversight Board (US), July 25, 2007. Online at: pcaobus.org/standards/auditing/pages/auditing_standard_5.aspx

Websites:
Chartered Institute of Internal Auditors (UK and Ireland): www.iia.org.uk
Institute of Internal Auditors (IIA): www.theiia.org

The Assurance versus Consulting Debate: How Far Should Internal Audit Go?
by Michael Parkinson

EXECUTIVE SUMMARY
- The internal audit function of most organizations contains highly qualified and experienced individuals who, over a number of years, develop a detailed understanding of the organization's risks and operations.
- Thus, when a complex business risk issue emerges, the internal auditors may be well placed to help address it.
- Under these circumstances, does the short-term advantage of using the internal auditors as consultants to address the problem outweigh the longer-term cost of potentially compromising the level of assurance provided to the board and top management?

INTERNAL AUDIT

Internal auditors have described their discipline as an "assurance and consulting activity." Such a definition immediately begs the question: what is the difference, and what should the balance be?

Assurance has been variously defined. The dictionary definition, "a statement or indication that inspires confidence," differs quite considerably from the statement to be found in Assurance Standards (quoted here from the Australian Assurance Standards Board): "[the level of] satisfaction as to the reliability of information provided. The degree of satisfaction achieved is determined by the nature and extent of procedures performed by the auditor, the results of procedures and the objectivity of the evidence obtained." The high standards of evidence and the limited range of reports that flow from this latter definition are a long way from the resource commitment and the kind of reports that most managers want from their internal auditors. Most managers are seeking something more akin to the first definition, but they want to retain the reliability provided by objective, evidence-based reviews.

Consulting, on the other hand, is generally accepted as meaning the provision of professional advice. It implies an underlying professional competence that is used in making judgments about a given situation and relied on by the user of the consultant's advice.

While the description of internal auditing set out above is widely accepted, it is not the only definition to be found. Many internal auditors omit "consulting" from their scope, believing that providing advice impedes their objectivity. Others assess their value to the organization by the volume of consulting requests that they receive from management.

There are two risks to the organization reflected in this issue: excess levels of consulting may compromise the assurance that the organization requires, but prohibiting consulting work may prevent the organization from using the skills and experience of the internal auditors to solve business problems.

ASSURANCE AND CONSULTING

There is a range of internal and external customers for assurance provided by internal audit. The primary customer is, classically, the audit committee of the organization. While it is often the case that internal audit reports elsewhere in the organization, most internal auditors say that they serve the organization through the stewards of its owners: the board, or its equivalent. (In mature organizations this is reflected in the internal auditor's reporting lines—to the audit committee for functional purposes and to the chief executive for administration.) The audit committee is the board's agent for assurance.

The Audit Committee has three basic sources for the assurance it needs: organizational management, who are resourced to run the organization, have (as a group) full knowledge of its operations and have a responsibility to account for their activity; the internal auditor, who should be resourced to examine the critical risks of the organization and is independent of management operations; and external audit, who are resourced to examine the financial statements of the organization and offer an opinion that is independent of both management and internal audit.

The mutual independence of the three arms of assurance is critical. In some circumstances, it is appropriate for the audit committee to seek confirmation from all assurance sources before making critical decisions. Any activity that might impair independence or objectivity will limit the value of the assurance provided and therefore limit the confidence of the audit committee—consulting activity can impair objectivity.

Most of the risks of the organization are beyond the scope of the external auditor. The reliability of the critical control systems for these risks is attested only by management and internal audit. In these circumstances any impairment to internal audit objectivity can be a serious issue.

Assurance

While management might see assurance as little more than a statement of comfort, from the auditor's point of view there are three components: a model of what ought to occur (the normative model); an evidence-based assessment of what is occurring; and an analysis of the difference.

For the internal auditor, identifying the normative model is often an arguable process; it is only occasionally provided by an external authority, such as accounting standards. Frequently the organization has not specified the manner in which it should operate, or even the mechanisms by which performance will be measured. The internal auditor's first task might therefore be to construct a normative model for the organization.

Even when the organization has a model of operation, it is the internal auditor's duty to consider whether that model adequately addresses the organization's risks. Internal auditors are required to apply their own judgment about whether the level of risk being accepted by the organization is appropriate. The assurance that comes from this process has a level of consulting implicit within it.

Many internal audit service providers, perhaps driven by fear of an increasingly litigious society, are unwilling to provide any form of assurance at all. This seems to arise from confusion between "assurance" as used by internal auditors and what an external auditor means by the word.

Consulting

As soon as the internal auditors provide recommendations to management, they have stepped from the area of assurance into that of providing advice. This is, strictly, consulting. Some internal auditors feel uncomfortable about providing recommendations because they believe that it will impair their independence should they review the same area again. However, when a process fault has been properly analyzed by the internal auditor, the next step—suggesting a solution—is logical. Often the solution will be jointly developed by the internal auditor and responsible members of management. It is, therefore, management's solution, but it is still delivered with the internal auditor's (implicit) approval.

The internal audit function of many organizations is a significant pool of talented individuals. These individuals, by the nature of their roles, can develop a deep understanding of the organization. When the introduction of new systems or processes is contemplated, internal auditors are in a position to provide sound advice, based on their knowledge of the organization and their skill in the analysis of control systems. This type of consulting activity is an extension of the assurance process. While it is in relation to an activity that has not yet commenced, and is in the form of strong advice, the commentary of internal audit should still be regarded as recommendations and not as instructions. Some organizations ask their internal auditors to sign off or approve the implementation of systems or processes. This act moves the internal auditor from the role of adviser to the role of manager and is extremely dangerous; it makes the internal auditor partially responsible for the system or process.

The conduct of consulting activities by internal auditors is still constrained by the internal auditing standards. This has a number of direct benefits, as all the conclusions and observations made by the internal auditor will continue to be based on robust evidence.

These same standards that make the work of the internal auditor valuable also mean that internal audit consulting cannot be a private service. If the internal auditors observe control faults, or risks that would be reported if the project were an assurance review, they are required to report these issues (or make sure that they are reported) to responsible management and the audit committee.

An extreme form of consulting is where an internal auditor is seconded to a line area for a defined period. During this time they are not operating as an internal auditor and the removal of this individual from the internal audit function must be transparently reported. Such a situation encompasses many of the same issues that arise when an internal auditor is given a consulting function.

ASSURANCE VERSUS CONSULTING

The most commonly cited drawback of using internal audit as a consulting service is the threat of self-audit. That is, those who rely on the assurance process ask whether they will be able to get assurance from either the internal auditors or management if the auditors have consulted with management in the development of the process. If the internal audit function has been asked to sign off the process, then this may be a real problem, but it is arguable that the internal auditor would have the same problem if management were to implement an extensive set of recommendations as the result of an assurance review.

This risk, while real, can be managed. The mechanisms devised for internal auditors to manage the impairment that arises from having worked in an area under review can be applied to this situation. The obvious step is to use an alternative internal auditor—either another individual within the function or one obtained from outside the organization. When this cannot be done, the impairment must be declared in the assurance process and the internal audit project should be thoroughly reviewed by someone who was not involved in the original consulting exercise. In this case, although the independence of the internal auditor is impaired, an acceptable level of objectivity can be maintained.

There is a greater difficulty in relation to service providers. It might occur that one unit of a professional services firm is providing consulting services at the same time that another unit is assisting the internal audit function. In this case, the tight financial interdependence of the units means that one unit cannot give objective assurance in relation to the other. In this scenario it may also be difficult to enforce the requirement that internal auditors providing advice must report adverse control findings through the audit committee.

The second serious risk to consider is the impact of consulting activities on the assurance program. An internal audit program will have been approved by the audit committee to achieve a desired level of assurance. If the use of internal audit resources in consulting activities is to effectively reduce the level of assurance provided, the permission of the audit committee should be obtained.

Internal auditors have an underlying responsibility to protect the organization. This does not mean that internal audit has a primary responsibility to management, nor the obligation to respond to whatever management requires. On the other hand, the internal audit function cannot stand outside the organization when it has skills that can be effectively applied to resolving issues. There is a need for the internal auditor to use judgment.

Internal audit consulting can help management make decisions that have the best control consequences for the organization, but following internal audit advice does not mean that the consequences of decisions taken belong to the internal auditors. The consequences, good or bad, of implementing internal audit recommendations belong to management. Internal audit should not take credit for good outcomes, and management should not blame the auditors for the bad ones.

CONCLUSION: FINDING THE BALANCE

Assurance is, perhaps, directed at minimizing loss; consulting at maximizing benefit. Both are valuable to an organization. However, consulting can be an excuse for putting internal audit in the position of management, or doing work that management should be doing. This must be avoided; internal audit should provide information, not take decisions.

Finding the right balance requires a conscious strategy. The audit committee must, on behalf of the organization, determine how much assurance is needed, plan it appropriately, and resource it.

The Audit Committee must determine the rules under which consulting will be offered and manage the amount of consulting that Internal Audit does. This involves requiring reports from all the work done by Internal Audit, whether it is consulting or assurance.

MAKING IT HAPPEN

The audit committee must determine the rules under which consulting will be offered and manage the amount of consulting that internal audit does:

- Specify the assurance responsibilities of internal auditors in an assurance program;
- Specify, in the internal audit charter, the consulting services that internal auditors may provide, and the circumstances under which they may be provided;
- Require reports to the audit committee for all the work done by internal auditors, whether it is consulting or assurance;
- Monitor achievement of the assurance program.

MORE INFO

Books:

Fraser, John, and Hugh Lindsay. *20 Questions Directors Should Ask about Internal Audit*. Toronto, ON: Canadian Institute of Chartered Accountants, 2007.

Reding, Kurt F., Paul J. Sobel, Urton L. Anderson, Michael J. Head, *et al*. *Internal Auditing: Assurance and Consulting Services*. 2nd ed. Orlando, FL: IIA Research Foundation, 2009.

Reports:

Institute of Internal Auditors (IIA). "International standards for the professional practice of internal auditing." Orlando, FL: IIA. Online at:
www.theiia.org/guidance/standards-and-guidance/ippf/standards

International Auditing and Assurance Standards Board. "ISAE 3000: Assurance engagements other than audits or reviews of historical financial information." International Federation of Accountants, 2003. Online at: www.accountability21.net/uploadedFiles/Issues/ISAE_3000.pdf

Should Internal Auditing Assess Board Performance? by Sridhar Ramamoorti

EXECUTIVE SUMMARY

- Internal auditors are increasingly being challenged to look at ways by which they might evaluate and improve the governance process.
- When properly leveraged, the internal audit function can play a critical role in promoting and supporting effective corporate governance.
- Internal auditors must understand and recognize that corporate governance is a politically charged area, managed by individuals at the top of the organization, including the board and its key committees.
- The governance audit encompasses: gaining consensus on a definition of governance, ascertaining whether an assurance and/or consulting engagement is more appropriate, scoping the project along with commensurate resource allocation decisions, and ensuring proper communication flow before, during, and after the engagement is concluded.
- Examples of assisting the nominating and governance committees, as well as auditing executive compensation and the compensation committee are discussed.
- The experience of Kaiser Permanente's efforts to "improve their governance processes" is described.
- The importance of changing the outlook of the internal audit function, making it more proactive and influential, is highlighted.

INTRODUCTION

"Ultimately, the overall responsibility for the organization and its assets, and for its perpetuation into the future, rests squarely with the board." Dr Thomas R. Horton, Former Chairman, National Association of Corporate Directors.

Internal auditors are increasingly being challenged to look at ways by which they might evaluate and improve the governance process. Given their competencies and expertise in the areas of governance, risk management, controls, and compliance, when properly leveraged the internal audit function can play a critical role in promoting and supporting effective corporate governance (Ramamoorti, 2003). Indeed, internal auditors' skills in risk management and their broad-based perspective of the organization uniquely position them as a valuable resource for facilitating superior corporate governance outcomes.

Auditing governance can be a daunting challenge simply because it represents uncharted territory, and much of how to go about it in practice is ill-defined, amorphous, and intangible. Typically, the goals of corporate governance reform include, first and foremost, ensuring the organization's survival (i.e. pre-empting or mitigating catastrophic risks), and then, when continued existence has been assured, to thrive, to grow, and to remain profitable. In other words, the core strategy for management is to exploit upside risks or opportunities consistent with the business model, while simultaneously managing downside risks or threats to organizational objectives. Internal auditors can provide assurance services to the board on how successfully such strategies are being implemented by management.

"Today internal audit should be as much about performance as it is about conformance," contends Christopher McRostie, CEO of the Institute of Internal Auditors—Australia. However, he concedes that this challenge is formidable, citing Niccolò Machiavelli's *The Prince*, written in 1513: "...there is nothing more difficult to plan, more doubtful of success, nor more dangerous to manage than the creation of a new system. For the initiator has the enmity of all who would profit by the preservation of the old institution and merely lukewarm defenders in those who would gain by the new one." McRostie adds: "At the end of the day we need conformance and performance—they are not mutually exclusive. Despite the headline-hogging Enron, HIH, WorldCom and like fiascos, more money is lost in corporate disappointment than in corporate collapse."

The internal audit function can provide the board objective assurance about the organization's governance, risk management, and control processes (Swanson, 2010). However, internal auditors must recognize that corporate governance is a politically charged area, managed by individuals at the top of the organization, including the board and its key committees (Marks, 2007). Hence, to audit the governance process not only requires internal auditors with the appropriate stature, independence, and objectivity, but also the credibility and the formal organizational mandate to engage in such activity. Clearly, assessing the effectiveness of governance activities requires access to highly confidential and sensitive information, with a corresponding need for discreet and delicate handling by the auditors.

Marks (2007) persuasively argues that "Audits of governance, whether assurance or consulting in nature, may not be easy and often carry political risk. However, they are clearly important and should be given strong consideration in the audit plan—not just because they are required by the Standards, but also because they add value to the organization."

With this background, there is no argument that internal audit can play an extremely important role in being tasked with assessing board performance. Indeed, such a mandate would be in line with the IIA's International Professional Practices Framework (2011a) and the Standards (2011b) related to governance.

It is abundantly clear from a quick reading of Standard 2110 that the IIA Standards expect internal auditors to make assessments of and recommendations for enhancing the governance process within their respective organizations.

EXCERPT FROM THE INTERNATIONAL STANDARDS FOR THE PROFESSIONAL PRACTICE OF INTERNAL AUDITING

2110: Governance

The internal audit activity must assess and make appropriate recommendations for improving the governance process in its accomplishment of the following objectives:

- Promoting appropriate ethics and values within the organization;
- Ensuring effective organizational performance management and accountability;
- Communicating risk and control information to appropriate areas of the organization; and
- Coordinating the activities of and communicating information among the board, external and internal auditors, and management.

2110.A1

The internal audit activity must evaluate the design, implementation, and effectiveness of the organization's ethics-related objectives, programs, and activities.

2110.A2

The internal audit activity must assess whether the information technology governance of the organization supports the organization's strategies and objectives.

Source: IIA (2011b).

THE GOVERNANCE AUDIT

The governance audit can focus specifically on the following key areas of corporate governance.

- The qualifications of directors, including their "unique value proposition."
- Responsibilities of the governance, nominating, compensation, and audit committees.
- The relation between the board and executive management.
- Board (self-)evaluations.

When planning either an assurance or consulting project around governance, internal auditors should have in mind the following.

- *Consensus on underlying concepts:* Agree on a definition of governance to enable proper delineation of the scope of the project.
- *Assurance and/or consulting engagement:* Ascertain whether the primary objective is to undertake an assurance or a consulting engagement, or a combination of the two, for the organization. The benefits of each option must be assessed.
- *Project scoping:* For instance, governance projects may be limited to reviews of selected activities rather than be a comprehensive assessment of corporate governance.
- *Resource allocation:* As noted earlier, such engagements are high-profile and require top-notch professionals because of the high degree of visibility to top management and the board. The maturity of the professionals who are assigned, as well as their stature, relationships, and credibility will matter greatly when they are interviewing top management and board members.
- *Communication flow:* Information and communications must be effectively managed throughout such engagements. It is critical that all engagement team members fully understand their roles and responsibilities. Ongoing feedback on interviews and the overall conduct of the engagement must be shared in a timely manner with all concerned. This is also important to navigate any "political landmines."

If a consulting project is performed, the auditor and management and/or the board should agree on the timing and form for presenting the results of the review. Questions to consider include the following.

- *Formality, timing:* Will recommendations be formally or informally communicated during the project, or only at its conclusion?
- *Recipient(s) of the report:* Who will receive the report? Who will act on the findings and recommendations?
- *Follow-up actions:* What follow-up is necessary to ensure appropriate consideration and action on the findings and recommendations?

Even before commencing such assurance and/or consulting engagements, it is important for the internal audit function and management and/or the board to reach consensus on the overall purpose of the engagement as well as the reporting protocols, including the following.

- *Form and content of the report:* What is the report's nature and scope? What will the report contain? What matters will be discussed verbally? Who are the parties involved, and who is responsible for follow-up actions?
- *Distribution of the report:* This is especially important if the report includes sensitive or confidential information. As a general principle, limited distribution is advisable unless there is a compelling reason to broaden the distribution list.
- *Follow-up:* There needs to exist a pre-established process for reviewing report results and obtaining responses, including action plans. Who will manage the implications of any noted ethical violations, illegal activities, or other problematic findings? For example, potential conflicts of interest or illegal activities may need to be reported to regulators, and culpable individuals may need to be fired.

ASSISTING THE NOMINATING AND GOVERNANCE COMMITTEES

Effective corporate governance is first and foremost predicated on whether the company has the right set of directors and whether they work well as a group. Hence, it is extremely important to review the qualifications of the board members critically, and to make replacements where necessary. Internal audit can be an independent, objective function to be given this task.

As described in *Corporate Governance and the Board: What Works Best* (PwC, 2000),

a personal inventory of what members of the board bring to their role can help to identify each board member's unique value proposition. In general, board members must possess a whole gamut of desirable characteristics, such as integrity, judgment, credibility, trustworthiness, capacity for strategic thinking, intuition, vision, industry knowledge, communication skills, decision-making ability, interpersonal skills, willingness to participate actively, and the ability to handle conflict constructively. No doubt this is a tall order. Which is why it makes sense to have an impartial review of board members' characteristics and potential to contribute to the organization in an oversight capacity by the internal audit function.

According to *Corporate Governance and the Board: What Works Best* (PwC, 2000), among many other attributes, effective board members must:

- have the expertise to ask insightful questions;
- have the courage and conviction to make tough decisions;
- treat all stakeholders (analysts, investors, the media, management, and staff) equally;
- respect the confidentiality of board service;
- bring insight, knowledge, judgment, and analytical skill to the board;
- establish a value-based culture through word and action;
- aggressively and constructively consider emerging customer preferences, technology risks and opportunities, quality issues, supply chain, e-commerce, and new product and market opportunities;
- differentiate and balance discussion, guidance, and directives;
- provide operational and tactical guidance to management;
- demonstrate ethical values at the board table and in contact with employees and stakeholders;
- validate management-supplied data using internal and external information and sources;
- rely on resources, such as internal auditors, for advice and counsel for everything from analysis of operations and assessment of risk to recommendations for improved corporate governance;
- specifically consider the ethical values of proposed transactions;
- continually assess management's plans to ensure future success;
- link the organization's performance to tactics, strategy, and drivers of real value;
- link personal performance to corporate

strategy and short- and long-term organizational and personal goals;
- measure board performance against financial and nonfinancial metrics and forward-looking measures such as benchmarking and best practices;
- pay more attention to the future than to the past;
- commit to the ongoing training and development needed to maintain and enhance individual and collective effectiveness;
- devote time to frequent offline interactions among members, management, and staff;
- have the capacity, desire, and commitment to carry out these responsibilities.

Internal audit may use a Likert-type scale to develop measurable criteria for each of these qualitative attributes. For each board member a composite score may be arrived at, and the nominating/governance committee should be kept apprised of any board members who fall below acceptable composite score thresholds.

AUDITING EXECUTIVE COMPENSATION AND THE COMPENSATION COMMITTEE

"By simply being willing to subject themselves to an executive compensation audit," assert Ramamoorti and Balakrishnan (2010), "compensation committees can do much to bring transparency to executive compensation design and disclosures." Accordingly, the executive compensation and benefits audit process will ensure that the resulting executive compensation packages have credibility and integrity.

An executive compensation audit can focus on one or all of the five key dimensions listed below.

- *Understanding organizational mission and objectives:* Internal audit must seek to link this understanding to corporate governance and enterprise risk management and how it relates to the design of executive compensation and awards.
- *Compensation committee:* Ensure that these board members are independent directors and do not have undisclosed conflicts of interest.
- *Compensation consultants:* Assess how compensation consultants are selected, and evaluate the independence as well as the competence of those so engaged.
- *Reasonableness of executive pay and perks:* A particularly delicate and challenging area to audit, this requires the highest degree of

sensitivity, confidentiality, and collaboration with the board members.
- *Regulatory compliance:* Ensure that all regulatory requirements are met (for example, compensation discussion and analysis) and that adequate disclosures have been included.

CHANGING THE INTERNAL AUDIT FUNCTION'S OUTLOOK

Linda Bardo Nicholls, president of the Victoria division of the Australian Institute of Company Directors, humorously points out that internal audit should change from the "department of *No* to the department of *Did you know*?". Nicholls envisions a more proactive, influential role for internal auditors, with practitioners providing insight and analysis.

"Over the last decade, internal audit was focusing on complying with Sarbanes-Oxley," says Richard Chambers, the IIA's CEO. "Then, as we wound out of the initial phase of SOX, and into the financial crisis, the concern was with very fundamental risks—the financial performance of companies, and business and strategic risks. But two years ago, we started to see a dramatic shift to looking at the significant risk that inadequate corporate governance poses to the enterprise, and to the effectiveness of the risk management function."

Functionally reporting to the audit committee is vital because it is the ultimate source of an internal auditor's independence. It provides extra assurance that the internal auditor can do his or her job free of coercion and interference from senior management. There is no doubt that access to the audit committee is crucial because senior management can become prone to conflicts of interest at times when the need for transparency is greatest—such as when the company is being poorly or dishonestly managed. Indeed, internal audit needs to be in a position to keep the Board apprised of any behavioral and integrity risks at the top echelons of management.

Nicholls perceptively observes that "Strategic mismanagement, poor execution, survival without success and chronic underperformance are more costly than collapse, and these are the areas where internal auditors who are focused on performance—on what must go right—can make a meaningful difference."

Should Internal Auditing Assess Board Performance?

CASE STUDY

Kaiser Permanente's Internal Audit Services

As reported by Overmyer and Purcell (2010), in 2005 Kaiser Permanente's internal audit function performed a detailed self-assessment in preparation for its first external quality-assessment review in 2006.

Their assessment of, first, how and to what extent internal audit was "bringing a systematic, disciplined approach to evaluate and improve the effectiveness of governance processes," and, second, of how internal audit was fulfilling its role to "assess and make appropriate recommendations for improving governance processes" led to some surprising findings and prompted a critical examination of their effectiveness.

As Overmyer and Purcell (2010) noted, like many internal audit groups Kaiser's internal audit function's past work had often been more routine, including assessments of the antifraud program, periodic audits of executive expense reports, and reviews of board meeting expenses and travel policy. The audit function clearly understood its role to assess and make recommendations for improving risk management and internal controls. However, the challenge to assess and make recommendations for "improving governance processes" appeared to be a formidable undertaking.

The auditor should ensure that top management or board support and sponsorship exists for any governance project (Swanson, 2010). The support should include a commitment to provide the auditor with the access required to necessary information, as well as to respecting the results of the audit. In some organizations it may be appropriate to work with the general counsel to provide attorney–client privilege for the work if the results are likely to be sensitive—for example, if there is a likelihood that a board committee has not performed its responsibilities effectively.

Overmyer and Purcell (2010) also furnish some key considerations for this sort of effort. For instance, where the board or management has requested an assessment of the entire set of governance policies and practices, the work should be split among several projects over time, with associated reports. In such circumstances the auditor should also work with the board and management to ascertain how best to aggregate individual reports to make the overall assessment.

MORE INFO

Books:

Institute of Internal Auditors (IIA). *International Professional Practices Framework*. Altamonte Springs, FL: IIA Research Foundation, 2011a.

Swanson, Dan. *Swanson on Internal Auditing: Raising the Bar*. Ely, UK: IT Governance Publishing, 2010.

Articles:

Marks, Norman. "Internal audits of governance: Assessing organizational governance can be complicated and may involve political risk, but it should still be given strong consideration in the audit plan." *Internal Auditor* (December 2007). Online at: tinyurl.com/6yjgqgx

Overmyer, Cindy, and Neal Purcell. "The quiet revolution: Kaiser's internal audit expands governance role." *Directorship* (October/November 2010). Online at: tinyurl.com/657lcp8

Ramamoorti, Sridhar, and Usha R. Balakrishnan. "Carrots and sticks: By auditing executive compensation and benefits, auditors can help their organization move from risk to rewards management." *Internal Auditor* (October 2010). Online at: tinyurl.com/5wt9nd5

Standards:

Institute of Internal Auditors (IIA). "International standards for the professional practice of internal auditing (Standards)." Rev. ed. Altamonte Springs, FL: IIA, 2011b. Online at: www.theiia.org/guidance/standards-and-guidance/ippf/standards

Internal Auditing's Contribution to Sustainability by Jeffrey Ridley

EXECUTIVE SUMMARY

- Start with an understanding of, and an internationally recognized and accepted definition of, sustainability in your organization.
- Relate this definition to your organization's vision statement, strategies, and key objectives.
- Relate this definition to your terms of reference for internal auditing. Sustainability should be there as part of your role to provide assurance in the management of risk and controls.
- In today's and tomorrow's internal auditing engagements, the sustainability of your organization and of the planet should always be among your assurance objectives.
- If your terms of reference include assurance of governance in your organization, you have a much wider contribution to make in sustainability programs at board level.
- Whatever your internal auditing assurance role is in sustainability, you have the challenge and opportunities to develop this into consultancy and teaching roles covering all aspects of sustainability, at all levels in your organization.
- Contributing to the sustainability of your organization is the pinnacle of added value from your best-practice internal auditing services.

INTRODUCTION

Sustainability programs have three aims: people, planet, and profit. Few organizations today, across all sectors, will be without some form of sustainable development program—be it for altruistic reasons, required by regulation, or to stay at the cutting edge in their competitive market places. There can also be strong economic, environmental, and social reasons for marketing sustainable products and services: for reputational reasons and to control energy costs, or, even more importantly, to attract and keep both staff and investment.

Sustainability means more than just the economic, environmental, and social challenges an organization faces in its everyday and future operations: it means the ethics in these operations, touching on all the lives of those in the organization, its stakeholders, and the planet. The objectives of all sustainable development programs must be measured, and the results reported in and outside the organization. Stakeholders and society need to be assured independently that such measures are recorded accurately and in timely fashion before being reported. There are opportunities for internal auditing to contribute its independent and objective assurance services as an auditor as well as a consultant and teacher. Such a contribution can take best-practice internal auditing to a high level of added value.

WHAT IS SUSTAINABILITY?

Most governments and many organizations now define sustainability widely to include current and future issues and possible events that can impact an organization's resources and stakeholders at community, national, and global levels. The Global Reporting Initiative's (GRI) 2002 "Sustainability reporting guidelines" defined corporate social responsibility (CSR) as part of sustainability, and sustainability as "one of the three ideas that are playing a pivotal role in shaping how business and other organizations operate in the 21st century." The other two ideas stated by GRI are accountability and governance. Linking sustainability into accountability and governance is an important statement for internal auditors in their assurance role. Sustainability programs should be a part of every organization's governance structure and practices in all sectors—private, public, and voluntary. This is now recognized globally. The now well-known GRI "triple bottom line" reporting of economic, social, and environmental performance has been adopted by many organizations as part of their annual reporting to stakeholders. The European Commission and national governments in Europe, if not the world, have been and are continuing to recommend triple bottom line reporting of performance. In some countries and for some companies this is now a legal/regulatory requirement.

Standards and awards for sustainable programs exist at national and international levels. At international level there are sustainability management and leadership standards for environmental, social, and risk (ISO 14000, 26000, and 31000, respectively), human rights (SA 8000; see SAI, 2008), ethics (GoodCorporation, 2010), and corporate responsibility and sustainable development (the AA1000 series published by AccountAbility). One example of national awards is the UK Business in the Community annual awards for corporate responsibility run in association with the *Financial Times* newspaper. These recognize and celebrate companies that have a presence in the United Kingdom and which have shown innovation, creativity, and a sustained commitment to corporate responsibility.

The United Nations Global Compact (UNGC) in its recent research "A new era of sustainability" (Lacy *et al.*, 2010) continues the reinforcement of economic, environmental, and social reporting with its definition of sustainability:

"Throughout this report, we use the term 'sustainability' to encompass environmental, social and corporate governance issues, as embodied in the United Nations Global Compact's Ten Principles. These ten principles [cover] areas of human rights, labour, the environment and anti-corruption..."

Consider how the following ten principles, published by the UNGC in 2004, are embedded in your own organization's strategies and operations and, more importantly, how they are audited.

Human Rights
- *Principle 1:* Businesses should support and respect the protection of internationally proclaimed human rights.

- *Principle 2:* They should make sure that they are not complicit in human rights abuses.

Labor Standards
- *Principle 3:* Businesses should uphold the freedom of association and the effective recognition of the right to collective bargaining.
- *Principle 4:* The elimination of all forms of forced and compulsory labor.
- *Principle 5:* The effective abolition of child labor.
- *Principle 6:* The elimination of discrimination in respect of employment and occupation.

Environment
- *Principle 7:* Businesses should support a precautionary approach to environmental challenges.
- *Principle 8:* They should undertake initiatives to promote greater environmental responsibility.
- *Principle 9:* They should encourage the development and diffusion of environmentally friendly technologies.

Anticorruption
- *Principle 10:* Businesses should work against corruption in all its forms, including extortion and bribery.

This wide definition of sustainability recognizes and reinforces the importance of an organization's sustainable strategy as being part of the ethical way it conducts its business. Questions every

---

CASE STUDY

What the AA1000 Series Means for Internal Auditors[1]

Internal auditors may find the AA1000 series standards formulated by AccountAbility useful when they are providing assurance or consulting services in the field of sustainability (i.e. ethics and corporate social responsibility). It is the managers of the organization who are responsible for establishing and implementing policies in this area. However, internal auditors may be in a position to facilitate their work by telling them about the AA1000 series and, in particular, the "AccountAbility principles standard" and the "Stakeholder engagement standard." As AccountAbility has designed AA1000 Assurance Standard (AA1000 AS (2008)) for external assurance providers, it is likely that internal auditors will never use it in full. However, the standard itself and its supporting guidance can assist internal auditors in conducting their own internal audit engagements in the area of sustainability. The IIA (2011) standards require internal auditors to establish criteria against which to evaluate the subject matter of the engagement. The AA1000 AS and its guidance are a good source of criteria for the area of sustainability. If the organization has engaged external providers to give assurance on sustainability reporting, the internal audit function will wish to coordinate and liaise with those providers. It will be useful to understand one of the principal standards that they may be following. Given that the AA1000 AS follows processes similar to those of the ISO standards, this area may provide a learning and development opportunity for internal auditors who are interested in sustainability and in working as external assurance providers.

board and internal auditor should ask are listed in the next section.

The answers will always lead sustainability risk assessments to controls, challenges, weaknesses, strengths, and improvements. The questions in the box are a benchmark for those every internal auditor should seek to answer.

HOW GOOD IS YOUR SUSTAINABILITY CONDUCT?

Is it:
- required by your regulators?
- led from the top—by style and values?
- embedded in all strategies, plans, and operations?
- seen in all structures and systems?
- communicated internally to everyone—staff and visitors?
- communicated externally to all stakeholders?
- known across all supply chains?
- included in all review processes?
- independently monitored?

Does it:
- create or reduce wealth?
- improve or reduce the quality of performance?
- increase or decrease the efficiency and effectiveness of all staff?
- increase or decrease customers' satisfaction?
- improve or lower the organization's reputation in society?
- increase or decrease competitive edge?
- consider or ignore all stakeholders' needs?
- encourage or discourage good behavior?

Do you have:
- a formal and published code of conduct?
- a procedure for dealing with all irregularities?
- a whistleblowing procedure?
- practical ethics training for all your staff?
- environmental, health, and safety policies?
- environmental, social, and ethical accounting, auditing, and reporting?

Source: Ridley (2008).

SUSTAINABILITY IN GOVERNANCE, RISK MANAGEMENT, AND CONTROL PROCESSES

In all economic, environmental, and social sustainability programs the Cadbury (1992) corporate governance principles of *openness*, *integrity*, and *accountability* should be seen and practiced. The linking of sustainability programs into corporate governance by the UNGC is essential if the challenges of sustainability are to be addressed successfully across the world. The UNGC research highlights today's need

"to embed environmental, social and corporate governance issues within core business" and "environmental, social and governance issues should be fully integrated into the strategy and operations of a company" (Lacy *et al.*, 2010). There is already evidence that these questions are being addressed and answered by law and regulation in many countries. For example, in the United Kingdom the Companies Act 2006 (Sect. 417) now requires publicly quoted companies to report annually on economic, environmental, and social issues raised by their operations, stating how these are being addressed strategically and how they are managed, measured, and monitored in every operation. Many organizations now do publish statements internally and externally on sustainability programs as a part of their good corporate governance, risk management, and control practices.

In 1992 the Commission of Sponsoring Organizations of the Treadway Commission (COSO) published its now internationally well-known integrated pyramid framework for internal control, which uses the following components:
- control environment;
- risk assessment;
- control activities;
- information and communication;
- monitoring.

This was followed in 2004 by a publication on enterprise risk management (ERM), defining this as "a process, effected by the entity's board of directors, management, and other personnel, applied in a strategy setting and across the enterprise, designed to identify potential events that may affect the entity, and manage risk to be within the risk appetite, to provide reasonable assurance regarding the achievement of objectives." ERM is now a process that must consider sustainability as a "potential event" in all its assessments of risk. It is considered to be the best guidance for risk management in organizations. The 2004 publication has been followed by other COSO statements on ERM, the latest being "Strengthening enterprise risk management for strategic advantage" in 2009.

Currently, the formality of risk management has been addressed by the Association of Certified and Chartered Accountants in its recent analysis of the elements of good risk management (Davies, Moxey, and Welch, 2010). This lists the essential requirement for "an independent assurance function that gives objective assurance, to the board or the non-executive directors." An internal audit function that complies with the Institute of Internal

Auditor's *International Professional Practices Framework* (IIA, 2011), with its defined "systematic, disciplined approach" to assurance, is in an ideal position to review and report on sustainability risks.

SUSTAINABILITY IS AN IMPORTANT FOCUS FOR PROFESSIONAL INTERNAL AUDITING

The IIA's first statement on the responsibilities of the internal auditor in 1947 described internal auditing as an "independent appraisal activity within an organization for the review of the accounting, financial, and other operations as a basis for protective and constructive service to management" (Brink, 1977). The objectives of internal auditing were stated as being:

"...to assist management in achieving the most efficient administration of the operations of the organization. The total objective has two major phases, as follows:

1 The protection of the interests of the organization, including the pointing out of existing deficiencies to provide a basis for appropriate corrective action.
2 The furtherance of the interests of the organization, including the recommendation of changes for the improvement of the various phases of operations."

These objectives have formed the foundation for all subsequent developments of internal auditing as it has changed from a service to a recognized international profession. Later, in 1981, the "service to management" was changed to "service to the organization," recognizing a changing role of reporting to the board as well as to management, and also a widening scope of assurance covering stakeholder influences and needs in the achievement of an organization's objectives. The IIA's national institute, the Chartered Institute of Internal Auditors, United Kingdom and Ireland (IIA UK and Ireland), published guidance on corporate social responsibility (CSR) auditing for internal auditors in the 1990s and early 2000s. In 2003 it published a statement discussing emerging social responsibility issues such as trust, materiality, and brand and the role of internal auditing (IIA UK and Ireland, 2003b):

"The internal auditor is a vital conduit to the creation of trust. The internal auditor is already contributing to a number of CSR and sustainability issues by keeping management informed on aspects of operational and compliance issues, which is part of their core function, as well as brand management audits and through participation in the stakeholder dialogue process. Also, the increasing importance of CSR and sustainability and its impact on risk management brings additional challenges involving the control environment, including the provision and installation of effective management and reporting systems, which will provide clarity and transparency, and therefore trust."

And:

"The internal auditor...has a key role to play in determining the materiality of the content of the CSR and sustainability report. This is a responsibility that can only increase with the burgeoning of CSR and sustainability reports, both in volume and size of content."

The services provided by many of today's professional internal auditors have developed into a wide scope of assurance, consulting, and teaching. There is clearly evidence in the past and today that internal auditing as a profession is being guided into being involved in the visions for sustainability programs—guided by, for example, the IIA to include this involvement in its annual planning and engagements into governance, risk management, and control implementation. Yet these internal auditing services are not evident in all organizations today, and they vary across those organizations where internal auditing has established a presence in sustainability. However, this involvement will grow in the future, both in practice and through the continuous development and improvement of internal auditing professional practices, fueled by board needs and regulation.

The IIA Research Foundation has promoted and sponsored international research into the internal auditing role in governance, risk management, and control, including their influence and impact on sustainability. Its research paper "Sustainability and internal auditing" (published in book form as Niewlands, 2006) develops *a* model of internal auditing relevant to sustainability in emerging markets. In a case study developed by the research, internal auditors are declared to have the following opportunities to demonstrate added value to their sustainable organization. The roles that auditors can play include:

- assisting in the design/implementation of the sustainability management system;
- assisting in creating sustainability awareness or training employees;
- performing audits of limited scope requested by top management;
- performing supply chain audits;

- performing compliance audits;
- advising on the appointment of outside assessors;
- coordinating audit activities by external assessors.

The IIA, in its latest statements on CSR and internal auditing, "Evaluating corporate social responsibility/sustainable development" (2010b), brings together and updates its past guidance for internal auditors in adding value to sustainability strategies in their organizations. In the introduction it emphasizes that:

"Internal auditors should understand the risks and controls related to CSR objectives. Where appropriate, the CAE [chief audit executive] should plan to audit, facilitate control self-assessments, verify results, and consult on the various subjects. Internal auditors should maintain the skills and knowledge necessary to understand and evaluate the governance, risks, and controls of CSR strategies."

This guide introduces two approaches to auditing sustainability—auditing by (CSR) element and auditing by stakeholder group. Elements are listed and discussed as: governance, ethics, environment, transparency, health, safety, security, human rights, work conditions, and community investment. Stakeholders are listed and discussed as: employees and their families, environment, customers, suppliers, communities, shareholders, and investors. Both approaches can be as separate engagements or as part of a functional/system engagement. When sustainability audit plans are developed, it suggests that the following questions should always be asked and developed into a program of assurance to be reported at board level.
· How well is CSR information communicated across the organization and its supply chains?
- Which CSR reporting standards have been adopted?
- How are CSR strategies and priorities established/communicated?
- Are organizational CSR responsibilities documented for all elements?
- Is the organization signatory to any CSR standards of performance?

In my book *Cutting Edge Internal Auditing* (Ridley, 2008), I develop the following *principium* for all internal auditors at the cutting edge of their profession:

"Internal auditing has a responsibility to contribute to the processes of assessing reputation risks and advising at all levels in their organizations on how reputation can be managed and enhanced through good corporate responsibility practices."

This statement is based on many years of research and observation of best-practice internal auditing. Sustainability should always be the foundation of every internal audit engagement.

Writing on the social responsibility audit in the 1970s, John Humble (1973) cited Peter Drucker's key areas in which an organization must set objectives as:
- business(es);
- profitability;
- innovation;
- market standing;
- productivity;
- financial and physical resources;
- manager performance and development;
- worker performance and attitude;
- public (though Humble preferred "social") responsibility.

Little has changed! All of these areas are a part of every organization's objectives today and require independent assurance. Humble viewed the challenge of social responsibility at that time as follows: "...one of the critical and difficult management tasks is balancing these objectives at any time, taking into consideration the changing requirements of stockholders, employees, customers and society generally." He went on to define social responsibility as one of the key areas of the business, one that is "typically concerned with the external environment problems of pollution, community and consumer relations, and the internal environment problems of working conditions, minority groups, education and training."

Chambers and Rand (2010) recommend the following environmental control objectives as those which require assurance by internal audit.
- Provision of an authorized and documented policy on environment issues as a framework for responsibly conducting related business activities.
- Minimization of the impact of the organization's activities on the environment.
- Ensuring that the organization's products are environmentally friendly.
- Ensuring that waste is minimized and properly disposed of.
- Avoidance of pollution and environmental contamination.
- The assessment, on an ongoing basis, of the environmental impacts of business operations and defining the requirements to be adhered to.
- Ensuring that alternative and potentially environmentally friendly processes and technologies are considered and implemented where justified.

- Minimization or avoidance of the use of scarce materials and non-renewable energy sources.
- Ensuring that harmful or hazardous materials and waste products are safely and responsibly transported and disposed of.
- Ensuring that all environmental legislation and regulations are fully complied with.
- Avoidance of adverse impacts on the organization's reputation and image.
- Ensuring that environmental issues are subject to monitoring and management.

CONCLUSION

The importance of all aspects of sustainability in organizations as part of risk management will continue to drive a need for assurance that the issue of sustainability is being addressed and controlled economically, effectively, and efficiently. Risk management, control, and independent monitoring are key to the successful implementation of all sustainability strategies. There is evidence in the past and today that professional internal auditing is being guided, is involved in, and is contributing to sustainability visions and programs at national and international levels. In practice that contribution will grow in the future through the continuous development of internal auditing professionalism and from the needs of the organizations in which internal auditors work. Sustainability strategies, programs, and reporting should always be a part of the scope and planning of all internal audit engagements.

MAKING IT HAPPEN

A Model of the Relevance of Sustainability to Internal Auditing
A model by Niewlands (2006) includes the following assurance, consulting, and teaching roles:
- Assistance in the design/implementation of the sustainability management system.
- Assistance in creating sustainability awareness or in training employees.
- Performing limited-scope audits requested by top management.
- Performing supply chain audits.
- Performing compliance audits.
- Advising on the appointment of outside assessors.
- Coordination of audit activities by external assessors.

Each of these actions can lead to one or more engagements in the internal auditing risk-based planning.

MORE INFO

Books:

Brink, Victor Z. *Foundations for Unlimited Horizons: The Institute of Internal Auditors 1941–1976*. Altamonte Springs, FL: IIA, 1977.

Chambers, Andrew, and Graham Rand. *Operational Auditing Handbook: Auditing Business and IT Processes*. 2nd ed. Chichester, UK: Wiley, 2010.

Humble, John William. *Social Responsibility Audit*. London, UK: Foundation for Business Responsibilities, 1973.

IIA. *International Professional Practices Framework (IPPF)*. Altamonte Springs, FL: IIA Research Foundation, 2011.

Nieuwlands, Hans. *Sustainability and Internal Auditing*. Altamonte Springs, FL: IIA Research Foundation, 2006.

Ridley, Jeffrey. *Cutting Edge Internal Auditing*. Chichester, UK: Wiley, 2008.

Reports:

Cadbury, Sir Adrian. "Report of the committee on the financial aspects of corporate governance." London, UK: Gee, December 1992. Online at: www.ecgi.org/codes/documents/cadbury.pdf

Chartered Institute of Internal Auditors (IIA UK and Ireland). "Sustainability, environmental and social responsibility assurance." 2002.

Chartered Institute of Internal Auditors. "Professional issues bulletin ethical and social; auditing and reporting—The challenge for the internal auditor." 2003a.

Chartered Institute of Internal Auditors. "Emerging corporate social responsibility issues: Trust, materiality and brand." 2003b.

Chartered Institute of Internal Auditors. "IIA risk based internal auditing tool." February 2006.
Chartered Institute of Internal Auditors. "Sustainability and the AA1000 series." 2009.
Committee of Sponsoring Organizations of the Treadway Commission (COSO). "Internal control—
    Integrated framework." AICPA, 1992.
COSO. "Enterprise risk management—Integrated framework." 2004. Online at:
    www.coso.org/ERM-IntegratedFramework.htm
COSO. Guidance on Monitoring Internal Control Systems. 3 vols. New York: AICPA, 2009a.
COSO. "Strengthening enterprise risk management for strategic advantage." Thought paper. COSO,
    2009b. Online at: www.coso.org/guidance.htm
COSO. "Effective enterprise risk management oversight: The role of the board of directors."
    Thought paper. COSO, 2009c. Online at: tinyurl.com/69q5hnu [PDF].
Davies, J., P. Moxey, and I. Welch. "Risk and reward: Tempering the pursuit of profit." Association
    of Chartered and Certified Accountants (ACCA), June 2010.
Global Reporting Initiative (GRI). "Sustainability reporting guidelines." G2 guidelines. 2002.
GoodCorporation. "The GoodCorporation Standard." Revised July 2010. 2010. Online at:
    www.goodcorporation.com/good-corporation-standard.php
Institute of Internal Auditors (IIA). "Evaluating corporate social responsibility/sustainable
    development." IPPF practice guide. February 2010b. Online at: tinyurl.com/6hd66n9
IIA UK and Ireland see Chartered Institute of Internal Auditors.
International Organization for Standardization (ISO). "ISO 14000 Environmental management."
    2004, 2007. Online at: tinyurl.com/68chdow
ISO. "ISO 31000:2009 Risk management." 2009. Online at:
    www.iso.org/iso/catalogue_detail.htm?csnumber=43170
ISO. "ISO 26000:2010 Guidance on social responsibility." 2010. Online at:
    www.iso.org/iso/catalogue_detail?csnumber=42546
Lacy, Peter, Tim Cooper, Rob Hayward, and Lisa Neuberger. "A new era of sustainability:
    UN Global Compact–Accenture CEO study 2010." Accenture, June 2010. Online at:
    tinyurl.com/2fk4x38 [PDF]
Organisation for Economic Co-operation and Development (OECD). "OECD guidelines for
    multinational enterprises." 2008.
Social Accountability International (SAI). "Social accountability 8000." SAI Standard SA8000. 2008.
    Online at: tinyurl.com/6x44g3f
United Nations Global Compact (UNGC). "The ten principles." 2004. Online at:
    www.unglobalcompact.org/aboutthegc/thetenprinciples
World Business Council For Sustainable Development (WBCSD). "Vision 2050: The new agenda for
    business." WBCSD report. 2010. Online at: tinyurl.com/6yf2ryw

Standards:
AccountAbility. "AA1000 series of standards." 2008. Online at: www.accountability.org/standards/

Websites:
AccountAbility: www.accountability.org
Business in the Community: www.bitc.org.uk
Chartered Institute of Internal Auditors: www.iia.org.uk
Committee of Sponsoring Organizations of the Treadway Commission (COSO): www.coso.org
European Confederation of Institutes of Internal Auditing (ECIIA): www.eciia.org
Global Reporting Initiative (GRI): www.globalreporting.org
GoodCorporation: www.goodcorporation.com
International Organization for Standardization (ISO): www.iso.org
Institute of Internal Auditors (IIA): www.theiia.org
Organisation for Economic Co-operation and Development (OECD): www.oecd.org
Social Accountability International: www.sa-intl.org
United Nations Global Compact: www.unglobalcompact.org
World Business Council for Sustainable Development: www.wbcsd.org

NOTES

1 Reprinted with permission from the IIA UK and
  Ireland (2009).

Considerations when Outsourcing Internal Audit by Peter Tickner

EXECUTIVE SUMMARY

- The key consideration is whether it is better to outsource internal audit, insource to support an existing function, or leave the function inhouse.
- Outsourcing is a valid option when cost or effectiveness is the single most important factor in considering the internal audit function.
- If the key consideration is efficiency, outsourcing may not be the best option.
- Outsourcing a small, existing internal audit function may be counterproductive.
- Outsourcing either a new internal audit function or a weak medium-to-large inhouse audit function is often an effective solution.
- Organizations should only consider outsourcing once they have evaluated the effectiveness of the existing inhouse function and have identified any improvements that they can implement. Only then can the merits of outsourcing be evaluated properly against those of retaining the inhouse function.
- Outsourcing can provide benefits by bringing skills not available to an inhouse team, but it can also risk losing the internal knowledge of the organization.
- A valid alternative for consideration is cosourcing (a partnership between inhouse and external provider), which may confer the advantages of outsourcing while keeping the effective parts of the inhouse function.
- Outsourcing can be to a specialist internal audit provider, a major organization with an audit arm such as one of the "big four" accounting firms, a specialist financial and business services provider, or a consortium formed from several internal audit departments in similar businesses.

INTRODUCTION

Outsourcing the internal audit function is a major step and one that should not be taken for the wrong reasons. Wrong reasons include a personality clash between the chief internal auditor and the person taking the decision to outsource, and a decision based on the perceived ineffectiveness of an under-resourced inhouse audit team that would struggle to perform well even if the most outstanding employees in the organization were assigned to it.

When deciding to outsource internal audit, three options should automatically be evaluated before a decision is taken. First, is the inhouse function fit for purpose? Second, is outsourcing a value-adding solution? Third, is a better option to cosource[1] where skills can be improved or cost savings made?

In some circumstances outsourcing can initially save costs and, in the long term, reduce the pension requirements of internal employees. Before taking such a step, the options must be weighed and a realistic evaluation of the consequences made. What may seem on paper a straightforward way of reducing internal audit costs and increasing the pool of expertise can have unexpected consequences if the starting position is not as the organization imagines it to be.

ASSESSING THE RISKS BEFORE OUTSOURCING INTERNAL AUDIT

For organizations with little or no existing internal audit resource there is often little risk associated with taking on an outsourced provider, particularly where the organization has a need for an effective internal audit function. This is not the case in organizations with any significant existing internal audit service. If the whole function is outsourced and employees, certainly initially, expect to transfer to the audit provider, the organization will need to ensure that the chosen provider can manage the transition and still provide the required level of service.[3]

One of the great mistakes in outsourcing so-called "noncore" services in the dogmatically driven "new management" 1990s was to end up handing over the existing staff to an external management regime that was driven only by its own desire to make as much profit as possible from the contract. This often had the dual impact of demotivating previously loyal staff who no longer felt wanted by the organization and therefore worked less loyally and less hard than before, while at the same time the organization ended up with fewer staff performing the work on the ground as the external management sought to extract maximum profits for their company.

CASE STUDY

Her Majesty's Treasury

In the 1990s the United Kingdom's HM Treasury embarked on a program of outsourcing noncore functions, including internal audit. An immediate and unexpected snag was hit when the head of internal audit pointed out that the inhouse function had been significantly under-resourced for several years. In order to outsource the function they would need to determine the true need for internal audit resources, as it would be unlikely that an external provider could give the levels of service required with the same or fewer staff than were currently employed. Also, an issue arose as to who was to ensure the quality of an outsourced service provider. The Treasury set standards for internal audit in government and could not be seen to fail to provide the right standard of service for itself. Leaving an outsourced contract to be evaluated by someone with no specific knowledge of the function would leave the Treasury exposed to external criticism. At the time, no senior finance staff outside of the audit department had any specialist knowledge of internal audit.

To ensure that there would be an adequate internal audit, the Treasury had an audit needs assessment prepared to go with the specification for the service to be outsourced. When senior management realized that a significant increase in staff and costs would follow, they opted for a cheaper compromise option of cosourcing specialist skills and retaining a core general audit team. Although this did not fully meet the identified audit need, it enabled the Treasury to demonstrate to external reviewers that it did take the level of resource needed for internal audit seriously. At the same time it enabled the Treasury to implement the extant UK government policy of using the private sector wherever that was the best placed to offer the appropriate skills and add value.

Lessons Learned from the Case Study

The decision to outsource has to be preceded by a thorough analysis of the data available about the existing service, both financial and structural. The 'political' decision in this instance backfired. Ultimately, management spent time and resources to end up with a more effective but more expensive audit service when the strategy had been to cut costs by outsourcing non-core functions. At the time of writing the Treasury's internal audit service is still largely in-house. It is unlikely that there is any meaningful benefit to be gained from outsourcing an existing small inhouse internal audit function. Almost certainly, the chief internal auditor or a senior audit manager will have to be retained to oversee the quality and performance of the outsourced function, and it is likely that the margin for making savings will be small if not nonexistent.[2]

Conclusions from the Case Study

In such circumstances the best option may well be to keep a small cadre of inhouse staff supplemented by an insourced external partner to provide one-off expertise and professional support, thereby avoiding the need to carry the costs of a full-time internal member of staff or a significant overhead to manage an outsourced function.

In similar organizational types—for instance public services such as the UK National Health Service, local authorities, and the police—it is not unusual to consider outsourcing to a consortium or a specialist internal audit provider rather than to one of the major accounting bodies.

Although the "big four" and those specializing in providing internal audit services among the larger players in the market place can often provide a lean, high-powered internal audit service, particularly for blue-chip and well-established commercial organizations, they are often a step too far for public bodies with tighter budgets and less flexibility about the existing workforce. Employees at major accountancy firms are generally better paid and rewarded than public sector equivalents, making genuine cost savings difficult. For some medium-sized and smaller players in the market it is not desirable to take on employees who are unlikely to add to their bottom line or marketability elsewhere. In effect, for many public bodies this can have a significant impact on any perceived savings from outsourcing internal audit, as more specialized, smaller organizations may feel unable to compete for the contract, leaving the field clear for a major player to bid at a less competitive price than might otherwise have been achieved.

MATCHING THE MODEL TO THE RIGHT CIRCUMSTANCES

Outsourcing based on reducing costs and inputs can make a tempting case for those on tight budgets, whether private or public sector, particularly in the current climate. It is important in such circumstances for an organization to think rationally about what it is seeking to achieve by outsourcing internal audit. Reducing costs can be achieved easily in the short term by reducing employees and/or their remuneration. Outsourcing can also help to reduce future pension costs. If the organization needs to pay lip service to an internal audit function only in order to keep its regulator or external stakeholders happy, then outsourcing based purely on lowest cost, regardless of quality, will achieve that objective.

If the existing inhouse service has come in for criticism and outsourcing is seen as the means to raise the internal audit bar, then cost becomes secondary to a visible improvement in quality of service. Here the change can be cost-neutral or even lead to a higher cost, but the decision to outsource will need to be based on the achievement of an expected standard of performance that is measurable and demonstrably better than the existing service, with outcome and output rather than input as the key drivers.

Getting the basket of performance measures right will be the key for most organizations. Defining an effective internal audit function is not as straightforward as at first it might seem. Describing performance in a rigid or mechanical way, such as an overly systematic approach through ISO standards and the like, can lead to a sterile audit service that fails to pick up the issues of most significance and risk to the organization. What use is an internal audit that routinely checks and reports on standard activities but fails to notice the hurricane waiting to blow the organization away?

UNDERSTANDING THE RISKS

Effective organizations will want an internal audit function that is on the ball and responsive to the "big ticket" issues of concern to top management while at the same time having its ear to the ground for those embarrassing problems that middle management often suppress to avoid blotting their copybook with top management and limiting their careers. There is no reason why a well-chosen outsourced provider cannot provide such a service, but there are risks that the organization needs to know are being effectively managed before they outsource.

First, will the outsourced provider have sufficient knowledge of the innermost parts of the organization? While any skilled internal auditor should be able to conduct a professional audit, half of the skill of an internal auditor is its ability to understand the business and read the people in the organization.

This is not so much a problem where the organization is one of many in a similar industry or public service, but it can be trickier if the organization is specialized or in a niche market with few players from which an outsourced service may have gained appropriate knowledge to understand the business.

Second, will internal audit employees be embedded within the organization? One of the great benefits of an inhouse service is that employees are there on a day-to-day basis and know the undercurrents within the organization. A service provider that sends employees in for one-off assignments or frequently changes the staff or management responsible for providing the outsourced audit is unlikely to retain any corporate inner knowledge of its client. Such organizations are far less likely to spot anomalies or major issues until it is too late.

Finally, will the outsourced provider be able to sustain an effective internal audit over the lifetime of the contract? Once an inhouse team has been outsourced or replaced by a higher-level or different audit function, it can be difficult to "reverse engineer" an inhouse audit team again. Outsourcing should be seen as an irrevocable step that is taken for the right reasons and with the organization's eyes wide open or it should not be taken at all.

Another consideration is to avoid conflicts of interest, either through appointing a contractor that already provides the organization with external audit services or through appointing one that provides an already outsourced financial activity that will be subject to its internal audit.

OTHER CONSIDERATIONS

There are other alternatives to a full outsource that need to be considered here as well. If the inhouse senior management of internal audit are seen as effective, why not look for the best of both worlds? Retain the effective management team but let them cosource skills and knowledge from a suitably priced leading provider of outsourced internal audit services. If the audit requirement is large or diverse enough, the organization can consider using more than one cosource partner to support the internal audit function. This can also often be an effective way to drive out costs and in efficiencies, by playing off the providers against each other for some of the available general audit work. Alternatively, the organization might consider retaining the more general internal audit work inhouse and outsourcing various specialist aspects to different specialist providers—for example IT auditors, treasury audit, investments audit, fraud auditors, or operational auditors.

In either of these partial alternatives to full outsourcing it is possible to try out options to find the best model for the work that can be unwound if a particular option doesn't work out in practice. Equally, if a successful model is found, consideration can be given to a more extensive outsourcing model.

Another alternative to inhouse, outsource, or cosource routes is the use of a consortium, whereby the inhouse team is encouraged to merge with similar inhouse teams in other organizations, creating economies of scale while providing an independent professional internal audit over several similar organizations. Such an approach has worked successfully in the British NHS and among health care providers in the United States, but it can be less viable between rival commercial organizations or those where research or other scientific or security matters could be put at risk by sharing services.

CONCLUSION

Outsourced and cosourced internal audit have worked well in many organizations in the private and public sector. It can ensure a refreshed skill set of professional internal auditors that an inhouse audit setup can find hard to maintain. At its best the organization gains a highly professional expert team to work alongside senior management, one that is proactive and produces clear, succinct reports that help the organization to move forward. At worst, it can lead to a disjointed service that fails to match the needs of the organization and produces meaningless reports that add little or no value, or which fundamentally damages the organization by failing to understand a key issue, missing signs of a catastrophic organizational failure/fraud, or unnecessarily consuming organizational time and resources and frustrating middle management.

MAKING IT HAPPEN

- Make sure that internal audit outsourcing is being done for the right reasons.
- The right reasons include: improving the skill set, being "meaner and leaner," reducing the cost for the same or better quality, reducing overheads such as pensions, and buying in specialist help and experience that isn't available inhouse.
- The wrong reasons include: cutting the costs regardless of the impact on the effectiveness of internal audit, looking only at inputs and not at outputs or outcomes, and a vendetta between a senior manager and the chief internal auditor.
- See what improvements can be made inhouse before going to the market place—or you may end up outsourcing the problem and not the solution.
- Where an existing substantial inhouse team will have to be outsourced, don't underestimate the potential damage to employee morale and performance.
- Pick an outsourcing partner that can understand your organization and empathize with its ethics and values.
- In choosing an outsourcing partner, avoid conflicts of interest that may compromise the independence of your external auditors or suppliers of business services that will be audited by the outsourced internal audit provider.
- If possible, try a trial outsourcing of a specialist skill or a one-off audit project before considering outsourcing the whole function.
- Make sure that there are robust management and performance arrangements in place, but don't become obsessed by meaningless minutiae that measure effort but not the value of what that effort has produced.
- Don't overlook alternatives to outsourcing, such as cosourcing and consortia arrangements.

Best Practice • In Practice

MORE INFO

Articles:

Anon. "Of the risk of internal audit outsourcing." *Free Papers Download Center* (December 1, 2010). Online at: eng.hi138.com/?i270596_Of_the_risk_of_internal_audit_outsourcing. A distillation of previous academic research on outsourcing internal audit by three separate Chinese authors.

Geiger, Marshall A., D. Jordan Lowe, and Kurt J. Pany. "Outsourced internal audit services and the perception of auditor independence." *CPA Journal* (April 2002). Online at: www.nysscpa.org/cpajournal/2002/0402/features/f042002.htm

Report:

Institute of Internal Auditors (IIA). "The role of internal auditing in resourcing the internal audit activity." IIA position paper. January 2009. Online at: www.theiia.org/download.cfm?file=66876

NOTES

1 By cosourcing I mean using an external provider to carry out some internal audit activities while leaving the function of internal audit under the control of a reduced inhouse team.

2 The 2009 IIA Position paper on resourcing the internal audit function (see More Info) emphasizes the need to consider how best to discharge the chief audit executive function.

3 This is always the case in the public sector and should be in many private sector organizations, where the Transfer of Undertakings (Protection of Employment) Regulations 2006, known universally as TUPE, apply to existing staff.

QFINANCE

Contemporary Developments in International Auditing Regulation
by Christopher Humphrey and Anne Loft

Best Practice • In Practice

EXECUTIVE SUMMARY
The contemporary development of international audit regulation is connected to the growing significance of international investors who demand financial reports that are prepared and audited in accordance with globally accepted international standards. International Standards on Auditing (ISAs) are set by the International Auditing and Assurance Standards Board (IAASB), an independent standard setting board working within the International Federation of Accountants (IFAC) and subject to public oversight by international regulators. ISAs have been adopted in many countries, but their practical impact depends centrally on how they are implemented and enforced. Recent years have seen a greater emphasis on such issues.

INTRODUCTION
The development of international audit regulation is closely linked to the development of international accounting regulation. Both have been significantly associated with the globalization of capital markets and growth in importance of international investors. Such investors expect the financial reports of the companies they are investing in to be fair and reliable, with auditors playing a critical role—famously categorized by Paul Volcker in 2002—as the "guardians of truth in markets."

Audit regulation is centrally concerned with the issue of ensuring that auditors are competent and independent. These attributes ensure that auditors are both capable of detecting significant errors and omissions in financial status (competent) and faithfully reporting these to investors/stakeholders in the enterprise (independence).

Broadly defined, audit regulation has the same four basic elements of any regulatory system—namely a concern and involvement with the setting, adoption, and implementation of standards and, through monitoring and enforcement processes, ensuring that such standards are applied in practice.

Following this introductory section, the chapter reviews the setting of international auditing standards (ISAs). This includes the role of international regulatory bodies in supporting this process and the demands they have made of the standard setting body and the international accounting profession more generally. In the third section, issues of compliance and oversight are discussed; including recent developments in international coordination through the

International Forum for Independent Audit Regulators (IFIAR). The fourth section examines the role of the big audit firms in international audit regulation, and the final section presents conclusions and some thoughts for the future.

SETTING GLOBAL STANDARDS
International Standards for Auditing (ISAs) are set by the International Auditing and Assurance Standards Board (IAASB), which is situated within the International Federation of Accountants (IFAC)—a private body whose member bodies are the national associations of professional accountants in each country. There are currently (December, 2009) 159 member bodies of IFAC, representing 124 countries and around 2.5 million professional accountants worldwide. IFAC recently celebrated its 32nd anniversary, having been formed in 1977, four years after the International Accounting Standards Committee (IASC), which was the predecessor body of the International Accounting Standards Board (IASB).

The members of the IAASB are a mixture of practicing professional accountants (especially members of the large audit firms) and persons from outside the profession. A number of important global organizations have supported the development and application of ISAs, which are now used in more than 100 countries around the world.[1] These include the Financial Stability Forum (FSF), a body set up by the G7 Finance Ministers and central bank governors in 1999 in the wake of the financial crisis in Asia in 1997/8—and re-established as the Financial Stability Board (FSB) in April 2009.[2] The objective of the FSF/FSB is to strengthen

QFINANCE

financial systems and ensure the stability of international financial markets, and as part of this remit it has designated 12 key standards and codes as most relevant to strengthening financial systems. Both International Accounting Standards (IASs/IFRS and ISAs are included in this group (the only private standard setters to be included).[3] These 12 standards and codes are seen as "best practices" associated with the legal, regulatory and institutional framework for financial systems.

The International Organization of Securities Commissions (IOSCO) is another important organization in this respect. Despite the FSF/FSB's inclusion of ISAs in its leading globally recognized standards and codes, the endorsement of ISAs by IOSCO has proved to be a more problematic and longstanding issue. A 1992 resolution by IOSCO's Presidents' Committee in support of the use of ISAs was subsequently suspended while "negotiations" continued with IFAC over issues such as the quality of ISAs and the degree of public oversight of the standard setting process.

The EU has also continued to review the feasibility of a formal EU endorsement of ISAs. In 2003, the European Commission issued a Communication entitled "Reinforcing the statutory audit in the EU," announcing that it intended that ISAs would apply to all statutory audits in Europe. It emphasized, though, that this required the public interest to be fully taken into account in the IAASB's standard setting processes, with a subsequent communication reiterating that the EU needs to be content that ISAs are "developed with proper due process, public oversight and transparency" and that IFAC's governance arrangements are adequate to ensure the pursuit of the public interest, specifically that the standards are "conducive to the European public good." In the Statutory Audit Directive issued on May 17, 2006, it repeated this message, whilst at the same time the text of the Directive indicated that it was expected that ISAs should become EU's auditing standards, ultimately to be legally binding in all Member States. The European Commission is currently analyzing the responses to its June 2009 formal public consultation on the adoption of ISAs for statutory audits required by European Community Law, having previously commissioned and published an independent study on the relative costs and benefits of adoption.[4] IFAC has moved towards satisfying such demands over its standard setting processes and governance arrangements by establishing,

among other things, an active Public Interest Oversight Board (PIOB) and developing ISAs through the IAASB's "clarity project." The members of the PIOB are selected by leading institutions in the international regulatory community, including IOSCO, the Basel Committee on Banking Supervision (BCBS), the International Association of Insurance Supervisors (IAIS), the European Commission, World Bank and the FSF/FSB. Included in the activities of the PIOB is the monitoring of all meetings of IFAC's public interest standard setting committees, making this a very active process of oversight. With this IFAC appears to have satisfied one of the requirements of the regulators for improving governance arrangements to bring in a clear consideration of the public interest, although it is worth noting that the effectiveness of such governance reforms is currently being evaluated by the above mentioned regulatory and international organizations (commonly referred to as the Monitoring Group.[5]

The IAASB's Clarity Project, started in 2004, and was completed in February 2009.[6] The project's aim was to ensure that ISAs have clear objectives and that each standard distinguishes what the auditor absolutely shall do when carrying out an audit from guidance on how to achieve this.[7] In the process of clarification, some standards were ultimately revised quite considerably (and more than was originally anticipated). In total, the clarity project produced 36 updated and clarified ISAs, together with a clarified International Standard on Quality Control (ISQC). The standards are to be applied to audits of financial statements for reporting periods beginning on or after December 15, 2009.

In June 2009, IOSCO issued a statement that formally encouraged[8] securities regulators to accept audits performed and reported in accordance with the clarified ISAs for cross-border purposes; "recognizing that the decision whether to do so would depend on a number of factors and circumstances in their jurisdiction" (IOSCO, 2009). In much the same way, IOSCO encouraged securities regulators to consider the clarified ISAs when setting auditing standards for national purposes.[9]

According to IFAC, currently 43 countries have adopted ISAs or are required to use them by law, with a further 28 countries having generally adopted them as national standards but with modifications (acceptable to the IAASB) for specific legislative and regulatory

Best Practice • In Practice

requirements.[10] While ISAs are pushing towards the position of being the global standards for auditing, a significant inclusion in the 55 "other/ remaining" countries surveyed by IFAC, is the United States of America—which, as yet, has not abandoned its own auditing standards. Up until 2002 the American Institute of Certified Public Accountants (AICPA) was responsible for setting US auditing standards but, in the wake of the Enron scandal, and others like it, this responsibility was given to a new independent body under the supervision of the Securities and Exchange Commission (SEC). This body, namely, the Public Company Accounting Oversight Board (PCAOB), has it its own processes for setting independent audit standards and also has extraterritorial powers of regulatory reach in relation to audits of US quoted companies. Recent speeches by SEC staff at the 2009 AICPA national conference on current SEC and PCAOB developments have confirmed that the PCAOB does maintain an active interest in ISAs and standard setting developments at the IAASB— and that, in their view, the momentum for international convergence in auditing standards is growing.[11] The chances of ISAs becoming truly "world standards" are also likely to be aided by the SEC's approach towards IFRS. The latest indications are that the SEC will shortly update its "roadmap" proposals for US listed companies to move to IFRS.[12] The international pressure on the SEC would seem to have increased recently, with the G20 in September 2009 notably calling for a "redoubling of efforts" by international accounting bodies to achieve a single-set of "high quality global accounting standards" and for the convergence process to be completed by June 2011.[13]

Finally, in relation to global (auditing) standards, it is important to point out that, while scandals such as Enron regularly illustrate the international significance of both auditor independence and competence, international independence standards remain some way off. While IFAC's Code of Ethics for Professional Accountants[14] provides a potential international regulatory solution in this area, the lack of international consensus on the issue of auditor independence is such that regulation here is more likely to be of national or regional orientation, influenced strongly by related legal structures.

COMPLIANCE AND REGULATORY OVERSIGHT

As was noted at the start of this chapter, a regulatory system is not just about standard setting but also the implementation and enforcement of such standards. Historically, issues of compliance with international auditing standards were not given enormous emphasis at the global level—reflecting a range of factors, including desires to grow the numbers of countries adopting such standards, a limited level of available resources, accepted traditions of self-regulation and professional peer review and the clear positioning of responsibilities for compliance, regulation, and oversight activities at the national rather than the international level.

One of the most active and visible initiatives in this area has been the ROSC (Reports on Standards and Codes) program set up by the IMF and World Bank in 1999, which examines the degree to which emerging and developing countries are using key standards and codes (defined to include ISAs and IASs as benchmark standards for each individual country's reports on accounting and auditing practices). The formal remit is to: "analyze comparability of national accounting and auditing standards with international standards" and "assist the country in developing and implementing a country action plan for improving institutional capacity with a view to strengthening the country's corporate financial reporting regime."[15]

IFAC has increased its focus on global compliance issues with the 2004 launch of its Compliance Program, overseen by the Compliance Advisory Panel (CAP), which seeks to ensure that member bodies are meeting their membership obligations. Formally, this program has three main elements, comprising: an assessment by each member body of their country's regulatory and standard-setting framework; a self-assessment questionnaire of the extent to which each member body is using its best endeavors to adopt international accounting and auditing standards and maintain quality assurance and enforcement regimes to ensure such standards are applied in practice; and the development of action plans to further the global accounting and auditing standards convergence process and address any issues/weaknesses identified in the self-assessment questionnaire. IFAC, "in the interests of transparency," has chosen to post all the responses received from member bodies for full public access on its website.[16]

These initiatives are dealing with the general issue of compliance, but not with the actual compliance of a particular audit firm with ISAs and other standards. In reaction to the problematic audits of Enron, Global Crossing

QFINANCE

and other large companies, in July 2002, the passing of the Sarbanes–Oxley Act replaced the self-regulation of the US auditing profession with the PCAOB-led system of independent inspection. Similar initiatives have followed in other countries and there is a whole new international emphasis on auditor oversight as an essential feature of audit regulation. This oversight is, for obvious reasons, done at local national level. However, the Sarbanes–Oxley Act did not exclude foreign registrants with US stock exchanges from the requirement from oversight by the PCAOB. This appears to have encouraged a number of (large) countries to establish their own auditor oversight systems in the hope that there will be mutual recognition of each other's systems. This, however, has only occurred to a small extent, resulting in a considerable amount of extra-territorial activity by the PCAOB audit inspectors.

The issue of public oversight has further developed on the international stage through the establishment in September 2006 of the International Forum of Independent Audit Regulators (IFIAR).[17] IFIAR is committed to sharing knowledge and experiences of the audit market and associated regulatory activities between independent national audit regulatory agencies. It seeks to promote collaboration and consistency in regulatory activity and to act as a platform for dialogue with other organizations with an interest in the quality of auditing. There are currently 36 independent national regulators who are members of this new international organization, including the PCAOB. Observers at IFIAR meetings include the FSB, IFAC's PIOB, IOSCO, IAIS, World Bank, European Commission and the Basel Committee, again reflecting the increasingly interlocking nature of international regulatory relationships (for more discussion, see Humphrey *et al.*, 2009).

The multi-layered nature of such regulatory arrangements is well illustrated by the fact that the European Union itself had previously established a European Group of Audit Oversight Bodies (EGAOB) in December 2005—with the specific remit of ensuring effective coordination of new public oversight systems of statutory auditors and audit firms within the European Union.[18] The press release announcing the EGAOB development cited the view of Commissioner McCreevy that this "group will help to make public supervision systems a reality in all 25 Member States, promoting practical day-to-day co-operation as it goes along. It is a key initiative in our drive to bring EU audit rules into the 21st century and restore faith in the profession." The European Commission reiterated its views on the importance of public oversight, with a Recommendation (May 13, 2008) on external quality assurance for the statutory audit of public interest entities. This expanded the responsibilities of public oversight boards and emphasized that they should play an active role in the inspections of audit firms.

THE GLOBAL REGULATORY INVOLVEMENT OF AUDIT FIRMS
An interesting development with respect to public oversight was the presentation by the CEOs of the six largest global auditing firms at IFIAR meetings in Norway (April 2008) and South Africa (September 2008) to consider global quality monitoring arrangements. This section of the chapter explores what is an evidently growing involvement of the large audit firms in international audit regulation.

During the last two decades, there has been a continued increasing concentration in the international auditing profession, with the large firms getting a greater share of the audit market. The Big Eight firms of the past have reduced to

---

MAKING IT HAPPEN

For international audit regulation to meet the claims laid out for it in terms of global scope and consistency of application requires a variety of actions and commitments on the part of the international financial regulatory community. Some of the more frequently mentioned priorities include:
- ISAs to be fully endorsed by international financial regulators;
- ISAs to be adopted globally for listed company audits;
- IFAC to continue to operate as an international organization acting in the global public interest;
- Greater global coordination of the work of audit regulatory and oversight bodies;
- Enhanced visibility of the quality and achievements of audit work.

the Big Four today of PwC, KPMG, E&Y, and Deloitte—with the next two largest firms, BDO International and Grant Thornton International, relatively speaking, being quite a lot smaller. Gradually, through a variety of pressures, often driven by major corporate collapses and financial crises, such firms have sought to ensure a greater global consistency in auditing practice, such that that an audit, for example, in China by PwC is equivalent to one conducted by the same firm in, say, Sweden. Through internal processes of regulation, they place pressure on parts of their network where audit quality and associated quality control procedures are apparently insufficient, and thus act as an "internal" or "self" regulatory pressure towards harmonizing standards.

The audits undertaken by the, then, Big Five[19] in Asia at the time of the crisis (1997–8) were sharply criticized by the World Bank, and it was this that stimulated the Big Five to set up a Global Steering Committee. One of the aims was to provide a body to deal, on a collective, global basis, with the common professional and regulatory issues they were facing. Another aim was to strengthen IFAC as the global audit standard setter. Under this initiative the large firms supported IFAC financially and were allocated seats on each of IFAC's standard setting boards. In the case of the newly established IAASB (previously the International Auditing Practices Committee) they had 5 seats out of a total of 18. This greater engagement of the Big Firms with IFAC continued to grow, especially in the wake of the Enron scandal and its aftermath, with the establishment of a new organization, the Global Public Policy Committee (GPPC).

The GPPC comprises the six largest international accounting networks and focuses on "public policy" issues for the profession. The GPPC has a Regulatory Working Group and a Standards Working Group and while much of its work is undertaken in private, it does issue policy papers where it expresses its commitment to working in the public interest and facilitating the functioning of global capital markets (see GPPS, 2006). The global firms' involvement in international regulatory affairs has also seen them expand the scale of financial support that they provide to IFAC, which now receives approximately one-third of its funding from the large firms. The firms can also be seen to making substantial efforts to further strengthen their own global organization. For instance, it was reported in the *Financial Times* (August 20, 2008) that a number of them had announced restructuring plans to align more tightly member firms within global structures/networks and introduce "enhanced" audit practice standards.[20] The current financial crisis has witnessed a continuing major involvement with global regulatory matters, driven by the direct consequences that auditing work could have for global financial stability through decisions relating to the valuation of "toxic" assets and the auditor's determination as to whether audited enterprises are "going concerns."

MAINTAINING PUBLIC INTEREST IN GLOBAL REGULATION

While the global audit regulatory arena is complex, it is possible to draw out a number of important characteristics. While contemporary audit regulation engages directly with audit practice at the national level, it is being driven primarily by events and strategic action at the global level. The development in this global regulation of audit has been rapid during the current decade and, associated with the identification of reliable financial reporting, is becoming an essential part of a wider international financial architecture. Significant strategic actions have been made by international organizations such as the EU, IOSCO, FSF/FSB, and the World Bank, to aid, support and increasingly mandate, the usage of international standards on auditing. While these organizations are primarily governmental in character, the main international audit standard setter, the IAASB—under the auspices of IFAC—is classified as private in nature, as are the large audit firms who are also closely involved, albeit in a less public way. This has placed particular emphasis and significance on the development of public oversight regimes as a way of ensuring that international audit standard setting processes are seen to be globally credible and sufficiently responsive to public interest demands (see IFAC, 2008; PIOB, 2008). The policy recommendations emerging from the November 2008 meeting of the G20 likewise have highlighted the importance of regulators serving the public interest and the global importance of making sure that financial markets operate in the most transparent of fashions. The current financial crisis is testing global regulatory structures to their limit, and it is pretty certain that auditing will remain a fascinating field—both to observe and to debate in an open and constructive fashion. It could be argued that serving the public interest deserves no less.

ABBREVIATIONS

ACCA	Association of Chartered Certified Accountants
AICPA	American Institute of Certified Public Accountants
BCBS	Basel Committee on Banking Supervision
CAP	Compliance Advisory Panel
EU	European Union
FSF/(FSB)	Financial Stability Forum/Board
GPPC	Global Public Policy Committee
GPPS	Global Public Policy Symposium
IAASB	International Auditing and Assurance Standards Board
IAIS	International Association of Insurance Supervisors
IFAC	International Federation of Accountants
IFIAR	International Forum of Independent Audit Regulators
IFRS	International Financial Reporting Standard
IMF	International Monetary Fund
IOSCO	International Organization of Securities Commissions
ISA	International Standard on Auditing
ISQC	International Standard on Quality Control
PIOB	Public Interest Oversight Board
PCAOB	Public Company Accounting Oversight Board
ROSC	Report on Standards and Codes (World Bank)
SEC	Securities and Exchange Commission

MORE INFO

Article:

Humphrey, Christopher, Anne Loft, and Margaret Woods. "The global audit profession and the international financial architecture: Understanding regulatory relationships at a time of financial crisis." *Accounting, Organizations and Society* 34:6–7 (August–October 2009): 810–825. Online at: dx.doi.org/10.1016/j.aos.2009.06.003

Reports:

International Federation of Accountants (IFAC). "Regulation of the accountancy profession." IFAC Policy Position 1. December 2007. Online at: tinyurl.com/2b3wa4e

International Federation of Accountants (IFAC). "International standard setting in the public interest." IFAC Policy Position 3. December 2008. Online at: tinyurl.com/27ohv6l

International Federation of Accountants (IFAC). "International Federation of Accountants 2008 annual report: Transitioning to a global financial system." February 2009. Online at: web.ifac.org/download/2008_AR_IFAC_Full.pdf

International Forum for Independent Audit Regulators (IFIAR). "Charter." Online at: www.frc.org.uk/images/uploaded/documents/IFIAR%20Charter1.pdf

Public Interest Oversight Board (PIOB). "Third public report of the PIOB." May 2008. Online at: tinyurl.com/23byvuu

Public Interest Oversight Board (PIOB). "Fourth public report of the PIOB." May 2009. Online at: tinyurl.com/29bm3q3

Technical Committee of the International Organization of Securities Commissions (IOSCO). "Contingency planning for events and conditions affecting availability of audit services: Final report." May 2008. Online at: www.iosco.org/library/pubdocs/pdf/IOSCOPD269.pdf

Website:

International Auditing and Assurance Standards Board: www.ifac.org/iaasb

NOTES

1 See web.ifac.org/download/2008_IAASB_Annual_ Report.pdf

2 See www.fsforum.org/press/pr_090402b.pdf

3 See www.fsforum.org/cos/key_standards.htm

4 ec.europa.eu/internal_market/auditing/isa/index en.htm#isastudy

5 www.iosco.org/news/pdf/IOSCONEWS162.pdf

6 See web.ifac.org/clarity-center/index

7 www.cnbv.gob.mx/recursos/iosco13.pdf

8 It is an interesting point of debate as to whether such "encouragement" on the part of IOSCO equates with the formal endorsement of ISAs sought, for example, by accounting firms and professional bodies such as PwC, IFAC, ACCA, and the Institut der Wirtschaftsprüfer in Germany—on the grounds that ISAs were already in widespread usage (see IOSCO, 2008).

9 www.iosco.org/library/statements/pdf/statements-7. pdf

10 web.ifac.org/isa-adoption/chart

11 See www.sec.gov/news/speech/2009/ spch120709amp.htm

12 The initial proposals suggested an adoption decision in 2011, with mandatory application for US issuers in 2014. The latest indications are that the SEC will announce its current thinking regarding IFRS adoption in early 2010 (see www.sec.gov/news/speech/2009/ spch120909ebw.htm).

13 www.pittsburghsummit.gov/mediacenter/129639.htm

14 www.ifac.org/Ethics/Resources.php

15 See www.worldbank.org/ifa/rosc_aa.html

16 See www.ifac.org/ComplianceProgram

17 IFIAR's formal charter can be found at www.frc.org. uk/images/uploaded/documents/IFIAR%20Charter1. pdf

18 europa.eu.int/rapid/pressReleasesAction.do?reference =IP/05/1596&format=HTML&aged=0&language=EN& guiLanguage=en

19 The Big Four plus, the now defunct firm of, Arthur Andersen.

20 See www.ft.com/cms/s/0/198b3e42-6edd-11dd-a80a-0000779fd18c.html?nclick_check=1

How Can Internal Audit Report Effectively to Its Stakeholders? by Andrew Cox

EXECUTIVE SUMMARY

- Internal audit has a range of stakeholders who rely on its work, seeking assurance that the organization is running well and that there are effective controls in place.
- Internal audit has a responsibility to its stakeholders to provide reports on the operation of the organization's risk management, control, and governance processes. It also has a responsibility to justify the value of its work and the organization's spending on internal audit resources.
- Internal audit can report on its work to its stakeholders by:
  - reporting on the outcomes of its internal audit work;
  - reporting on the quality of its internal audit work.
- Together, these elements combine to provide stakeholders with an overall view of the effectiveness of internal audit; one without the other will only provide a partial reporting structure.

INTRODUCTION

Internal audit has a variety of stakeholders who rely on its work. These include: the board of directors; the audit committee; the chief executive officer; senior executives such as the chief financial officer, chief information officer, chief risk officer, etc.; the external auditors; in some cases, regulatory bodies; and stockholders—who, in the case of government organizations, could be the public.

All these stakeholders are seeking assurance that the organization is running well, and that effective controls are in place and operating properly. Internal audit has an important role to play in providing assurance to these stakeholders, but the trick is how to report the results of its work to them effectively.

ASSURANCE MODELS

Assurance can be equated with the term governance, the four pillars of a good corporate governance framework being—according to the Institute of Internal Auditors—executive management, the audit committee, external audit, and internal audit. Each of these elements relies to an extent on the others, and they all need to be operating effectively to provide overall assurance to stakeholders.

The board of directors will generally want to see a combined assurance model in place for the organization that provides three lines of defense, as shown in Table 1. This demonstrates the interdependencies between the four pillars of good corporate governance and the three lines of defense that go to make up a combined assurance model.

Table 1. Combined assurance model with three lines of defense.
(*Source*: **National Australia Bank, with amendment**)

First line of defense	Second line of defense	Third line of defense
Management controls	Management of risk	Independent assurance
Real-time focus	Real-time focus + review focus of 1st line	Review focus of 1st and 2nd line
Elements Policies and procedures Internal controls	Elements Risk management Legal department	Elements External audit Internal audit
Role Review compliance Implement improvements	Role Confirm compliance Recommend improvements	Role Independently confirm compliance Recommend improvements

REPORTING ON THE OUTCOMES OF INTERNAL AUDIT WORK

A model for reporting the outcomes of internal audit work could be based on the following four elements: internal audit reports, recommendations for improvement, a communication strategy, and an annual internal audit report. These are discussed below.

Internal Audit Reports

Internal audit reports are the most important part of the work of an internal audit function. The report is the culmination of the effort directed toward an audit of a part of the organization. Internal audit can be a costly resource, so reports of its work should demonstrate its value to the organization. Internal audit reports need to be:

- Timely: reports should be issued in a timely manner.
- Accurate: reports should contain accurate information.
- Logical: reports should be logical and valid.
- Clear: reports should be clearly written and easily understood.
- Purposeful: reports should state why the internal audit was performed.
- Written with the audience in mind: reports should be written to suit the intended reader.

The power of a tick cannot be underestimated—it provides balance to an internal audit report. People do not go to work to do a bad job, and they appreciate recognition of good work. What they do not appreciate is an audit report that is negative by exception, says nothing positive, and effectively just gives them stick. So, acknowledge good work, and always say something positive in the report—and not begrudgingly.

Internal audit reports need to tell a story and be insightful. Merely telling people what is wrong cannot be seen as a good use of internal audit resources. That is the easy work, and does not reflect well on internal auditing as a profession. The real value of the work of internal audit comes from an emphasis on cause and effect. It is easy work to find the effect, but much more difficult to ascertain the root cause. Because of this, many internal auditors take the easy way out and just report on what has been found to be operating ineffectively.

Many internal audits could provide additional value to the organization if there was more emphasis on efficiency, effectiveness, economy, and organizational outcomes, with a view to assisting the organization further to improve and streamline business processes.

Recommendations for Improvement

Internal audit reports need to contain recommendations for improvement if they are to have any point. And the recommendations need to be targeted at correcting the root cause.

Locating the cause provides information on accountability relationships, and provides the basis for making improvements. It is important not just to find that something is wrong, but to work out what caused it to be wrong. This can prevent similar problems from happening again. Each recommendation needs to include:

- Whether it is agreed with or not by the audit customer (and if not, why not).
- What the audit customer is going to do about it (action plan).
- By what date the action will be implemented and completed.
- Who will be responsible for implementing the recommendation.

Recommendations contained in internal audit reports also need to be risk rated. In this way, management with the responsibility to implement remedial action will know which recommendations are most important and should be implemented first.

An important task of the internal audit function is to ensure that agreed recommendations arising from internal audit reports are satisfactorily actioned within a reasonable time-frame. If this is not done, its work will be virtually worthless. Many internal audit functions adopt an approach whereby:

- Agreed recommendations from internal audit, external audit, and regulatory bodies are entered into a tracking system and monitored on an ongoing basis by internal audit and the audit committee.
- Management responsible for implementing the recommendations is required to advise internal audit when this is complete, or to provide periodic reports on progress where this may be over a longer period of time.
- Overdue recommendations are reported to the audit committee.
- Internal audit periodically follows up to ensure that implementation has occurred as reported by management. This can be by 100% follow-up, by following up only those recommendations of higher risk, or by following up on a sample basis. A full follow-up audit is not generally necessary.

One point worthy of consideration is the necessity to cover off risks if recommendations are not actioned within a reasonable time-frame. Where a recommendation relates to a higher-risk problem and is not dealt with quickly, the chief audit executive should ask:

- Why has it not been actioned?
- Should the risk rating assigned to the recommendation be increased?
- What fall-back or interim risk management procedures have been put in place to mitigate the risks associated with nonimplementation of the recommendation?
- Should management make a statement accepting the risk associated with nonimplementation of the recommendation?

This information should be reported to each meeting of the audit committee.

Communication Strategy

To develop and maintain a profile within an organization, internal audit should take steps to improve its communication in order to make itself more visible to the wider organization. Some ways in which internal audit might do this include:

Raising awareness

- Have information about internal audit and its achievements posted on the organization's intranet.
- Distribute a small brochure about internal audit, what it does, and its achievements.
- Further develop relationships with stakeholders by making presentations on the work of internal audit to groups within the organization's corporate environment.
- Prepare an annual internal audit report on its activities.

Engaging management

- Consult with internal audit customers prior to the commencement of each internal audit, and request their input to the objectives and scope of the audit.
- Facilitate a risk workshop with internal audit customers in the planning phase of each internal audit.
- When conducting internal audits, internal auditors should spend most of their time in the work areas of their internal audit customers, rather than in the internal audit work area.
- At the completion of internal audit fieldwork, hold a workshop with the audit customer to discuss and agree possible improvement options.
- Provide a balanced reporting format by reporting on what management is doing well, in addition to identifying opportunities for improvement.

Providing value-add

- Plan for each internal audit with a wider view by encompassing objectives relating to efficiency, effectiveness, economy, and organizational outcomes.
- Have involvement in working groups related to strategic developments within the organization in an observer/adviser capacity. It is considered best practice for internal audit to contribute to such forums by providing opinions, and ensuring that controls are considered and built-in to projects and systems under development, rather than after the event via post-implementation reviews, without necessarily compromising the integrity of later audits.

Annual Internal Audit Report

In some organizations, best practice extends to providing the audit committee and management with an annual report of internal audit activities featuring:

- Achievements in the year.
- Analysis of systemic issues identified through the work of internal audit.
- An opinion on the organization's overall risk management, control, and governance environment.

This can provide additional assurance to the audit committee, as well as being beneficial in alerting management to issues and risks identified in internal audits but which may also be occurring in other business areas.

REPORTING ON THE QUALITY OF INTERNAL AUDIT WORK

A model for reporting on the quality of internal audit work could be based on the following four elements: a quality assurance and improvement program, performance measures, review by external audit, and review by regulatory bodies.

Quality Assurance and Improvement Program

The "International Standards for the Professional Practice of Internal Auditing" issued by the Institute of Internal Auditors requires every internal audit function to operate a quality assurance program:

"The chief audit executive must develop and maintain a quality assurance and improvement program that covers all aspects of internal audit activity."

A quality assurance and improvement program is designed to enable an evaluation of internal audit's conformance with the Definition of Internal Auditing and the Standards, and an

Best Practice • In Practice

QFINANCE

evaluation of whether internal auditors apply the Code of Ethics. The program also assesses the efficiency and effectiveness of internal audit and identifies opportunities for improvement.

This program should include both internal and external assessments. Internal assessments comprise: ongoing monitoring of the performance of the internal audit activity; and periodic reviews performed through self-assessment or by other persons within the organization with sufficient knowledge of internal audit practices.

External assessments must be conducted at least once every five years by a qualified, independent reviewer or review team from outside the organization. The chief audit executive must discuss with the board the need for more frequent external assessments; and the qualifications and independence of the external reviewer or review team, including any potential conflict of interest. The chief audit executive must communicate the results of the quality assurance and improvement program to senior management and the board.

Performance Measures

Best practice in internal auditing suggests that, like most business units in an organization, internal audit should have performance measures or key performance indicators (KPIs) in place to demonstrate its own level of performance. Best practice also suggests that performance measures need to be specific (clear and concise), measurable (quantifiable), achievable (practical and reasonable), relevant (to users), and timed (having a range or time limit). For more on this, see the case study.

Review by External Audit

As part of its annual external audit of an organization, the external auditors will usually assess the internal audit function on such matters as its organizational status, scope of function, technical competence, and due professional care exercised in its work.

Review by Regulatory Bodies

In many countries, regulatory bodies review the competency and work of internal audit as part of their periodic regulatory review of an organization. These are generally restricted to particular industry groups, for example financial institutions.

CONCLUSION

Internal audit has a responsibility to its stakeholders to provide reports on the operations of the organization's risk management, control, and governance processes. It also has a responsibility to justify the value of its work and the organization's spending on internal audit resources.

Internal audit can do this in two ways:
- By reporting on the outcomes of its internal audit work.
- By reporting on the quality of its internal audit work.

CASE STUDY

Measurement of the Internal Audit Function

The chief audit executive of an organization in Brisbane Australia was seeking ways to measure the work of his internal audit function. He knew that internal audit was doing a good job, but he did not have the evidence to prove it. In thinking how to address this problem, he designed KPIs against which his internal audit function could demonstrate its performance to the audit committee and the organization (Table 2). After all, internal audit assesses the performance of other areas of the organization, so why should it be exempt from having its own performance examined?

The chief audit executive considered these to be the KPIs the audit committee would be interested in to provide an overall assessment of the work of internal audit, and when he asked the audit committee, they agreed. He discounted KPIs such as the number of internal audit recommendations, or the number of internal audit hours delivered, since these can be manipulated and would therefore have little credibility with the committee.

How Can Internal Audit Report Effectively to Its Stakeholders?

Table 2. KPIs prepared by the chief audit executive to assess internal audit.
(*Source*: National Australia Bank, with amendment)

Key performance indicator		Measure	Target	Frequency
1. Completion of Internal Audit Plan				
1.1	Complete planned internal audits as per the approved *Internal Audit Plan* (subject to approved plan amendments)	% of planned internal audits completed within the financial year	95%	Annually
1.2	Complete special and ad hoc management-initiated internal audits and investigations in addition to scheduled internal audits (an allowance for this is contained in the *Internal Audit Plan*)	% of allowance utilized for unplanned ad hoc and management-initiated internal audits and investigations	95%	Annually
1.3	Approved *Internal Audit Plan* to be completed within the approved internal audit budget	% variance from approved budget for the financial year	5%	Annually
2. Implementation of internal audit recommendations				
2.1	Internal audit recommendations accepted by management	% of recommendations accepted by management (subject to internal audit independence being maintained)	95%	Annually
2.2	Monitor the implementation status of internal audit recommendations by management and report outcomes to the audit committee	Updated status obtained from responsible managers and reported to the audit committee	Quarterly status reports delivered	Quarterly
3. Formal survey feedback				
3.1	Results of customer feedback surveys following each internal audit	% of survey responses of good or better (averaged)	90%	Annually
3.2	Result of annual feedback survey of members of the audit committee	% of survey responses of good or better (averaged)	90%	Annually
4. Independent quality review of internal audit				
4.1	Result of external quality assessment of internal audit in accordance with *The International Standards for Professional Practice of Internal Auditing*	Report issued detailing results of review	Consistent with better practice	Five-Yearly

Best Practice • In Practice

QFINANCE

MAKING IT HAPPEN

The chief audit executive should develop effective reporting mechanisms with the audit committee and other stakeholders. Key reporting tools include:

- Insightful internal audit reports.
- Monitoring of internal audit recommendations, and periodic follow-up to ensure that recommendations have been implemented effectively and in a timely way.
- An internal audit communication strategy.
- An annual internal audit report that covers achievements in the year, an analysis of systemic issues identified through the work of internal audit, and an opinion on the organization's overall risk management, control, and governance environment.
- A quality assurance and improvement program that incorporates both internal and external assessments.
- Key performance indicators measuring the performance of internal audit.
- Periodic review of internal audit by external auditors and, where applicable, regulatory bodies.

MORE INFO

Books:

Reding, Kurt F., Paul J. Sobel, Urton L. Anderson, Michael J. Head, *et al*. *Internal Auditing: Assurance and Consulting Services*. 2nd ed. Orlando, FL: IIA Research Foundation, 2009.

Sawyer, Lawrence B., Mortimer A. Dittenhofer, and James H. Scheiner. *Sawyer's Internal Auditing: The Practice of Modern Internal Auditing*. Altamonte Springs, FL: IIA, 2003.

Report:

Australian National Audit Office. "Public sector internal audit: An investment in assurance and business improvement." Better Practice Guide. September 2007. Online at: www.anao.gov.au/uploads/documents/Public_Sector_Internal_Audit.pdf

Standards:

Institute of Internal Auditors. "International standards for the professional practice of internal auditing." October 2010. Online at: www.theiia.org/guidance/standards-and-guidance/ippf/standards

Websites:

Institute of Internal Auditors (IIA): www.theiia.org
Institute of Internal Auditors—Australia: www.iia.org.au

Has Financial Reporting Impacted on Internal Auditing Negatively?
by Andrew Chambers

EXECUTIVE SUMMARY

- At the turn of the millennium, the internal auditing profession sought to formally broaden its role for internal audit by embracing "consulting services" that went beyond its traditional assurance role. This move was almost immediately challenged by the collapse of Enron and other large corporations, which led to stockholders and boards demanding more focus not only on the internal audit assurance role but also, more specifically, on the assurance of internal control over financial reporting—at the expense of assurance on operational effectiveness and efficiency and assurance on compliance with laws, regulations, and policies.
- Since then, internal audit has often been commandeered into discharging what should be management's role—for instance, to comply with Section 404 of the Sarbanes–Oxley Act (2002)—whereas the proper internal audit role should be to audit the compliance work that management has done. A better balance is now being achieved, not least as the Sarbanes–Oxley compliance requirements become bedded into companies as well as becoming slightly less onerous.
- The storm that hit the US corporate sector at the turn of the millennium was a salutary reminder of the importance of effective assurance auditing and the need for this to be done in depth. However, it is not only (or even primarily) in financial and accounting matters that assurance is needed. Entities achieve their objectives mainly in the operational areas of their businesses, and they need assurance that operations are effective and efficient. They also need assurance that laws and regulations are being complied with, for instance with regard to the security of personal data in IT.
- Entities can also benefit from the consulting services that internal audit is able to offer, but internal audit is still neglecting these activities by focusing disproportionately on the internal control of financial reporting.

INTERNAL AUDIT'S CONSULTING ROLE

It was unfortunate that The Institute of Internal Auditors (The IIA) released its first consulting implementation *Standards*, to add to its already existing assurance *Standards*, at exactly the time when Enron collapsed. "Implementation Standards" set out how the "Attribute Standards" and "Performance Standards" should be applied in the context of either assurance or consulting work. In 2007 The IIA announced that it had no plans to release further sets of "Implementation Standards."[1]

In spite of its bad timing, the release of the consulting *Standards* was a natural development in the evolution of internal auditing, albeit not one that gained universal approval. This development was the principal driver behind the release in 2000 of a completely revamped set of *Standards* (effective January 1, 2002) to replace The IIA's original *Standards* that had remained unaltered, except in one or two minor details,

since their first release in 1978. The main need for new *Standards* arose from a widely held perception that the old *Standards* had ceased to describe either what constituted contemporary best practice in internal auditing or, indeed, how internal auditors spent much of their time. Faced with this challenge, the IIA set out to determine the nature of internal auditing as it currently was. Prior to developing the new *Standards* the IIA invested much effort, including two exposure drafts, in achieving an agreed new definition of internal auditing. The new *Standards* were then modeled around this new definition (see "Optimizing Internal Audit," pp. 71–75).

"Internal auditing is an independent, objective assurance and consulting activity designed to add value and improve an organization's operations. It helps an organization accomplish its objectives by bringing a systematic, disciplined approach to evaluate and improve the effectiveness of risk management, control, and governance processes."[2]

Prior to this definition and prior to the new *Standards*, internal auditing had been perceived as an assurance service, but now "consulting activity" was added. Some say this definition gives the consulting role equal weight to the assurance role (for example, "the definition gives equal consideration to both assurance and consulting activities.")[3] The fundamental challenge was to determine whether all the non-assurance activities that engaged internal auditors' time should continue to be regarded as noninternal audit work or whether they should be brought within the definition of internal auditing. The latter was decided upon. This was hardly surprising as throughout the 1990s there had been some skepticism as to the value of internal auditors' assurance work and a view that their role in providing consulting services was much more constructive and added much more value.

SWING TO MORE EMPHASIS ON THE ASSURANCE ROLE

Then came the spectacular collapses of Enron, Tyco, WorldCom, and others. Almost immediately the pendulum in the internal audit role swung away from offering consulting services toward providing stronger assurance. Audit committees and boards arrived at the painful realization that they had been starved of the independent assurance they needed and they looked to their internal auditors, among others, to provide them with that assurance.

The IIA's Global Auditing Information Network (GAIN) survey found that 36% of a total of 341 respondents fully supported the idea of internal auditors doing consultancy work. Of the remainder, 41% agreed with the statement: "consulting is usually the way to go, but you have to be careful; sometimes it is not a good idea," 7% considered that internal auditors should rarely or never do consulting work, and 16% thought that in theory consulting sounded good, but in practice it was a bad idea more often than not.

An *AuditWire* article[4] quoted two contrasting views about the place of consultancy services in the internal auditor's repertoire:

Against:

"The Andersen debacle drove home the risks to maintaining our independence when we auditors neglect or stray from our primary mission, which should be providing internal control assurance.

When my audit team is approached by management for a consulting project, four red flags are raised in my mind:

- If management is asking the audit group for help, there must be a control concern. As an auditor, my first responsibility is to decide whether an audit or investigation is warranted.

CASE STUDY

This case illustrates how internal audit focus has been skewed by recent demands for extra assurance of internal control over financial reporting.

One of the top ten global multinationals came to Sarbanes–Oxley compliance rather later than it should have done. At the time it already had difficulties with the regulatory authorities, in particular the SEC. It was determined not to fail in its compliance with Section 404, having already risked the ire of the SEC with respect to its disclosures under Section 302. The multinational's approach to Section 404 compliance was to set up a dedicated Section 404 compliance team within its internal audit function. The head of this team, recruited from outside, had been a partner at one of the "Big Four" accountancy firms. Worldwide, the company had some 250 internal auditors and 70 became Section 404 specialists, many being recruited from outside. In addition, the company bought in supplementary Section 404 compliance resources from one of the Big Four. These overhead costs for management compliance with Section 404 did not of course include the extra fees paid to the external auditors for their own attestation work under Section 404. Typically, Section 404 has doubled the cost of the external audit.

The team's approach was first to develop a plan, with dates, for rolling out the project. It then identified and documented all the processes that could have a material impact on the multinational's financial statement assertions. This included identifying and documenting the key controls within these processes, and then developing and documenting a program to test the functioning of these controls. The results of all this work were recorded in process maps, narrative writeups and spreadsheet-based control registers.

Following the successful implementation of this part of Section 404 compliance, the emphasis then become to transfer this compliance work to line management, so that line managers themselves became responsible for running the compliance program in the future.

- If there is no control concern, I must wonder whether the manager considers the project too risky for his or her own people to do or whether it's of too little value to engage a third party on the project.
- If it's too risky for the manager's own people to tackle, does this indicate that the manager has the wrong people on staff or not enough people? If the project has insufficient value to warrant hiring a third party, why would I want to associate our audit group with the project?
- Finally, I must ask myself whether I believe that I have been so successful in my assurance role that internal auditing has no other risk-based priorities to pursue. If so, the audit group must be overstaffed."

In favor:

"Consulting is one of the most important services we provide for management. We have found a direct correlation between our time spent on consulting and the decrease that we have in investigations. So, when I do my audit plan at the beginning of the year, I save a certain amount of time to do the consulting projects that aren't part of the risk-based audit program …

"We have an incredibly wonderful, comfortable relationship [with management]. People see the audit staff as peers and feel very comfortable calling and asking them questions …

"In the next couple of months, I'll be developing an online conflict-of-interest training course, which our federal researchers will be required to take. We'll be doing that with our new whistleblowers policy as well."

The corporate governance debacles at the turn of the millennium, of the United States in particular but of Europe and elsewhere too, therefore heralded a relative swing away from an internal audit emphasis on consulting services back to the more traditional assurance role. As we will see later in this chapter, internal auditors were to prove not entirely effective in this assurance role. There are many internal audit functions, including some of the largest, that reject a consulting role entirely. The heavily revised 2009 *Standards* of The IIA will make that harder, if not impossible, to sustain while still applying the *Standards*.

INTERNAL AUDIT FOCUS ON ASSURANCE OVER FINANCIAL REPORTING

The impact of the corporate governance debacles has been even more extreme than stated above: Not only have management and the audit committee tended to place more stress on the assurance role of internal audit, but beyond that, they have often required internal audit to focus on assurance about financial and accounting matters rather than assurance on operational and other matters. The standard definition of internal control gives three objectives of internal control, and internal audit functions have recently been asked to focus more on providing assurance on the second of these:

"Internal control is broadly defined as a process, effected by the entity's board of directors, management and other personnel, designed to provide reasonable assurance regarding the achievement of objectives in the following categories:

- Effectiveness and efficiency of operations;
- Reliability of financial reporting;
- Compliance with applicable laws and regulations."[5]

and

"Internal control can be judged effective in each of the three categories, respectively, if the board of directors and management have reasonable assurance that:

- They understand the extent to which the entity's operations objectives are being achieved.
- Published financial statements are being prepared reliably.
- Applicable laws and regulations are being complied with."[6]

That the assurance needs of boards extend across all three objectives of internal control and also risk management is illustrated well by a provision within the United Kingdom's corporate governance code:

"The board should, at least annually, conduct a review of the effectiveness of the group's system of internal controls and should report to shareholders that they have done so. The review should cover all material controls, including financial, operational and compliance controls and risk management systems."[7]

IMPACT OF SARBANES–OXLEY ON INTERNAL AUDITING

The Sarbanes–Oxley Act of 2002, itself a direct result of the Enron debacle, has turned the screw further as far as internal audit is concerned. It has been emulated outside the United States with equivalent laws now in Canada and Japan. The Sarbanes–Oxley Act catches US quoted companies, overseas subsidiaries, and operating units of US quoted companies and companies registered elsewhere with secondary listings in the US. Draconian criminal sanctions contained within the Act mean that the criminalization of breaches of corporate governance has arrived in a serious way, and executives across the world are mindful of the global reach of the US Department of Justice. Section 906 on "Corporate Responsibility for Financial Reports" of the Sarbanes–Oxley Act sets out criminal penalties with fines of up to one million dollars or imprisonment of up to 10 years, or both, for chief executive officers and chief financial officers (or equivalent thereof) who certify financial reports in the knowledge that they do not comport with all the requirements; or if the false certification were willful, the penalties may be up to five million dollars or imprisonment for up to 20 years, or both (see "Implementing an Effective Internal Controls System," pp. 29–34).

The key certification requirement is set out in Section 404. Subsection (a) requires that each annual report contain an internal control report, which states the responsibility of management for establishing and maintaining an adequate internal control structure and procedures for financial reporting. The annual report must also contain an assessment by management, as of the end of the most recent fiscal year of the issuer, of the effectiveness of the internal control structure and procedures of the issuer for financial reporting. Subsection (b) requires that, with respect to that internal control assessment, each registered public accounting firm that prepares or issues the audit report for the issuer shall attest to, and report on, the assessment made by the management of the issuer in accordance with *Standards* for attestation engagements issued or adopted by the Public Companies Accounting Oversight Board (PCAOB). Such an attestation shall not be the subject of a separate engagement. Section 302 of the Act requires a similar assessment and certification by management of internal control over other disclosures made in the annual report.

"The Sarbanes–Oxley Act was designed in a panic and rushed through in a blinding fervour of moral indignation." *The Economist*.

"Sarbanes–Oxley has provided a bonanza for accountants and auditors, the very professions thought to be at fault in the original scandals." Tony Blair.[8]

Very frequently, internal audit has been drafted in to undertake much of the assessment work on behalf of management with respect to Sections 302 and 404 compliance, diverting internal audit from other work. This was particularly the case when companies were initially seeking to comply with the Sarbanes–Oxley Act. Over time, companies have been endeavoring to transfer this compliance work to line management,

freeing up internal audit to provide assurance that this work is being done effectively rather than doing the work itself.

Measures by the SEC and PCAOB[9] (in 2007), sometimes termed "SOX-Lite," have helped to make compliance less onerous. The definitions of "significant deficiencies"[10] and "material weaknesses"[11] in internal control—both of which have to be reported by management—have been relaxed, and the so-called "triple audit" by the external auditors under Section 404 has now become just a "double audit," though it is the least costly element that has been abandoned under PCAOB Auditing Standard No. 5.[12]

Following the delisting of British Airways in the United States, and thus the end of its requirement to comply with the Sarbanes–Oxley Act, the company's annual report for the year ended 31 March 2008 showed a reduction in external audit fees from £4.3 million to £3 million, and further savings of £1.27 million associated with other costs primarily pursuant to complying with the Sarbanes–Oxley Act.

THE WALKER REVIEW

It is interesting to speculate why internal audit emerged virtually unscathed from the financial crisis that hit the world economy towards the end of the last decade. Was it because they did a good job, or that there were low expectations about their remit? In the wake of this crisis, the Walker Report addressed corporate governance in UK banks and other financial entities. Its analysis and recommendations have much wider relevance than just for the UK. That this report saw internal audit as no part of the solution speaks volumes. The report says:

"Some concern was also expressed at the very limited discussion of audit, in particular internal audit, in the July consultation paper—though this in fact reflected judgement that the principal failures that afflicted problem banks did not principally arise under the rubric of 'audit' ... Discussions in the context of this Review process suggest that failures that proved to be critical for many banks related much less to what might be characterised as conventional compliance and audit processes, including internal audit, but to defective information flow, defective analytical tools and inability to bring insightful judgement in the interpretation of information and the impact of market events on the business model."[13]

On the contrary, we take the position that "defective information flow, defective analytical tools and inability to bring insightful judgement in the interpretation of information and the

Financial Reporting Impacted on Internal Auditing Negatively?

impact of market events on the business model" are mainstream issues for internal audit to comment upon. It follows that internal audit was ineffective in its assurance role at communicating persuasively to top management and the board the risks that financial institutions were running. Internal auditors in nonfinancial entities were ineffective at communicating to their top managements and boards the risks that those entities were running through their excessive dependence on precarious financial institutions.

MAKING IT HAPPEN

Key "learning" points for finance professionals, as well as ideas and issues for action or further consideration:

- Take compliance requirements seriously.
- Consider the costs of compliance when deciding whether to list or delist in the US.
- Don't leave new compliance requirements to the last moment.
- Consider using your internal audit function in the initial stages of implementing new compliance obligations.
- Remember that internal audit should be independent of the activities upon which It provides assurance.
- In time, transfer compliance responsibilities to line management and away from internal audit.
- Accept that internal audit adds value when assurance over operational efficiency and effectiveness along with assurance of compliance with laws, regulations, and policies are both "in scope"—not just assurance of control over financial reporting.
- Accept that internal audit also adds value when it is available to provide consulting services to management.
- Consider whether internal audit is sufficiently independent of management to provide valuable assurance to the board and its audit committee.

MORE INFO

Reports:

Financial Reporting Council. "The Combined Code on Corporate Governance." June 2008. Online at: www.frc.org.uk/documents/pagemanager/frc/Combined_Code_June_2008

Financial Reporting Council. "Internal control—Revised guidance for directors on the Combined Code." October 2005. Online at: www.frc.org.uk/documents/pagemanager/frc/Revised%20Turnbull%20Guidance%20October%202005.pdf

Financial Reporting Council. "The Turnbull guidance as an evaluation framework for the purposes of Section 404(a) of the Sarbanes–Oxley Act." December 2004. Online at: www.frc.org.uk/documents/pagemanager/frc/draft_guide.pdf

Public Companies Accounting Oversight Board (PCAOB). "Auditing Standard No. 5: An audit of internal control over financial reporting that is integrated with an audit of financial statements." 2007. Online at: www.pcaobus.org/Standards/Standards_and_Related_Rules/Auditing_Standard_No.5.aspx

US Securities & Exchange Commission. "Commission guidance regarding management's report on internal control over financial reporting under Section 13(a) or 15(d) of the Securities Exchange Act of 1934." June 20, 2007. Online at: www.sec.gov/rules/final/2007/33-8809.pdf

Website:

Institute of Internal Auditors: www.theiia.org
This Florida-based website is a fund of information. In particular "Sarbanes–Oxley Section 404: A guide for management by internal controls practitioners" (2nd ed, January 2008) at www.theiia.org/download.cfm?file=31866 [PDF]. The Institute's bimonthly membership newsletter, AuditWire, is available in electronic form to IIA members and subscribers on its website and via e-mail. The IIA runs Global Audit Information Network (GAIN)—a very effective and economic online benchmarking service for internal audit functions. More information at www.theiia.org/guidance/benchmarking/gain

NOTES

1 Further sets might, for instance, have been in the areas of fraud investigations, IT auditing, governmental internal auditing, and auditing in financial institutions.

2 The IIA's definition of internal auditing, to be found within its *Standards*.

3 Brune, Christina. "Consulting: Friend or foe?" *AuditWire* 25:1 (January–February 2003).

4 Quotes from Peter Rodgers (vice president and general auditor of BISYS Group Inc. in Columbus, Ohio) as being against consulting services, and Geraldine Gail (director of internal audit, the University of California, Santa Cruz) as being in favor, in: Brune, Christina "Consulting: Friend or foe?" *AuditWire* 25:1 (January–February 2003).

5 Committee of Sponsoring Organizations (COSO) (www.coso.org). *Internal Control—Integrated Framework*. AICPA, 1992. (Available at www.cpa2biz.com).

6 Executive Summary to *Internal Control—Integrated Framework*, p. 4.

7 Financial Reporting Council (2010): The UK Corporate Governance Code, 2010, Code Provision C.2.2 (www.frc.org.uk).

8 Speech on compensation culture delivered at the Institute of Public Policy Research, University College, London, on May 26, 2005. www.number10.gov.uk/output/Page7562.asp

9 In particular, PCAOB Auditing Standard No. 5 replacing the more demanding Standard No. 2.

10 PCAOB Auditing Standard No. 2 (2004): "A control deficiency (or a combination of internal control deficiencies) should be classified as a *significant deficiency* if, by itself or in combination with other control deficiencies, it results in more than a remote likelihood of a misstatement of the company's annual or interim financial statements that is more than inconsequential will not be prevented or detected." This statement has been replaced by PCAOB Auditing Standard No. 5 (2007): "A *significant deficiency* is a deficiency, or a combination of deficiencies, in internal control over financial reporting that is less severe

than a material weakness, yet important enough to merit attention by those responsible for oversight of the company's financial reporting."

11 PCAOB Auditing Standard No. 2 (2004): "A significant deficiency should be classified as a *material weakness* if, by itself or in combination with other control deficiencies, it results in more than a remote likelihood that a material misstatement in the company's annual or interim financial statements will not be prevented or detected." This has been replaced by PCAOB Auditing Standard No. 5 (2007): "A *material weakness* is a deficiency, or a combination of deficiencies, in internal control over financial reporting, such that there is a *reasonable possibility* that a material misstatement of the company's annual or interim financial statements will not be prevented or detected on a timely basis … A material weakness in internal control over financial reporting may exist even when financial statements are not materially misstated."

12 Until 2007, the PCAOB interpreted Section 404 as requiring a "triple audit"—(1) the traditional audit of the financial statements, (2) an attestation that management have done what they are required to do under SEC rules to assess and certify the effectiveness of internal control over financial reporting, and (3) the external auditor's own assessment of the effectiveness of internal control over financial reporting. In fact, a careful reading of Section 404 indicates that the Act only required (1) and (2). Post 2007 requirements under the SOX-Lite regime mean that PCAOB Auditing Standard No. 5 continues with (1) and (3) (above)—a surprising interpretation by PCAOB, but one that preserves a maximum of the extra fee-earning opportunity that Section 404 has given external auditors.

13 HM Treasury. "A review of corporate governance in UK banks and other financial industry entities—Final recommendations." (Walker Report). November 26, 2009. pp. 90, 93. Online at: www.hm-treasury.gov.uk/d/walker_review_261109.pdf

Internal Audit and Partnering with Senior Management by Bruce Turner

Best Practice • In Practice

EXECUTIVE SUMMARY

- The business world is constantly changing. Internal auditors increasingly need to embrace ongoing changes to the business. They also need to understand changes to key drivers, such as the regulatory environment, the profession, and the social and political landscape.
- To do so, internal auditors must maintain a meaningful dialog with senior management, so as to understand their changing needs and expectations.
- An internal audit work plan that aligns neatly with the primary risk concerns of senior management and other key stakeholders ensures that the audit effort is directed at the areas that are likely to add the greatest value to the organization.
- Because of the increasing complexity associated with running an organization, internal auditors must ensure that their recommendations translate into improved business processes and effective risk management, governance, and control arrangements.
- Internal auditors need to have the capability to deliver a product that meets or exceeds the expectations of senior management.
- Internal auditors must also be able to tell their story to maintain their influence, relevance, and credibility within the organization.

THE CHANGING ENVIRONMENT

"The internal audit function has evolved from corporate cop to that of a savvy in-house consulting service."[1]

Internal auditing in the twenty-first century imposes even greater demands on the professional internal audit staff, whose role has expanded to combine both an assurance and a consulting service to management. Internal audit charters have been broadened considerably to reflect these demands.

The chief executive of the Institute of Internal Auditors in Australia (Christopher McRostie) has reflected:

"In rapidly changing and increasingly complex business and regulatory environments the internal audit function has evolved from corporate cop to that of a savvy in-house consulting service that not only reports problems, but that also gives constructive suggestions to line managers about how to improve the performance of the business."[2]

Internal audit staff are being increasingly relied on to provide organizational expertise in risk management, internal control, and governance processes as a consequence of the emergence of stronger corporate governance demands across the world. Internal auditors need to have strategies in place that allow them to remain abreast of trends and emerging issues within their organization and the broader business community.

Contemporary internal auditing practitioners need to apply a strategic approach to understanding the key organizational value drivers and positioning themselves to meet the expectations of senior management.

Internal auditors are well placed to influence senior management in setting the right tone at the top. This, in turn, is a powerful way to nurture an organizational culture that is consistent with the values, risk tolerance, and strategies of senior management and the board.

WHAT SENIOR MANAGEMENT WANTS

"The Chief Audit Executive should effectively manage the internal audit activity to ensure it adds value to the organization."[3]

Senior management trusts internal auditors to "tell it as it is" by reporting without fear or favor. One company chairman[4] observed that "senior management want much more immediate and informal input on how the corporation is doing ... I'd rather have the internal auditor on my doorstep telling me what I need to know so I can act on it now." His main suggestions for internal auditors were:

- Don't be distracted from good business practice.
- Understand your customer.
- Avoid being too production-oriented.
- Prioritize your activities and coordination role.
- Speak up when others may not.

Senior management is looking for assurance that current business activities meet regulatory and legislative obligations. They are also looking for ideas that drive better business performance

QFINANCE

143

in line with their overarching strategies and business model.

Internal auditors are best placed to meet senior management's expectations when they apply a sense of urgency to their work, apply a win–win mindset, and consistently deliver on commitments made. It is imperative that the integrity and credibility of their activities is undoubted, and that they nurture a professional and constructive relationship. The chief audit executive should undertake surveys of senior management to measure the quality of the service and determine how well the internal audit activity is serving their needs.

See below for a perspective on senior management's priorities in one organization in relation to internal auditing.

The chief audit executive ought to maintain regular conversations with senior management with the objective of understanding their business perspectives and expectations of the internal audit activity. This helps to shape the planning, objectives, and scope of individual audits. The relationship should be based on cooperation, collaboration, and mutual respect.

A structured stakeholder relationship program is a useful mechanism to ensure that regular contact is maintained and that the conversations and commitments are appropriately tracked. It needs to be tailored for the business environment by recognizing the areas that need the greatest level of contact.

By way of example, a three-tier stakeholder relationship program schedule might have:
- Quarterly contact with senior managers, such as the chief financial officer and chief risk officer.
- Half-yearly contact with business leaders in remote locations.
- Annual contact with managers of relatively low-risk activities like marketing.

Because of the heavy workload of many senior managers, it may be difficult to get time in their diaries. Get to know who their gatekeepers are and build relationships with them. That can sometimes help to unlock the doors in a more timely manner.

Some larger agencies establish audit liaison officers or champions across their business lines or regional offices as contact points for the internal audit activity. These people can also facilitate audit planning and the conduct of audits, and provide periodic updates on the status of previous audit recommendations.

There are benefits in establishing an internal auditor alumni. Most internal auditors retain their passion for the profession when they leave the area. They represent a fertile avenue across the organization for keeping abreast of what is really going on in the business.

SENIOR MANAGEMENT PRIORITIES
- Accurate reporting, which reflects a business perspective, is well-written, easy to follow, and is consistent with the facts.
- Practical, constructive, and actionable recommendations.
- Proper consideration of business concerns and perspectives.
- Clear communication of objectives and scope at the start of the audit.
- Disruption to daily business operations is minimized.

PLANNING THE INTERNAL AUDIT EFFORT TO DELIVER VALUE
"Begin with the end in mind."[5]

The internal audit effort is underpinned by effective planning that directs audit effort to the higher-risk areas of the business. It is imperative that senior management and other key stakeholders are engaged in the development of the internal audit plan to ensure that it is relevant and consistent with the organization's risk profile.

In addition to looking for feedback on the adequacy and effectiveness of risk management, governance, and internal controls, senior management want recommendations that help to improve business processes. They are no longer satisfied with receiving just the results of individual audits, though these remain important. Senior management are increasingly looking for the internal auditors to provide additional analyses of the results of audits to identify systemic issues and provide insights into the corporate culture of the organization. One way of meeting these expectations is to set "themes" for the various audits contained in the internal audit plan. This facilitates high-level reporting to senior management against each of the themes.

Internal auditors can provide the greatest value to senior management when they:
- Align their activities to their organization's goals and objectives, and periodically review the role of internal audit in the light of changes to the business and global events.
- Understand the business, the key drivers, the impact of developments on the organization's risks, and the mood of senior management.
- Consult effectively with senior management, staff, and other key stakeholders, and contribute ideas and advice on an ongoing basis.

Best Practice • In Practice

CASE STUDY
Misguided Auditing Efforts
On reviewing the audit coverage of the retail loan portfolio of a commercial bank, an auditor discovered that there was broad coverage of personal loans which averaged about US$30,000. The auditors were doing a very thorough audit of the personal loans in line with the content of the internal audit plan, their sampling techniques were effective, their work papers were well-constructed, and the resultant audit report was well written.

However, the auditor also found that there was absolutely no audit coverage of foreign currency loans, although the average loan was around US$750,000 and had a far greater inherent risk. The reason was simple. Foreign currency loans had been introduced the previous year, and internal audit planning had not kept pace with the changing loan product and risk profile of the commercial bank. Consequently, the internal audit effort was misdirected and proved to be of little value to senior management in the overall context of their loan portfolio.

- Elevate the focus of their activities to strategic decision-making and broader risk management strategies and mitigation, while maintaining an appropriate balance with traditional compliance and operational and financial auditing.
- Provide broader information and a deeper insight into emerging governance, risk, and control issues in a timely manner.
- Deliver what they promise.

MAXIMIZING INTERNAL AUDIT'S CAPABILITY
"The vision of the director of auditing and the high expectations of management are merely wistful wishes without the right staff to do the job."[6]

It is the capability of internal audit staff that often determines the level of credibility, trust, and respect that the internal audit activity has within the organization.

Ensure that senior management and the audit committee are kept apprised of the talent within the internal audit activity. Periodically produce a staff profile that sets out the skills, experience, qualifications, and years of audit experience of the internal auditors. This helps to establish or retain credibility, especially when it is combined with benchmarking of other internal audit activities.

At a time in our history when there is a global shortage of professional internal audit practitioners, coupled with a broader internal audit charter, it is imperative to position the internal audit activity as an employer of choice.

To attract the right people, use the results of the periodic external quality assessment reviews to differentiate your internal audit activity from others (these reviews are mandatory under professional internal auditing standards).

Elements that could be considered in building greater internal capability include the following.
- Develop a recruitment strategy based on a skills gap analysis. This will ensure that you have the right multidisciplinary capability to undertake the broad range of audits in the internal audit plan.
- Establish internal audit as a learning environment and encourage innovation. This is a point of differentiation from others that will help to cater for the needs of talented and ambitious individuals.
- Produce a professional development plan for internal auditors that incorporates both a top-down and a bottom-up approach. There are typically three elements: develop the current capability; extend the capability to broaden the circle of influence; and identify future disciplines. The top-down analysis will help to close the gap between current and future staff capability needs. It should also promote continuous learning by encouraging postgraduate studies and the pursuit of professional certifications. The bottom-up element reflects the specific developmental needs of individual internal auditors.
- Recognize that internal auditors must have exceptionally strong communication skills across all areas (especially written, reading, oral, listening, body language, and presentation).
- Promote professional internal auditing standards. Use the results of the periodic external quality assessment reviews to differentiate your internal audit activity from others.
- Build greater awareness of the internal audit activity across the organization, as this will help to attract fresh talent to the area. For

QFINANCE

instance, many large organizations have a structured graduate recruitment program, which is potentially a rich breeding ground. But graduates often do not understand the nature of internal auditing beyond the basic technical aspects they learned at university.

- Establish a policy that encourages subject matter experts to spend some time in internal audit on a secondment (typically three to six months). Tailor this to attract people with high potential, on the basis that what they learn in internal audit will help them throughout their career.

TELLING THE INTERNAL AUDIT STORY

"The balanced scorecard can help internal auditing directors achieve superior performance by focusing on value-added services, corporate strategies and priorities."[7]

The internal audit activity influences the business in many different ways, quite apart from producing the traditional audit reports. To this end, it is important that the chief audit executive takes the time to tell the internal audit story.

The balanced scorecard is a contemporary reporting structure that helps to paint a picture of how effectively the internal audit activity is partnering with senior management and driving value for the organization. In addition to periodic reporting throughout the year, the balanced scorecard approach provides a solid foundation for producing an annual report on internal audit aimed at better informing internal stakeholders. The balanced scorecard typically focuses on four elements: partnering with the audit committee; supporting senior management; managing internal audit processes; and managing people and their development.

There is an emerging interest in what internal audit is doing outside the organization. A recent trend has been to include a section in the balanced scorecard on professional outreach (for example, activities with professional associations, presentation of papers at external conferences, and published articles).

There are a range of communication channels that the chief audit executive can use to help build the "audit brand." The strategies will vary depending on the size of the organization. A good starting point is to develop a marketing plan or communication strategy. The intention is to influence people across the organization to embrace appropriate governance and risk management techniques, and to promote an effective control environment. In doing so, it helps to raise awareness about the internal

MAKING IT HAPPEN

The chief audit executive must set the right direction for the internal audit activity in consultation with the audit committee and senior management. This will be reflected in an internal audit charter that outlines the role and responsibilities of the internal audit activity, as well as its vision and mission. The internal audit plan will reflect where internal audit resources are best applied.

At a time when the expectations of senior management and other stakeholders are getting higher, successful internal auditing demands the right people. These people will be intelligent, passionate, and innovative. They will have the knack of communicating well with senior managers and other stakeholders and responding to their needs, without compromising their independence of mind. Their research will alert them to the "next big risk."

Ideas for Further Consideration

There is a strong parallel between factors that result in highly credible internal auditing and those at the heart of a successful small business. Internal auditors will be well placed to partner with senior management when they think like a manager and apply business concepts similar to those outlined below. They are nine easy steps that underpinned a successful franchise business:[8]

- Try different things.
- Try to do everything you do better, and improve what you do in every possible way.
- Try to be more cost-effective.
- Try to keep overheads down.
- Try to give better service to your clients, make them happy, and focus on them.
- Be persistent and never give up.
- Look after your customers obsessively and worry about how you can look after them better.
- Give maximum service for the least cost.
- Listen a lot. Listen all the time. Listen. Listen. Listen.

audit activity, which, in turn, helps to garner cooperation and support for internal auditors in the conduct of their work.

Elements that could be included in a communication strategy include:

- Active participation in presenting key messages at the organization's induction, training, and other corporate programs.
- Articles in staff newsletters.
- An interesting, useful, and informative internal audit intranet site.
- Establishment of a network of business unit champions as a conduit for regular communications on audit matters.
- Taking an interest in the organization's graduate programs, so as to help promote ambassadors for internal audit in future leaders.
- Brochures on the internal audit activity.

ELEMENTS OF AN ANNUAL REPORT ON INTERNAL AUDIT

The content of an annual report will be dictated by the needs of senior management and the nature of the internal audit charter. Typical headings include:

- Foreword;
- Summary of internal audit activities;
- Overall conclusion;
- Activity headings.

For each balanced scorecard element there should be:

- A performance summary;
- A meeting attendance summary;
- Highlights;
- Areas for continuing focus.

Best Practice • In Practice

MORE INFO

Books:

Covey, Stephen R. *The 7 Habits of Highly Effective People: Powerful Lessons in Personal Change.* London: Simon & Schuster, 2004.

Fraser, John, and Hugh Lindsay. *20 Questions Directors Should Ask about Internal Audit.* Toronto, ON: Canadian Institute of Chartered Accountants, 2004.

Frigo, Mark L. *A Balanced Scorecard Framework for Internal Auditing Departments.* Altamonte Springs, FA: Institute of Internal Auditors Research Foundation, 2002.

Pickett, K. H. Spencer. *The Internal Auditor at Work: A Practical Guide to Everyday Challenges.* 2nd ed. Hoboken, NJ: Wiley, 2004.

Sawyer, Lawrence B., Mortimer A. Dittenhofer, and James H. Scheiner. *Sawyer's Internal Auditing: The Practice of Modern Internal Auditing.* 5th ed. Altamonte Springs, FL: IIA Research Foundation, 2003.

Report:

Australian National Audit Office. "Public sector internal audit: An investment in assurance and business improvement." Better Practice Guide. September 2007. Online at: www.anao.gov.au/uploads/documents/Public_Sector_Internal_Audit.pdf

Websites:

Australian National Audit Office (ANAO): www.anao.gov.au
Canadian Institute of Chartered Accountants (CICA): www.cica.ca
Corporate Executive Board: www.audit.executiveboard.com
Institute of Internal Auditors (IIA): www.theiia.org

NOTES

1 LexisNexis. *Risk Management* 48 (2008): 12.

2 *Ibid.*

3 Pickett (2004), pp. 60–61.

4 Thomas, R. L. "A chairman's view of internal audit." *Bank Management Journal* (May/June 1996): 28–29.

5 Covey (2004), chapter on habit 2.

6 Sawyer, Lawrence B. *Sawyer's Internal Auditing.* 3rd ed. IIA, 1988, p. 785.

7 Frigo (2002), pp. 43, 50 (slightly edited).

8 Meltzer, G. "Someone else's slip-ups—Minding their own business." *Daily Telegraph (Sydney, Australia)* (October 16, 2001): 34 (edited).

QFINANCE

How Internal Auditing Can Help with a Company's Fraud Issues by Gail Harden

EXECUTIVE SUMMARY

- Fraud risk exposure should be assessed periodically by an organization to identify specific potential schemes and events for which it needs to have controls in place to mitigate risks.
- Internal audit serves as a critical defense against the threat of fraud, with a focus on assessing and monitoring controls designed to prevent and detect fraud.
- Internal auditors can be part of fraud deterrence by examining the adequacy of the system of internal controls.

INTRODUCTION

Regulatory oversight is increasing, as are penalties. A passive attitude in an organization toward oversight and the topic of fraud, antifraud programs, and controls would be a strong indicator of a significant deficiency in its system of internal controls.

Economic factors can increase the occurrence of fraudulent practices. When the economy is in a downturn the risk of fraud increases due to personal financial pressures, the stagnation of compensation, and corporate stabilization strategies.[1] Problems associated with corporate stabilization strategies include:

- fewer personnel and fear of downsizing;
- increased workloads;
- less accuracy;
- less time to make decisions;
- shortcuts taken to circumvent controls;
- low morale;
- likelihood of "cooking the books" to meet performance goals.

Additionally, corporations expand into foreign markets to reduce costs, which can lead to less transparency, stretched resources, and corrupt practices.

FRAUD AND FRAUD RISK ASSESSMENT DEFINED

Fraud is defined as the use of dishonesty, deception, or false representation in order to gain a material advantage or injure the interests of others. Types of fraud include false accounting, theft, third party or investment fraud, collusion between employees, and computer fraud. Fraud risk assessment is a structured approach to identify and analyze fraud risk and controls in an organization, and to assess whether those controls are working as intended. PricewaterhouseCoopers (PwC) explained:

"Fraud risk assessment expands upon traditional risk assessment. It is scheme and scenario based rather than based on control risk or inherent risk. The assessment considers the various ways that fraud and misconduct can occur by and against the company. Fraud risk assessment also considers vulnerability to management override and potential schemes to circumvent existing control activities, which may require additional compensating control activities."[2]

WHY SHOULD INTERNAL AUDIT PERFORM FRAUD RISK ASSESSMENT?

The Institute of Internal Auditors (IIA) sets forth professional standards that require internal auditors to assess the risks facing their organizations. Furthermore, internal audit is expected to evaluate whether the company's controls sufficiently address identified risks of material misstatement in financial reporting due to fraud.

Internal audit participates in fraud deterrence by examining and evaluating the adequacy of internal controls. By merely asking such questions, internal audit makes it known that it is on the lookout for possible fraud schemes. Internal audit reports to the audit committee and management on the functioning of internal controls in relation to fraud risk, thus facilitating adherence to financial reporting and corporate governance responsibilities.

The audit committee has responsibilities of fiduciary oversight to consider:

- the process utilized to identify, document, and evaluate fraud risk;
- types of fraud identified;
- the level of likelihood and significance of fraud;
- appropriate action taken to close any gaps in the existence and operation of controls;
- opportunities for override of controls by management.

Figure 1. The fraud risk assessment process

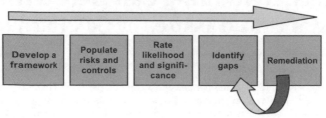

PROCESS OVERVIEW

The fraud risk assessment process is a structured method to identify possible fraud schemes, identify internal controls that help to prevent or detect identified fraud schemes, document the results of testing the controls, and implement corrective action plans where needed. The objective of this process is to identify the existence of controls and how they operate, not necessarily to seek out fraud. Adequate controls reduce the opportunities for fraud to be committed. The assessment considers the various ways in which a company can be subjected to fraud and misconduct, along with its vulnerability to management override and other potential schemes to circumvent existing controls.

Fraud risk assessment is a continuous process, as shown in Figure 1.

Process Steps
The steps in the process are:
- develop a framework (i.e. a format);
- identify risks and controls;
- rate the likelihood and significance of the risks;
- identify gaps;
- plan and implement remedial measures.

The process should follow the approach recommended by the Committee of Sponsoring Organizations (COSO).[3] This includes:
- setting the "tone at the top," instituting a code of ethics, and setting up a whistleblower hotline;
- monitoring effectiveness;
- communication;
- identifying risks;
- linking risks and controls.

CASE STUDY

To understand the process better, consider the following approach taken by a specific company.

Develop a Framework
Development of a framework consists of selecting the business processes to assess, determining the automation tool to use, and setting up the layout using such a tool. The layout should include the identified potential fraud schemes, an evaluation of the likelihood and significance of the risks, controls to prevent or detect the risks, the type of control, whether the control has been tested, the date of the test and the results, and corrective action plans. Table 1 shows an Excel worksheet utilized by the company in our case study.

The business processes assessed by this company were financial reporting, business development, sales, billing, accounts receivable, cash receipts, purchasing, accounts payable, payroll, inventory and shipping, officers' expenses, and entity level controls. Revenue recognition and management override controls are of particular concern, and they fall under financial reporting controls. All processes were also assessed and organized according to the business location to which the processes have been decentralized.

Balance sheet and expense accounts should be identified as they relate to each of the business processes. Mapping accounts to the processes can be useful in determining the financial impact of a particular process by business location. For example, locations with higher revenue have a higher financial impact on the Revenue Recognition Process.

Identify Risks and Controls
The next step is to populate the framework with fraud schemes (risks) and controls. To identify potential fraud schemes and best practice controls requires extensive research. Examples of resources are, but are not limited to, seminars and conferences, articles and white papers from experts such as the Institute of Internal Auditors, Deloitte, KPMG (or other CPA (certified public

Table 1. Example of a fraud risk assessment framework

Fraud Risk Assessment
Accounts Receivable
Process Owner: <Insert Process Owner Name>

Fraud Risk	Likelihood	Significance	Control Activity	Preventive or Detective	Has Audit tested Control?	Date tested	Result	Action Plan
Theft of cash receipts and written off as bad debts.	High	High	Reconciliation of bad debt expense reserve with supervisory review.	Detective	Yes	1/10/06	OK	
			Person posting receivables does not also have system access to make journal entries to bad debt expense.	Preventative	Yes	1/10/06	OK	
			Procedure exists and is followed to turn over delinquent accounts to a third-party collections agency.	Preventative	Yes	1/10/06	OK	
			Accounts receivables reconciled to the general ledger by individual with no conflicting duties.	Detective	Yes	1/10/06	OK	
			Accounting Manager authorization required to write off uncollectible accounts.	Preventative	Yes	1/10/06	OK	
Rebilling of past due items to change the # of days past due (To change DSO's for example).	Medium	Medium	Policy disallows cancelling and rebilling invoices unless the original was billed to the wrong client, or some other extenuating circumstances.	Preventative	Yes			
			All credits require the use of a request form and approval from management according to an authorization matrix.	Preventative	Yes	1/10/06	OK	
			Duties to input billing and credits to the AR system, approvals for credits, and collections activities are segregated.	Preventative	Yes	1/10/06	OK	
Kiting – writing checks against insufficient funds or unavailable funds and hoping the funds are deposited or become available before the checks clear the account.	Medium	Low	The Accounting Manager has a "cash card" where cash receipts and disbursements are logged. He monitors the cash level and transfers money from savings when necessary to cover disbursements. The Controller approves the disbursement batches and also has access to monitor the daily cash position.	Preventative	Yes	1/10/06	OK	
			ZBA Accounts – type of bank account where funds are transferred from a deposit account to a disbursement account as disbursements are presented for payment.	Preventative				Company does not currently use ZBA accounts.
			Positive pay set up with the bank. This is a practice where the company sends a file to the bank of all the disbursements generated and the bank will only pay those that are on the file.	Preventative				Company is in progress to set up this type of arrangement.

In Practice • Best Practice

accountant) firms—these were used in the case example), business periodicals and journals, and the American Institute of Certified Public Accountants (AICPA).

It is important to choose controls that can be tested. For example, a third-party control cannot be tested. Reliance on external audit to find an error, or customer complaints, are examples of inadequate controls. No controls exist that provide absolute assurance against fraud. Individuals who are sufficiently motivated will find a way to override or circumvent controls. Even so, controls are a vital part of fraud deterrence. Auditors should continually ask themselves: "How could someone get around this control?" The general expectation of internal auditors is that they have sufficient knowledge to identify indicators of fraud, but they are not expected to have the expertise of a person whose primary responsibility is detecting and investigating fraud.

Rate the Likelihood and Significance of Risks
Risks should be rated by likelihood and significance. The objective of a risk rating is to narrow down and prioritize the controls to test. Process owners/managers should be interviewed or surveyed to evaluate risk ranking.

Likelihood can be assessed based on three levels: "remote," "more than remote/reasonably probable," and "probable." Likelihood could be evaluated based on previous experience and past audit results.

Significance can be determined by using the standards "inconsequential," "more than inconsequential," and "material." Materiality can be based on financial impact, reputation risk, and/or shareholder or lender considerations. Management determines the organization's risk appetite—the amount of risk the company is willing to accept as a consequence of doing business.

In our case study, the described levels equated to "low," "medium," and "high."

In our case study, the company rated likelihood and significance on a scale of 1 to 5, 1 representing the least risk or significance. The chart shown in Figure 2 was used to display the rating results graphically. Risks falling in the gray blocks require higher priority. In this example, risk #7, Orders for personal supplies, had a rating of 1 for likelihood and 1 for significance, thus placing it in the lower left-hand corner. Risk #4 had a rating of 4 under likelihood and 4 for significance, and so on. Risks falling closer to the top right-hand corner are the highest risks and should receive highest focus and priority.

Identify Control Gaps
Risks and controls have been identified and populated into the spreadsheet. The next step is to identify control gaps and weaknesses. Identifying control gaps and weaknesses meets the COSO element of "monitoring effectiveness." Generally, the information needed to document whether the controls exist and are working as intended comes from operational internal audits, external audits, direct testing, or any other regulatory testing.

Remediation
Remediation plans meet the COSO element of "communication." Missing controls, or controls not working as intended and the related corrective action plans, are communicated to the process owners and company management, as well as to the audit committee. The case example tracks all the corrective action plans utilizing a Microsoft Access database. Action plans not completed by the due date are reported to the audit committee.

Refer to Table 2 for an example of the section of the fraud risk assessment worksheet (Table 1) related to the testing of controls and setting out corrective action plans for remediation.

Ongoing Monitoring
In order to meet the COSO element of "monitoring effectiveness," the content of the framework should be regularly revisited to determine whether there are any new weaknesses, risks, or controls, and to take into account any changes in the internal and external environments. In conjunction with operational audits and other testing of controls, current data are entered for test results and corrective action plans.

Figure 2. Rating the likelihood and significance of risk

Likelihood and significance
(gray = higher risk)

Risks
#1 – Shell company scheme
  #2 – Overpayment scheme
  #3 – Phony contractor scheme
  #4 – Personal travel expenses
  #5 – Fraudulent auditor/
      inspector expenses
  #6 – Check tampering
  #7 – Orders for personal
      supplies

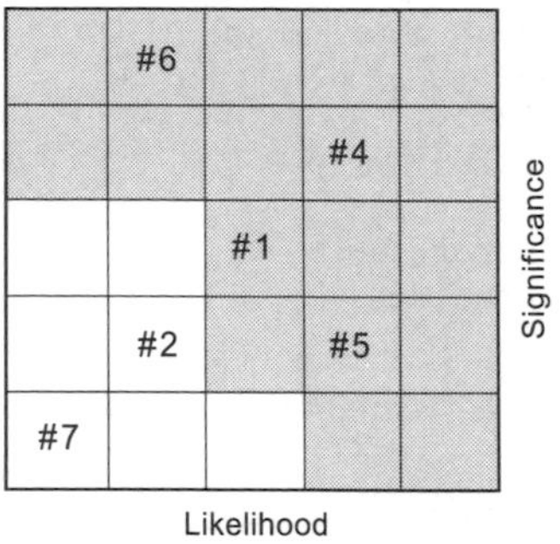

Table 2. Identifying control gaps and recommending remediation plans

Control Activity	Preventive or Detective	Has Audit Tested Control?	Date tested	Result	Action Plan
Reconciliation of bad debt expense reserve with supervisory review.	Detective	Yes	1/10/2006	Failed	No supervisory review, effective April 11, 2008, now have supervisory review.
Person posting receivables does not also have system access to make journal entries to bad debt expense.	Preventive	Yes	1/10/2006	OK	
Procedure exists and is followed to turn over delinquent accounts to a third-party collections agency.	Preventive	Yes	1/10/2006	OK	
Accounts receivable reconciled to the general ledger by individual with no conflicting duties.	Detective	Yes	1/10/2006	Failed	AR account reconciled but contained variances. Account to be reconciled and reviewed by August 31, 2008. Owner: Corporate Controller.
Accounting manager authorization required to write off uncollectible accounts.	Preventive	Yes	1/10/2006	OK	
Policy disallows cancelling and rebilling invoices unless the original was billed to the wrong client, or some other extenuating circumstances.	Preventive	No			

OTHER FRAUD PREVENTION AND DETECTION ACTIVITIES

The following control activities meet the COSO element of "tone at the top," a code of ethics, and whistleblower hotlines:

- company ethics and anti-fraud policy/program;
- fraud response policy and procedure;
- active participation and support from management and the board of directors;
- conducting background investigations prior to employment for senior and sensitive positions;
- ethics and fraud awareness training.

These topics and other related controls constitute what is referred to as "entity level controls." Table 3 shows the fraud risk assessment for entity-level controls.

Table 3. Fraud risk assessment for entity-level controls

Fraud Risk Assessment
General Fraud Controls—"Entity Level"
Process Owner: Board of Directors

Control Activity	Preventive or Detective	Has Audit tested Control?	Date tested	Result	Action Plan
Code of Ethics—communicated, training, monitoring	Preventive	Yes	2/1/2007	OK	
Background investigation when hiring	Preventive	Yes	2/1/2007	OK	
Ethics hotline and whistleblower program	Detective			OK	
Defined process for investigation of alleged fraud	Detective				
IT controls—system access, fraud detection & monitoring, controls to prevent inappropriate computer modifications and overrides by IT	Both	Yes	Annual	NI	IT Strategic Plan
Documented antifraud policies and procedures, Code of Ethics/Conduct, and hiring and promotion standards	Preventive		2/1/2007	OK	
Promoting antifraud programs through the organization's communication programs	Preventive				
Segregation of duties	Preventive				
Audit Committee is actively overseeing fraud prevention programs and incident investigations	Preventive	Yes	2/1/2007	OK	
Internal Audit assess and tests controls for fraud risk in the organization	Detective	n/a	n/a	n/a	

NI: Needs improvement

How Internal Auditing Can Help with a Company's Fraud Issues

Best Practice • In Practice

MAKING IT HAPPEN
The following are keys for success:
* A planned and documented approach, based on COSO recommendations, that integrates fraud risk assessment with operational and other audits.
* Active involvement from management.
* Consideration of specific potential fraud schemes for each business process and for general ledger accounts.
* Mapping of fraud risks and schemes to control activities.
* Assessment of fraud risks by likelihood and significance.
* Making fraud risk assessment an ongoing process.

CONCLUSION
An article in *Business Finance* in May 2008 (Skalak, 2008) stated that the average cost of one incident of fraud is US$3 million. Fast-growing companies are more susceptible to fraud. As they expand into new markets, acquire new operations, and enter joint ventures these companies become more vulnerable.

Internal audit is in a key position to lead the fraud risk assessment process as it has extensive knowledge of the company and direct lines of communication with management and the audit committee, as well as experience, training and a structured approach to identify and evaluate. Internal audit has a responsibility to assist the audit committee to carry out its fiduciary duties. Fraud risk is a key area of responsibility of the audit committee. According to a PwC white paper:

"For internal audit, this environment poses both opportunities and challenges. Corporate auditors who move quickly to develop antifraud action plans will find ample ways to provide added value to their organizations. Conversely, internal audit directors who fail to address rising stakeholder expectations jeopardize their relevance and imperil their job security."[4]

Internal audit's work on fraud risk assessment can add value to the organization. The following comment was cited in a *Business Finance* article in August of 2007. Larry Harrington, Vice-president of Internal Audit at Raytheon, was quoted as saying:

"We're building relationships within the engineering, supply chain, contracts, and other areas of the company that we might not otherwise have worked with that often, and folks who did not work with us that often might have had a perception of internal audit as the people who stab the wounded and beat up the dead. When you work with the rest of the business on a project like this, they see our talent, energy, and passion in a much more positive light."[5]

MORE INFO
Articles:
Krell, Eric. "The awakening." *Business Finance* (August 2007). Online at: businessfinancemag.com/article/awakening-0801
Skalak, Steven. "Up for grabs." *Business Finance* (May 2008). Online at: businessfinancemag.com/article/grabs-0503
Wells, Joseph T. "New approaches to fraud deterrence: It's time to take a new look at the auditing process." *Journal of Accountancy* 197 (February 2004). Online at: tinyurl.com/ycpd7f2

Reports:
Deloitte Forensic Center. "Ten things about fraud control: How executives view the "fraud control gap'." November 2007.
KPMG. "Fraud risk management: Developing a strategy for prevention, detection, and response." 2006.
PricewaterhouseCoopers. "Key elements of antifraud programs and controls." White Paper. November 2003.
PricewaterhouseCoopers. "The emerging role of internal audit in mitigating fraud and reputation risks." 2004.

QFINANCE

155

In Practice • Best Practice

Websites:

AICPA antifraud/forensic accounting resources:
fvs.aicpa.org/Resources/Antifraud+Forensic+Accounting

Deloitte "Dbriefs" webcasts (US): www.deloitte.com/us/dbriefs. Especially those on "Fraud detection, deterrence, and prevention: Are you doing enough?" (April 11, 2006) and "Fraud risk management: Whose job is it anyway?" (April 9, 2007).

IIA Member Exchange: www.theiia.org/memberexchange

PricewaterhouseCoopers: www.pwc.com

Protiviti risk and business consulting: www.protiviti.com

NOTES

1 "Financial fraud: Does an economic downturn mean an uptick?" Deloitte webinar, July 16, 2008.

2 "Key elements of antifraud programs and controls." PwC, December 11, 2003, p. 12.

3 The Committee of Sponsoring Organizations of the Treadway Commission (COSO) is a US private-sector initiative, formed in 1985. Its major objective is to identify the factors that cause fraudulent financial reporting and to make recommendations to reduce its incidence. COSO has established a common definition of internal controls, standards, and criteria against which companies and organizations can assess their control systems.

4 "The emerging role of internal audit in mitigating fraud and reputation risks." PwC, March 16, 2004, p. 3.

5 "The awakening." *Business Finance* (August 2007).

Internal Audit Planning: How Can We Do It Better? by Michael Parkinson

EXECUTIVE SUMMARY

- Internal auditing is widely promoted as a critical component in the governance of organizations. Yet many directors and top managers are concerned that they are not getting maximum value from this resource.
- Although in many organizations internal audit is under-resourced or under-qualified, the most common problem is that it is poorly used by the organization.
- Poor planning leads to application of internal audit activity in the wrong places and the delivery of irrelevant reports.

INTRODUCTION

Internal audit is an information service. Internal auditors do not—indeed, must not—make decisions for the managers of organizations. They are a highly skilled and expensive resource that exists to serve the best interest of the organization and yet, on the surface, they do not directly contribute to organizational performance. They examine processes and produce reports; they attempt to capture good practice and identify poor; and they design controls to address identified risks. It is the information they convey to the managers of an organization that makes internal auditors valuable.

Information is valuable when it is reliable and relevant. To be reliable it must be objectively based on evidence and well argued. The internal auditing standards provide the basis for the production of reliable information, as they require the application of appropriate techniques by suitably qualified individuals. Reliability comes from discipline and competence.

Relevance means providing information that is needed, when it is needed. Relevance can only be achieved by sound planning—planning that identifies the needs of the organization and enables the delivery of internal audit results at a time when they can be acted on. Planning is a process that must involve not only the professional input of the internal auditor, but also the strategic input of the board and top management of the organization.

Internal auditing will be ineffective if it does not ask, or is not asked, the right questions.

GAINING CONTEXT: A STRATEGY FOR INTERNAL AUDIT

The top level of planning for internal audit needs to consider the users of the information that internal audit is to provide. The users might include a wide range of interests: clearly, the direct managers of areas reviewed will use the reports, but users will also include top management, the audit committee, and, in many cases, a variety of stakeholders external to the organization.

Two levels of program planning are warranted:

- a strategy for internal audit developed as part of a wider strategy for assurance;
- an annual program of internal audits that considers both the requirements for strategic assurance and the need for more immediate advice.

Focus on Risk

Internal audit must address the risks the organization faces. These are of two basic kinds – risk to conformance and risk to performance— and neither type should be addressed to the exclusion of the other. Setting the balance is a crucial strategic decision that must be taken at board level.

The most useful information usually relates to the most significant risks that an organization faces. Some organizations still use rotational programs (programs that consider each part of the organization in turn), but these are of limited value as the assumption is that the risks are static. Planning of internal auditing must be based on a current assessment of the organization's risks.

An internal audit might develop ways of better addressing a risk, might provide assurance that a significant risk is being well controlled, might advise that a significant risk is not being well controlled, or might advise that risks have been misrepresented. During the internal auditor's strategic planning process, the issue to consider is whether a particular risk is important to the organization. Whether organizational management believes the risk to be well controlled is a lesser issue. False belief that a significant risk is well controlled can be a dangerous assumption.

It is not the role of internal audit to second-guess management, but it can be its role to hold a mirror to management representations. Internal audit has a role to challenge assumptions and to test processes. In this context it can be healthy for disagreements about risk exposures or appropriate levels of control to be fully explored.

The chief audit executive (CAE), in consultation with the audit committee and top management, should design an assurance strategy that meets the assurance requirements of the organization and its stakeholders. This strategy should consider: mechanisms for delivery of assurance across the full set of organizational risks; the structure of the organization; reasonable restrictions on available resources; and the contribution of the full range of possible assurance providers.

While an unacceptable risk might be the responsibility of management, internal audit might have skills that can assist in addressing it. Such a risk cannot wait for attention from a routine assurance program (there may be little assurance to provide), and internal audit may have the know-how to contribute to the design and implementation of improved controls. The assurance strategy should, therefore, allow for the application of internal audit resources to such issues. This type of activity needs careful handling within the organization—the internal auditing standards warn against allowing the approved assurance program to be compromised by diversion of resources into management activity.

Coordinating with Other Review Bodies

The internal auditing standards require the CAE to coordinate internal audit review activities with other assurance providers. This is responsible use of resources and involves confirming the quality and reliability of other internal review activities and then appropriately using their results. It also involves considering the extent to which internal auditing can, without compromising the integrity of its work, support the activity of external review bodies. It must be remembered here that the scope of activity of the internal auditor is much wider than the area of interest of the financial statement auditor or any regulator.

Internal reviews that should be considered include regulatory compliance activities, control self-assessments, and quality assurance activities such as ISO 9000 processes. In a well-

coordinated assurance environment the work of the internal auditor can contribute to the maintenance of an organization's formal quality certifications. On the other hand, internal audit should not *become* the quality assurance program. This wastes the skills of the function and allows line managers to abrogate their supervision and management responsibilities.

A coordinated set of review programs ensures that overlap of review activity is deliberate and contributes to improved assurance rather than wastes resources. Ideally, this coordination is achieved as part of strategic planning, but some will inevitably be a response to particular circumstances.

Getting it right requires awareness and flexibility within a well-structured framework. The organization must be sure that the assurance provided by internal audit is sufficient in the context of other assurance providers and the needs of the organization, and must ensure that resources are sufficient to provide all necessary coverage.

APPLYING INTERNAL AUDIT RESOURCES: THE INTERNAL AUDIT WORK PLAN

At least once each year the CAE should develop a work program from the assurance strategy. It has been traditional to do this only once a year, but it is increasingly being undertaken more regularly. A balance between responsiveness and planned coverage must be maintained. An internal audit program driven by short-term issues risks missing underlying problems with longer-term implications.

This work program will be informed by the current risk profile of the organization. If an organization has a mature risk management regime in place, this information will be readily available; in its absence the internal auditor will be reliant on advice from line managers and budget bids. An organization with a formulaic approach to the internal audit budget may provide resources based on history, or on an average organization, rather than on real needs. This will not provide an optimal result.

Activities that warrant immediate or proactive attention from the internal audit activity will be planned for the organization. The provision of proactive advice enables an organization to design processes correctly before implementing them. This is significantly more effective than relying on *post-hoc* criticism, which can lead to a requirement to modify processes after implementation. In particular, it has been established that changes made to computer systems become more expensive as development proceeds. A fundamental control fault detected after the implementation of such a system can be extremely costly.

Internal audit activity must be scheduled and resourced to allow work to be completed while the information is still relevant. This requires close cooperation between management and the internal audit activity. There is little value in keeping the internal audit work plan secret; making it public allows, and should oblige, managers to keep internal audit aware of issues that might be relevant to the timing of the review activity.

The CAE must have scope within the work plan to respond to issues as they arise. This enables organizational management to obtain advice about issues that concern them, and allows the internal audit work plan to respond to issues of concern as they are identified. This, clearly, should not be a license for the CAE to do as he or she wishes, and departures from the approved plan should be reported to the audit committee for their ratification.

The Individual Internal Audit Project

Scope and objectives for an internal audit project are likely to have been approved by the Audit Committee a considerable time before the review commences. They should not be adopted without consideration of changes in conditions since the planning. Often, the initial scope of the project will be broadly stated and needs to be further developed and expanded as the internal audit is conducted.

The CAE must have scope within the project to modify its focus. There will be issues of particular concern to the line manager; there will be matters that, in the judgment of the CAE, need attention. The internal audit must remain the instrument of the Audit Committee but it needs to address the realities of the organization.

As planning for the project proceeds, the internal auditor will consider the risks of the process in greater detail. Risk registers maintained by the organization facilitate this process, but the internal auditor needs to validate this information. It is also useful to involve relevant management in this risk assessment process. In this way, any differing views about risks, and the controls to address them, can be identified early in the project.

To be sure that there is no ambiguity in the final scope, the internal auditor might consider phrasing the information to be obtained as a question. A focusing question enables the internal auditor to know whether the results of the internal audit have been achieved—they will be able to answer the question.

Disciplined planning ensures that internal audit activity is directed at review objectives. Working from a question to be answered makes the relevance of any proposed audit procedures absolutely clear. Complex questions are analyzed during planning to produce simpler questions that remain relevant to the outcome. A focusing question enables the auditor to differentiate activity that is relevant—i.e. contributes to answering the question—from that which is not. The internal auditor can identify the information needed to answer the questions and can determine whether expert help is needed to do this.

Inability to phrase the internal audit scope as a question suggests that the task has been defined ambiguously. Scope ambiguity leads to waste and failure.

MAKING IT HAPPEN

The steps to success are:
- Formally align internal audit with risk management activity.
- Build a strategy to address the assurance needs of the organization.
- Build a medium-term internal audit work plan that is both consistent with the strategy and aligned to current needs.
- Clearly state the information outcomes needed from internal audit projects.
- Follow disciplined processes consistent with the internal auditing standards.

In Practice • Best Practice

MORE INFO

Book:

Picket, K. H. Spencer. *Audit Planning: A Risk-Based Approach*. Hoboken, NJ: Wiley, 2006.

Article:

Parkinson, Michael. "A strategy for providing assurance: Audit committees can gain assurance from many places." *Internal Auditor* (December 2004).

Reports:

Australian National Audit Office. "Public sector internal audit: An investment in assurance and business improvement." Better Practice Guide. September 2007. Online at:
www.anao.gov.au/uploads/documents/Public_Sector_Internal_Audit.pdf

Institute of Internal Auditors—Australia, Standards Australia, and Standards New Zealand. "Delivering assurance based on AS/NZS 4360:2004 risk management." No. HB 158-2006. Standards Australia, 2006. Available from:
infostore.saiglobal.com/store/Details.aspx?ProductID=568727

Professional Accountants in Business (PAIB) Committee. "Enterprise governance: Getting the balance right." International Federation of Accountants, February 2004. Online at:
tinyurl.com/6jskduw [PDF].

Standards:

Institute of Internal Auditors. "International standards for the professional practice of internal auditing." October 2010. Online at:
www.theiia.org/guidance/standards-and-guidance/ippf/standards

Incorporating Operational and Performance Auditing into Compliance and Financial Auditing by Andrew Cox

EXECUTIVE SUMMARY
- Almost every audit can also be an operational or performance audit.
- With a bit of creativity, it is not too difficult to include a value-adding element to a compliance or financial audit.
- Operational and performance auditing can provide added value to your organization.
- Including an operational or performance auditing element in your audits can enhance the image of auditing for those being audited and also for management.
- Auditors can increase their job satisfaction through operational and performance auditing.
- The 3Es of economy, efficiency, and effectiveness should be integral components of the internal auditor's work.

INTRODUCTION
"The truth is, "audit gets no respect." Quite frankly, if the audit department in question is using yesterday's approach in today's company, has not manoeuvred top management and the board into focusing on the company's top five or ten risks, has not caused management to quantify these risks, and has not succeeded in developing authorized bounds of risk tolerance, then it doesn't deserve any respect." Larry Small, President, Fannie Mae, 2000.

This is a great quote, but what a pity it was not applied in recent times when this company got into serious financial difficulty. Perhaps a greater focus on operational and performance auditing might have helped.

What are the big risks for management? Are they likely to be immaterial accounting mistakes, a missing signature on a form, an immaterial asset that cannot be located, people not following a procedure exactly, or perhaps petty cash missing?

Or maybe management is more concerned with making sure the organization is running properly, which means focusing on economy, efficiency, and effectiveness—better known as the 3Es.

OPERATIONAL AND PERFORMANCE AUDITING
What is the difference between operational and performance auditing?
- *Operational audit.* Sometimes called program or performance audits, these

examine the use of resources to evaluate whether those resources are being used in the most efficient and effective ways to fulfill an organization's objectives. An operational audit may include elements of a compliance audit, a financial audit, and an information systems audit. This term is mainly used in the private sector.
- *Performance audit.* This is an independent and systematic examination of the management of an organization, program, or function to identify whether the management is being carried out in an efficient and effective manner and whether management practices promote improvement. This term is mainly used in the public sector and may be the same as or similar to an operational audit.

While there may be purists who will argue there is a difference, the reality is that they seek to achieve the same objective. Although operational and performance auditing are generally applied to public sector auditing, and operational auditing is usually applied to private sector auditing, both seek to achieve organizational improvement of the 3Es.

THE AUDIT CONTINUUM
The audit continuum is shown in Figure 1. As we move from basic compliance auditing to more complex forms of auditing such as operational and performance auditing, the complexity of the audit and the difficulty in getting agreement to the audit objectives from the audit customer increases.

161

Figure 1. The audit continuum

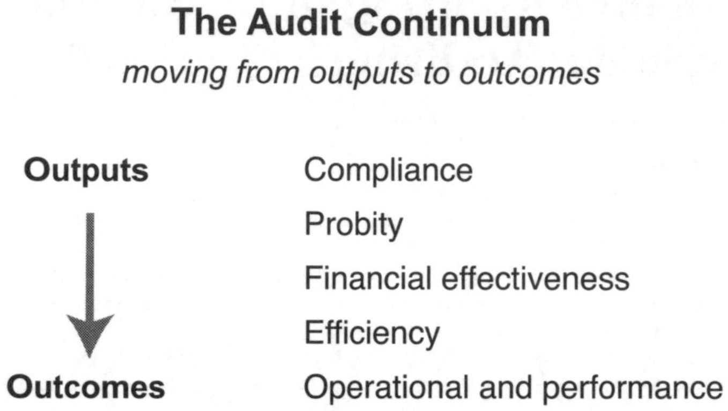

The Audit Continuum
moving from outputs to outcomes

Outputs	Compliance
	Probity
	Financial effectiveness
	Efficiency
Outcomes	Operational and performance

THE DIFFERENCES

The differences between operational and performance auditing, and compliance and financial auditing, are shown in Table 1. The real difference is that operational and performance auditing will genuinely add value and seek to improve the bottom line of an organization. Compliance and financial auditing cannot make this assertion, since their focus is generally on whether things are being done in accordance with legislation, regulations, policies, and procedures. Important though this aspect may be, it is unlikely to have the same improvement objective as operational and performance auditing.

ECONOMY, EFFICIENCY, AND EFFECTIVENESS

What are we seeking to achieve by using performance and operational auditing? The aim is to find out whether business operations are being managed in an economic, efficient, and effective manner; whether procedures for promoting and monitoring the 3Es are adequate; and, importantly, whether improvements can be made.

Economy is concerned with minimizing the cost of resources used (people, materials, equipment, etc.), having regard to the appropriate quality required: i.e., keeping the cost of inputs low without compromising quality. An example could be where healthcare supplies or services of a specific quality are purchased at the best possible price.

Efficiency is concerned with the relationship between goods and services produced (outputs) and the resources used to produce them (inputs): i.e., getting the most from available resources. An example could be where the cost of providing healthcare has been reduced over time. Efficiency is about "doing things right."

Table 1. Differences between operational and performance auditing, and compliance and financial auditing. (*Source*: The State Audit of the United Arab Emirates)

	Operational and performance auditing	Compliance and financial auditing
Purpose	Does performance meet the 3Es?	Is there compliance?
Focus	The organization and its objectives	Accounting transactions
Academic base	Economics, political science, sociology, etc.	Accounting
Methods	Methods vary from audit to audit	Standardized methods
Assessment criteria	Unique for each audit	Standardized criteria
Reports	Varying format	Standardized format

Effectiveness is concerned with achieving predetermined objectives (specifically planned achievements) and having the actual impact (output achieved) compared with the intended impact (objective): i.e., achieving the predetermined objective. An example could be where disease rates have fallen as a result of the healthcare provided. Effectiveness is about "doing the right things."

WHAT MANAGEMENT WANTS

Although there are many internal auditors who still believe their job is to tell management what is wrong but not how to fix it, many more enlightened internal auditors have worked out what management is really seeking. This includes such things as:
* help in reducing risk;
* help in improving the business;
* assurance that appropriate governance is in place and working properly;
* internal audits that are relevant and timely;
* internal audits that genuinely add value;
* more value for the money spent on internal audits.

THE STEPS IN PERFORMING AN OPERATIONAL OR PERFORMANCE AUDIT

The sequence of an operational or performance audit is likely to be:
* establish what should be done;
* establish what is being done;
* compare "what should" with "what is";
* investigate significant differences;
* assess the effects of the differences;
* determine the cause of the differences;
* develop audit findings and value-adding options and recommendations.

While the initial steps may not be very different from a compliance or financial audit, the crucial and value-adding steps are: determining the cause of the differences; and developing audit findings and value-adding options and recommendations.

These are the difficult parts. Most compliance or financial auditors can work out an effect, but trying to isolate the cause can be much harder. Hence, many internal auditors find it easier just to report on what is wrong and avoid trying to identify the root cause of a problem.

Often an internal audit recommendation will be something like "Employees should follow the procedures." This is lazy internal audit work and not a particularly enlightened recommendation—it is more of a throwaway line. There may be many reasons why an employee is not following procedures. But not many employees will deliberately disobey a procedure unless it is a bad procedure, or something else is preventing them from complying with it.

PARTNERING WITH MANAGEMENT

There are a number of ways in which internal auditors can promote their services—in particular the benefits of operational and performance auditing. These may include:
* Develop an engagement model and get management buy-in.
* Closely align your internal auditing with the business.
* Plan a risk-based internal audit program developed with management.
* Aim to become an integral part of the organization and to help management improve the business.
* Plan each internal audit with management.
* Facilitate a frank risk assessment with management and stakeholders for each internal audit.
* Formulate insightful objectives for each internal audit, not just "throwaway lines."
* Ask management to agree and sign off the terms of reference for each internal audit.
* Consider using technical experts where internal auditors may not have all the necessary skills for an internal audit.
* Facilitate a workshop with management and stakeholders at the conclusion of an audit to discuss and agree possible improvement options.

REPORTING

As mentioned previously, the real value in an internal audit report is in determining the cause of the differences between "what is" and "what should be," and developing audit findings and value-adding options and recommendations. This is the essence of what operational and performance auditing is all about.

By working closely with management and stakeholders at the conclusion of the audit to discuss improvement options, possibly using a facilitated workshop approach, a much better outcome can be achieved. After all, the people doing the job know a lot more about it than the internal auditor!

Best-Practice Approaches to Internal Auditing

In Practice • Best Practice

CASE STUDY
It is not difficult to turn a compliance audit into a performance audit. In fact, almost every audit can also be an operational or performance audit. And, by being creative, internal auditors can make their internal audit work more interesting and satisfying.

This case study comes from an internal audit conducted in a utilities company that provides electricity, gas, and water to the community. In this company, field staff work overtime. (Overtime is time worked beyond an established limit: i.e., hours worked in excess of the working hours prescribed in the employment agreement.)

The objectives of the audit were to:
- determine who had responsibility for overtime and assess whether this arrangement was working effectively;
- identify the key risks involved with overtime and the mitigation strategies and controls currently in place to manage those risks;
- identify the extent of overtime worked and test whether the key controls were working effectively to manage the identified risks;
- ascertain whether overtime requirements were being effectively communicated to managers and staff;
- review whether management regularly received and acted on feedback on the need for overtime and periodically examined cost-effective alternatives.

The audit covered all the regular auditing matters such as compliance with policy and procedures, sampling and testing overtime calculations, etc., as you would expect in a compliance audit.

Since it found that overtime payments were being made correctly in accordance with policies and procedures, the audit was a nonevent. But, with some extra work, analysis of the data showed that:
- most overtime was worked in the electricity division;
- overtime was being worked by around a third of employees, with the number of employees who worked overtime increasing;
- the overall amount of overtime had been steadily increasing in absolute and payroll percentage terms across the organization over the previous four years;
- the electricity and water divisions had overtime budgets for the next year that were below the budgets for the current year (almost certainly optimistically).

Analysis of the causes revealed that:
- there was a countrywide shortage of line workers, resulting in the electricity division being unable to recruit sufficient numbers of people with these skills;
- the electricity division pole replacement program was difficult to run with the number of line workers currently employed by the organization;
- a serious wildfire had destroyed substantial electricity assets.

Once the causes had been identified, the audit recommendations suggested that the organization consider such things as:
- developing a longer-term perspective when formulating future industrial plans for the workforce;
- extending human resources employee self-service to the field employees;
- extending mobile computing to the field for human resources activities and job costing;
- further annualizing salaries to include an overtime component;
- changing the rostering of work crews to true shift work arrangements over 24/7/365.

This added real value to the audit, rather than being a simple compliance audit approach—which would have merely reported that overtime calculations were being made correctly.

CONCLUSION
With a bit of creativity, it is not too difficult to include a value-adding element in a compliance or financial audit:
- Almost every audit can also be an operational or performance audit.
- You can do operational and performance auditing to provide added value to your organization.
- Including an operational or performance auditing element in your audits can enhance the image of auditing with the people being audited and with management.
- You can increase your job satisfaction through operational and performance auditing.

QFINANCE

164

MAKING IT HAPPEN
- Develop an engagement model for your internal auditing, and get management buy-in.
- Closely align your internal auditing with the business, plan a risk-based internal audit program developed with management, and aim to become an integral part of the organization in order to help management improve the business.
- Plan each internal audit with management, and facilitate an up-front risk assessment with management and stakeholders at the commencement of each internal audit—this is a quick and cost-effective way to determine the business processes, risks, and control procedures in place, as well as getting management buy-in.
- Ask management to agree and sign off the terms of reference for each internal audit—be sure that the objectives of an operational or performance audit are insightful and are not just throwaway lines.
- Consider using experts in technical subject areas where internal audit may not have all the skills required for an internal audit.
- Measurement criteria need to be developed; this is much more difficult than a compliance or financial audit and needs to be objective, understandable, comparable, complete, and acceptable.
- Learn the difference between "hard controls" (existence of policies and procedures, documents, payment approvals, segregation of duties, etc.) and "soft controls" (focus on ethics, integrity, competency, relationship building), and learn how to audit soft controls.
- Go outside the organization to get information and consult with external stakeholders.
- Keep the audit focused and timely, if not properly managed operational and performance audits can take on a life of their own and can end up taking a long time to complete.
- Engage and communicate with management throughout the internal audit.
- Convene a peer review challenge session within internal audit for the draft report; also do this for service providers who perform internal audits for you.
- Get the report "as right as it can be" before taking a draft to management.
- Facilitate a workshop with management and stakeholders at the conclusion of the audit to discuss and agree possible improvement options.

MORE INFO

Books:
Reding, Kurt F., Paul J. Sobel, Urton L. Anderson, Michael J. Head, *et al. Internal Auditing: Assurance and Consulting Services.* 2nd ed. Orlando, FL: IIA Research Foundation, 2009.

Sawyer, Lawrence B., Mortimer A. Dittenhofer, and James H. Scheiner. *Sawyer's Internal Auditing: The Practice of Modern Internal Auditing.* 5th ed. Altamonte Springs, FL: IIA Research Foundation, 2003.

Standards:
Institute of Internal Auditors. "International standards for the professional practice of internal auditing." October 2010. Online at:
www.theiia.org/guidance/standards-and-guidance/ippf/standards

Websites:
Australian National Audit Office (ANAO): www.anao.gov.au
Institute of Internal Auditors (IIA): www.theiia.org
International Organization of Supreme Audit Institutions (INTOSAI): www.intosai.org
Office of the Auditor-General of Canada: www.oag-bvg.gc.ca

Training Courses and Postgraduate Qualifications:
Institute of Internal Auditors. "Performance based auditing in the public sector." Details online at:
www.theiia.org/training/index.cfm?act=seminar.onsitedetail&semID=76

Institute of Internal Auditors. "Operational auditing: An introduction through advanced." Details online at: www.theiia.org/training/index.cfm?act=seminar.onsitedetail&semID=209

University of Canberra. "Graduate certificate in performance audit and evaluation." Details online at: www.canberra.edu.au/courses-units/gc/business/domestic-only/842aa

New Assurance Challenges Facing Chief Audit Executives by Simon D'Arcy

EXECUTIVE SUMMARY

- Internal audit's *raison d'être* is to provide assurance on the effectiveness of the management and control of significant risks.
- Assurance can only ever be reasonable but not absolute—continuing corporate failure due to inadequate risk management and control challenges the value of such reasonable assurance.
- Chief audit executives can use objective criteria to demonstrate the integrity of their reasonable assurance propositions.
- Objective criteria include completeness, frequency, future orientation, explicitness, objectivity, and subject matter knowledge.
- A key challenge for CAEs is that of a shift of mindset away from just doing audits, to auditing actually providing assurance of demonstrable integrity.

INTRODUCTION

Looking back over the last 15 to 20 years, it does seem that at one time the biggest challenge facing the profession of internal auditing was whether the unique scope and contribution of internal audit was clearly defined, understood, or indeed actually needed. Much of the thought leadership around internal auditing in recent years has focused on this challenge. Two publications by PricewaterhouseCoopers in 2007,[1] and a heads of internal audit summit "The Future of Internal Auditing Starts Here" in May 2008[2] jointly facilitated by the Institute of Internal Auditors and Deloitte, have all concluded that internal audit's primary role is clearly to provide assurance on the effectiveness of risk management. In fact, in many organizations internal audit already clearly does this, as demonstrated in Protiviti's June 2007 publication *Internal Auditing Around the World*.[3] It is clear—and has been since Turnbull (1999),[4] if not before—that boards have a duty to get themselves assured on the effectiveness of their systems of internal control. There is no doubt that chief audit executives see that their raison d'être is to provide such assurance, and many will claim, with some justification, that they have provided and will continue to provide this assurance. Therefore, on the face of it, CAEs have responded to their most fundamental challenge.

THE PROBLEM WITH ASSURANCE

If Turnbull (1999) marks the turning point in corporate governance, it has nevertheless not marked a turning point in the steady stream of corporate failures and disasters, which are often due to ineffective risk management and control.

The role of internal audit in these scenarios has been, if not quite exonerated, then at least found not liable, by virtue of one of the basic precepts of internal audit assurance—that it can only ever be reasonable and not absolute.

However, with the market turmoil of 2007 and 2008, the steady stream of failures has become a torrent of biblical proportions— initially, at the time of writing (September 2008), sweeping away the foundations of some major global financial institutions and likely to spread to other sectors as systemic market and recessionary risks crystallize. Accompanying the unfolding disasters is a damning commentary from governments and media on the hopelessly inadequate risk assessment and management capability of those corporates. The spotlight has been on the managers of risk and the attitude of senior executives to the assessment and management of risk. However, it will not be long before the spotlight moves toward the assurers of the effectiveness of risk management, and whether those assurers were in any way culpable. Rightly or wrongly, many will assume that reasonable assurance from internal audit should have identified and reported on the inadequacies of the risk management process, or at least been capable of doing so.

There is now a new challenge facing CAEs—that they are able to demonstrate that their assurance propositions have integrity and can withstand scrutiny against some key criteria. Internal audit assurance involves judgment, and there is an inherent imperfection in a process that relies on judgment. However, there is a difference between an omission or oversight based on accepted fallibility, and one where the scope of assurance was too narrow, where assurance conclusions lacked clarity, or were delivered too infrequently, or where work undertaken lacked sufficient knowledge or objectivity. Assurance delivered on the basis of a flawed proposition is indeed unreasonable assurance.

Therefore, in rising to meet that challenge, CAEs have been aspiring to create assurance propositions that are:
- Complete: They cover all significant risks.
- Frequent: They provide assurance with sufficient frequency.
- Explicit: They give assurance outcomes that are clear and unambiguous.
- Future-oriented: They offer assurance that controls will continue to be effective in the future, not just that they have been effective in the past.
- Objective: They provide objective assurance based on sound knowledge.

DEMONSTRATING THE INTEGRITY OF ASSURANCE IN A POST-CREDIT-CRUNCH WORLD

Most CAEs I have spoken with on the topic are in agreement that the above are valid criteria against which to assess assurance to demonstrate that the assurance given has integrity. However, there is no formulaic result or correct answer that the assessment should derive. Some CAEs are quite clear that their current risk-based methodologies score quite favorably in the assessment. The following is an amalgam of my own thoughts, assessments, and actual solutions, developed across four financial services organizations in the past decade in trying to respond to the challenge.

Completeness

First, were all significant risks in scope for my internal audit function? How sympathetic would or should a stakeholder be if the explanation was "sorry, out of scope" for not providing any assurance coverage on a significant risk area where a major issue had arisen. The default position is for "everything" to be in scope, because that is where assurance adds the most value. However, my experience is that "everything" means different things to different people, and it still leads to mismatches between expected assurance coverage and actual audit coverage. The cry of "where were the auditors?" when something goes wrong is less rhetorical and more actual than you might imagine. It served my function to define "everything" up front, rather than have to explain omissions retrospectively. This is becoming even more sensible in an environment where many point to the least tangible risk areas, such as strategy, sustainability, and culture, as those where assurance is most needed. (In fact, many respected observers are pointing to poor culture and behavior as being what has led to the economic meltdown, rather than policy or process failure.) If something is going to be agreed as out of scope, it is better to be in a position to have clearly defined and agreed it, even if by doing so you are reducing the value of your assurance proposition.

The best method I have found for creating an assurance universe, and to use as a basis for an assurance contract with the organization, is to list the significant risks (there are normally around 20, and such a list is often referred to as a risk map or significant risk register) as recognized and agreed by the board. What is clear is that the

Figure 1. The assurance spectrum

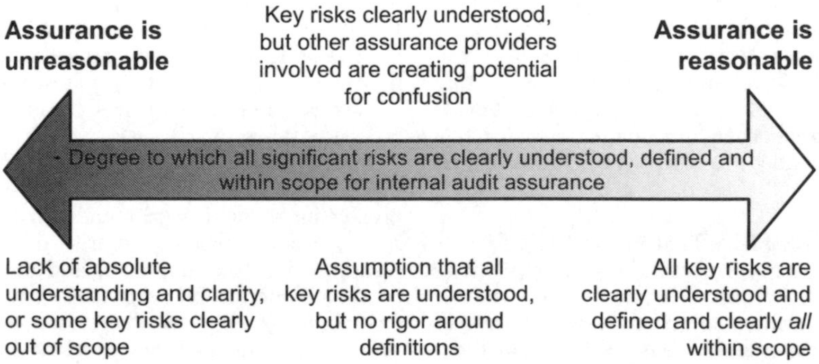

Assurance is unreasonable — Key risks clearly understood, but other assurance providers involved are creating potential for confusion — **Assurance is reasonable**

Degree to which all significant risks are clearly understood, defined and within scope for internal audit assurance

Lack of absolute understanding and clarity, or some key risks clearly out of scope | Assumption that all key risks are understood, but no rigor around definitions | All key risks are clearly understood and defined and clearly *all* within scope

significant risk register must include all financial, strategic, and operational risks as a minimum, including liquidity and sustainability risks. The internal audit profession is now turning its attention to the new paradigm risks that have been made painfully clear by the credit crunch—systemic/globalization risk, behavioral risks, and supply chain risks.

Frequency
The Combined Code on Corporate Governance, which sets the rules for FTSE-listed companies and is also recognized as a benchmark by nonlisted and public sector companies in the United Kingdom, implies a minimum annual assessment of the effectiveness of internal control (as a proxy for the effectiveness of management of significant risks).

However, a once-a-year assessment—even if it is about all the risks—does not appear to be frequent enough. The organizations for which I have worked have generally used a very compelling risk-based approach that prioritizes the assurance requirement over three years. But with this scenario it seemed to me that even a once-a-year assessment can only cover one-third of the assurance requirement (accepting that it would always include the highest-priority areas). I have posed the frequency question many times to senior managers, board members, and audit committee chairs. Their answer tends to be in the negative—i.e., it would be unreasonable that a major risk management breakdown should go unnoticed by internal audit until it was too late because the CAE's view of that risk was out of date, because it had not been looked at for six months or more, and was not due to be looked at again for another six months or more.

In fact, the best frequency would be if CAEs were in a position to provide a complete opinion all of the time. Logistical and practical constraints make this impossible. However, I have been able to produce more frequent assessments by focusing on each of the risk categories for which assurance is required and creating a strategy for delivering the outputs that I need so that I can stand in front of an audit committee once a quarter and deliver conclusions that have demonstrable integrity. Such strategies comprise combinations of continuous assessment techniques, ongoing reviews, and revisions of conclusions previously arrived at, as well as baseline assessments.

REVIEWS AND ASSESSMENTS
Baseline reviews are undertaken where management of the risk is relatively stable. These are time-framed, in-depth reviews of established controls and processes. The conclusions from such reviews may have a long shelf life and, if stability continues, may only need a light refresh to remain valid.

Continuous assessments involve regular or continuous reviews of a range of information and activity that indicate whether controls are operating as intended. They are used where conclusions have previously been established but more certainty is required to ensure that those conclusions remain valid between baseline reviews. They include a review of the output of other risk and control functions—for example, compliance.

Ongoing reviews are used where projects and other business initiatives may bring changes to the risk and control framework and reduce the value of reviewing preexisting processes and controls, or where control environments are unstable/immature and action is being undertaken to establish or remediate controls.

Orientation
In thinking about frequency challenge, I also started to think about the orientation of assurance. By orientation, I mean whether the assurance is just focused retrospectively, on things that have happened in the past, or whether it can and should look to the future. The Combined Code implies that the annual assessment will be a retrospective view of the previous year, much like the external auditor's opinion on the financial statements. However, in much the same way as external auditors consider the going concern aspects of firms, it seemed to me that my conclusions should have some element of future proofing.

Again, I considered the value of assurance that was anchored in the past (especially when it could refer to an event as long as 364 days in the past). If a risk had already crystallized, any assurance was old news and irrelevant. If controls were effective, for how long would they continue to be effective? I felt that my assurance would be more reasonable if I could "future proof" it.

But how much future proofing can and should be given? I achieved this by attaching a shelf life to quarterly conclusions. This is a concept where I vary how long my assurance conclusions are likely to remain valid, depending on certain broad criteria. For example, if the control environment is either currently unstable or will be subject to some major change in the near future, the validity of any conclusions will be short-lived. If the area is stable and likely to remain so, then a long shelf life can be given—and easily refreshed using the continuous assessment technique. In the organizations where I have employed this approach, in any set of quarterly conclusions the shelf lives given have varied considerably across risk categories. In fact, the more I have used this approach, the more I find that the fact that an explicit view on shelf life has been given has become as important as the actual length of time which is stated.

Explicitness

The requirement (by boards) for CAEs to give opinions on the effectiveness of the system of internal control and risk management is one of the biggest areas of debate and challenge facing the profession at the moment. Because of the legal implications of opinions, many CAEs will not give them, and will only report issues as they arise. Some CAEs who are prepared to give opinions do so without much thought of the consequences, or do so in the vein of "everything is effective apart from the following issues."

Setting aside the legal status argument, in my experience such approaches are potentially flawed. The default position of the recipients of assurance is one of assuming that all other controls and risk management activities across the enterprise are effective and will continue to be so, unless they have specifically been told otherwise. Unless that was truly the intended message, the assurance that is being provided is misleading. That is why I have worked on providing separate conclusions (as opposed to opinions, to avoid the legal connotation) for each significant risk category (and sometimes at a risk subcategory level) each quarter. My preference has been to go for a binary conclusion, where "this risk is effectively managed" is signaled by a green symbol, and "this risk is not effectively managed" is represented by a red one.

For a "green" conclusion nothing further is required in the way of explanation other than an indicator of the breadth and depth of coverage used to reach the conclusion. For a "red" conclusion the list of supporting issues, as well as the reliability indicator, are described.

My experience is that the binary approach is a step too far for some, so I have also employed a three-level and a four-level approach, where the conclusions range from "well controlled," through "acceptable level of control" and "controls require improvement," to "insufficient control." The point is that it is the explicitness of the conclusion (at the level of significant risk) and the reliability indicator which provide the assurance that is intended, rather than the summary of issues reported. The approach encourages much greater challenge and scrutiny—but I have found that to be a good thing.

Objectivity and Subject Matter Expertise

These are not new concepts or challenges for CAEs, but the challenge is to rethink them in the framework of the new assurance paradigm. Many cite independence of opinion as an end

MAKING IT HAPPEN

- It is most important that you have a solid anchor or hook on which to hang your assurance. Ideally this should be the board-defined risk exposures. If your organization does not have these, help your organization to define them.
- It will take several quarters to build rhythm and momentum, and up to 18 months to achieve a baseline assurance for all of the risks of equivalent requisite quality.
- If you already know something, and are confident in that knowledge, do not waste valuable resources on proving something you already know. Reliable knowledge, however gained, contributes to your assurance.
- If you set off down this path, there will be many naysayers. They will challenge whether you can realistically deliver all the work that is necessary, claiming that you can only scratch the surface. Stay focused. The best way to convince naysayers is with the outputs and outcomes. The number of audit man-days has always been, and always will be, an input measure, and is no guide to whether good, bad, or indifferent assurance is produced.
- Less—in terms of number of issues—is definitely more. The number of audit issues in any one organization should genuinely reflect the competence of risk management and not the number of auditors
- You will need to spend as much—if not more—time converting your own people to the cause. Old habits die hard. The only way to do this is to be persistent and unwavering in your assurance strategy. Be prepared to repeat...and repeat and repeat.
- Make use of early converts and use them shamelessly to help spread the message.

in itself, but it is only valuable if it enhances objectivity. After all, in any walk of life, not just in internal audit, we tend to be more convinced by the conclusion of someone who has no vested interest in what that conclusion is. Similarly, we tend to be more convinced by a conclusion if it is given by someone who really knows the subject to which it relates. Therefore, regardless of the completeness, frequency, future orientation, or explicitness of a conclusion, it can only provide reasonable assurance if we have confidence in the objectivity and expertise in the subject matter of the person giving it. Therein lies the challenge, as sometimes one element can only increase at the expense of another. In meeting this challenge, I have found that it is the recognition of the dynamic relationship between objectivity and subject matter expertise which allows dynamic management of it.

CONCLUSION

In common with many disciplines, the challenge for CAEs is not one of technique or technical development, but one of focus. In many ways, the biggest challenge is one of a shift of mindset away from planning to deliver some audits, toward planning to deliver an assurance outcome of demonstrable integrity. However, I believe it is a challenge that must be met, so that assurers have a stronger chance of helping their organizations to avoid corporate calamity due to risk management and control failure.

MORE INFO

Periodicals:

Internal Auditing, published monthly by the Chartered Institute of Internal Auditors: www.iia.org.uk/en/Publications/IA_and_BR_Magazine
Internal Auditor, published monthly by the Institute of Internal Auditors: www.theiia.org/intauditor

Articles:

Chambers, Andrew. "The board's black hole—Filling their assurance vacuum: Can internal audit rise to the challenge?" *Measuring Business Excellence* 12:1 (2008): 47–63. Online at: dx.doi.org/10.1108/13683040810864387
D'Arcy, Simon. "Bubble trouble—The wrong attitudes to risk." *Mortgage Finance Gazette* (February 4, 2009). Online at: www.mfgonline.co.uk/article/Bubble-trouble-the-wrong-attitudes-to-risk-228895.html
Perry, Michelle. "Weathering the storm." *Financial Services Review* (May 2008): 10–12. Online at: tinyurl.com/6zzt9pb [PDF].
Piper, Arthur. "A matter of opinion." *Internal Auditor* (June 2007). Interview with Alec Richmond, then President of IIA UK and Ireland.

Report:

Turnbull, N. "Internal control: Guidance for directors on the Combined Code." Institute of Chartered Accountants in England and Wales, September 1999.

NOTES

1 PricewaterhouseCoopers (PwC). "Internal audit 2012: A study examining the future of internal auditing and the potential decline of a controls-centric approach." 2007; also PwC. "State of the internal audit profession study: Pressures build for continual focus on risk." 2007. Both downloadable from www.pwc.com (search on titles).
2 Institute of Internal Auditors (UK and Ireland) in association with Deloitte. "Towards a blueprint for the internal audit profession." London: IIA, 2008. Online from: www.iia.org.uk.
3 Protiviti, *Internal Auditing Around the World*.

Four volumes published between 2005 and 2008 with profiles of internal audit functions at leading international organizations. The series tells the stories of 16 successful internal audit functions and examines common denominators that separate these leaders from their peers. Available from the Protiviti website: www.knowledgeleader.com.
4 "Internal control: Guidance for directors on the Combined Code" (the Turnbull Guidance) was originally published by the Institute of Chartered Accountants in England and Wales in 1999 and was followed by a number of subsequent revisions.

Checklists

Core Principles

The Accounts Filing Process and Its Importance

DEFINITION

Every business is required to file accounts on an annual basis with the relevant authorities. These accounts should detail items of expenditure and revenue and outline the profit on which tax is payable. There are various issues that a business owner must be aware of when filing accounts. Accounts must be filed by a particular date, and this is usually determined by the accounting reference dates, which determine which period the accounts cover and identify the financial year-end—normally accounts must be submitted by a set date after the year-end. Missing this deadline can result in penalties.

Many companies also have their accounts audited, perhaps because this is required by a bank or lenders, or by national legislation. If accounts are audited, the auditor's report must be included with them when they are submitted to the relevant authorities and shareholders. Company directors may appoint auditors to hold office until the first general meeting. After this, the auditors are normally appointed at a general meeting at which accounts are considered. The auditor must be a member of a recognized supervisory body and eligible under the rules of that body to act as a company auditor.

ADVANTAGES

- Auditing the accounts gives shareholders and managers a clear financial overview of a business and its various departments, thus highlighting problems that need to be addressed.
- Auditing helps to prevent and to detect fraud. An audit can uncover fraud and mistakes, while staff are deterred from committing fraud if they know that a regular audit is conducted.
- Carrying out a regular audit helps to ensure that the records are up-to-date at all times.

DISADVANTAGES

- Conducting an audit can be time-consuming and costly, particularly for a small firm.
- By interrupting the work of key staff, an audit can delay the provision of services and goods to clients.
- Conducting an audit is not a guaranteed way of exposing fraud because staff may manipulate the information supplied to the auditor.

ACTION CHECKLIST

✓ Establish whether your business needs to be audited. Many lenders are happy to accept formal accounts supported by an accountant's report. Small companies are usually exempt from audit requirements.

✓ Select an auditor carefully. Establish whether they have experience of the industry in which you are operating and look at several auditors to verify costs.

DOS AND DON'TS
DO

- Continually evaluate whether you need to conduct an audit. Your requirements and those of the authorities and lenders can change.
- Contact a tax consultant immediately if the tax authorities decide to audit your business.
- Understand the purpose and scope of the audit. This is critical to passing the audit, the scope and purpose of which can vary significantly from one auditor to another.

DON'T

- Don't forget that your accounts must be up-to-date and accurate if the audit is to prove effective.

MORE INFO

Books:
Rittenberg, Larry E., Karla M. Johnstone, Audrey A. Gramling, and Bradley J. Schwieger. *Auditing: A Business Risk Approach*. 7th ed. Mason, OH: South-Western Cengage Learning, 2010.
Soltani, Bahram. *Auditing: An International Approach*. Harlow, UK: Pearson Education, 2007.

The Chief Audit Executive's (CAE) Roles and Responsibilities

DEFINITION

The CAE has an in-depth knowledge of the business and is concerned principally with its systems for internal control and efficiency of operations, the reliability of its financial reporting, and its observance of relevant laws and regulations.

Corporate accounting scandals and the resultant outcry for transparency and honesty in reporting have led to a progressively more important role for the CAE. A CAE has two important and sometimes conflicting functions within an organization. The first is to examine and evaluate the organization's systems of internal control, as part of the requirement for stricter corporate governance. The second is to be fully cognizant of the risks, goals, policies, and processes of the organization while maintaining autonomy from management direction and control.

The CAE normally reports directly to the management and audit committee and is responsible for producing an annual assessment of the effectiveness of the organization's risk management and processes for control and governance, as set out by the board or management. Risk management deals with the way an organization sets goals, then recognizes, interprets, and reacts to risks that could affect its ability to realize those goals. Processes for control and governance deal with the effectiveness and efficiency of operations, the reliability of financial reports and conformity with appropriate rules and laws.

ADVANTAGES

- CAEs improve business organization and risk management by providing reassurance on the effectiveness and efficiency of operations, the reliability of financial reporting, and compliance with applicable laws and regulations.
- CAEs provide management with an in-depth and unbiased understanding of the risks that the organization may be facing, allowing for pre-emptive planning.
- CAEs give company officers and directors forewarning of ethical and legal issues that the organization may be facing.

DISADVANTAGES

- Although CAEs are meant to be independent and impartial, they are paid by the company and are an integral part of the company's management. This can lead to conflicts of interest.
- CAEs' judgments, estimates, and interpretations are not always objective because of their close relationships with the organizations for which they work.
- A CAE's relationship with the management of a company is generally informal and the CAE's position does not carry the power to change processes.
- Although there are international bodies such as the Institute of Internal Auditors (IIA), CAEs as a profession are unregulated.

ACTION CHECKLIST

- ✓ Has the CAE previously worked in related business fields? If so, for how long and what did they achieve?
- ✓ How good is the CAE's track record on risk assessment and planning for contingencies?
- ✓ In assessing business processes, how up-to-date is the CAE with information audit technology controls?
- ✓ To which internationally recognized standards-setting body, such as the IIA, does the CAE belong?

DOS AND DON'TS

DO

- Allow CAEs unrestricted access to information to enable them to evaluate risks, management activities, and personnel better.
- Take into account that CAEs are not responsible for carrying out company activities; their role is solely advisory.
- Consult with the CAE if there are any implications where ethical or legal issues may be involved.

DON'T

- Don't involve CAEs in decisions that might compromise their autonomy as independent internal auditors.

MORE INFO

Websites:

Institute of Internal Auditors (IIA): www.theiia.org

KnowledgeLeader: www.knowledgeleader.com

Corporate Governance and Its Interpretations

DEFINITION

Corporate governance is the system by which organizations are directed and controlled. The defects of poor corporate governance have recently been very visible in financial institutions around the world. Since the endorsement of Sarbanes–Oxley, companies have set up audit committees, added financial experts to their boards, improved financial whistle-blowing capacity, and enhanced corporate transparency in financial statements and shareholder disclosures. However, are there any benefits from all of these requirements and best practices, and do they pay any dividends?

For good corporate governance to work, open and honest communication is necessary, with transparent policies and practices, clear lines of authority, and strong internal controls and audit functions, backed by a board that can act with clear independence from management.

A board has to identify with the business and its competition, focus on strategic problems and risk management, and establish high, yet pragmatic, standards of performance. The board directs the plans of the company but does not manage the company. The board must pick first-rate people to run the business while retaining its role to confront, evaluate, and hold managers accountable.

To do this, the board must develop and approve a strategic plan, establish specific and measurable goals, establish risk parameters (which should be reviewed regularly in light of the strategic objectives), encourage and preserve open lines of communication, select competent management, measure managers' performance, and hold management responsible using compensation and continued employment.

In contrast, management has the responsibility to implement the board's strategy, risk tolerances, and policies; keep directors fully informed; deal with the day-to-day operations of the business and its staff; and operate the information systems, procedures, and reports that keep the lines of communication open.

The costs of poor corporate governance have been very evident in the present financial crisis. Firms that engage in unscrupulous and risky behavior will generally fail, while those that have enhanced corporate governance will have higher valuations, greater profitability, and better sales. The recent market turmoil suggests that buying shares in firms that score highly in corporate governance may yield positive returns.

ADVANTAGES

- Good corporate governance is part of good risk management. It brings problems and concerns to light, allowing them to be addressed promptly.
- Good corporate governance helps businesses to focus on strategic issues and risk management, and establishes realistic standards of performance.
- Decision-making is improved by thorough analysis under good corporate governance. Management is held accountable, and management compensation is linked to shareholder value.
- The board can select good managers to run the business while maintaining its role to challenge, measure, and hold managers responsible.

DISADVANTAGES

- A board that lacks independence may not be willing to address poor performance by a line of business or even hold the management accountable.
- The dual loyalty that many board members feel to the management and to the institution is normally resolved in favor of the institution.

ACTION CHECKLIST

- ✓ Risks need to be reviewed periodically in light of the strategic objectives and margins of the business.
- ✓ How strong is the audit committee, and does the audit committee charter reflect the committee's areas of competence?
- ✓ Conduct a self-assessment periodically to help match expectations and actions.
- ✓ How effective is the risk-assessment program, how successful is the internal governance control, and are managers held accountable?
- ✓ Does the board and/or audit committee receive adequate and timely information from the internal and external audit staff?
- ✓ Does the relationship between board and management reflect their independent roles?

QFINANCE

DOS AND DON'TS

DO

- Set up an effective and independent corporate governance program.

DON'T

- Don't cut back on good corporate governance programs because of reduced margins—objective opinions may help to resolve problems.

MORE INFO

Books:

Colley, John L., Jr, Jacqueline L. Doyle, George W. Logan, and Wallace Stettinius. *What Is Corporate Governance?* New York: McGraw-Hill, 2005.

Mallin, Christine A. *Corporate Governance*. 3rd ed. Oxford: Oxford University Press, 2010.

Monks, Robert A. G., and Nell Minow. *Corporate Governance*. 4th ed. Chichester, UK. Wiley, 2008.

Article:

Causey, Dawn. "The worth of good corporate governance." *Community Banker* (August 2008): 50–52.

Websites:

Financial Services Authority (FSA; UK): www.fsa.gov.uk

Securities and Exchange Commission (SEC; US): www.sec.gov

The IIA Code of Ethics

DEFINITION

Established in 1941, the Institute of Internal Auditors aims to provide global leadership for the profession. Based in Florida, the Institute is the internal auditing industry's recognized authority across the world and is keen to promote the profession through improved education. The Institute's membership base covers 165 countries, with members spread across professions such as risk management, corporate governance, information-technology auditing and education, as well as mainstream internal auditing.

The objective of the Institute's code of ethics is to create an ethical culture throughout the profession. The Institute's members aim to help organizations to achieve their objectives through disciplined and highly systematic efforts to strengthen their governance, control, and risk-management procedures. The code of ethics not only covers the core activity of internal auditing but also extends to cover principles relevant to the profession, as well as the rules of conduct to which practitioners should adhere.

ADVANTAGES

- The code of ethics helps to ensure the objectivity of internal auditors, aiming to assist them to assess all relevant factors without being unduly influenced by others or by their own interests.
- By defining the standards expected of internal auditing professionals, the code helps to reinforce the trust that forms the main foundation of the profession. The code also aims to ensure that individual internal auditors have the required competencies to cover the particular task they are expected to perform.
- The confidentiality element of the code aims to make certain that internal auditors always appreciate the value of information. It underlines their requirement to safeguard information at all times, subject only to legal or professional obligations.
- The Institute has disciplinary procedures in place for instances where members are accused of violating the code of ethics, helping to ensure that members can be trusted to act in a consistently professional manner.

DISADVANTAGES

- Ethical standards in business can vary widely from country to country. Therefore, auditing professionals in some countries may have to work harder than those in other countries to fully achieve all the standards expected of a global code of ethics.
- Cultural differences between companies could also put more pressure on internal auditors in some organizations to adhere to the consistently high standards demanded by the code.

ACTION CHECKLIST

✓ In joining the Institute, professionals commit to the highest standards of integrity and professionalism, offering a high level of reassurance to clients.

✓ By encouraging employees to become members, companies help their internal auditors in areas such as self-development, potentially significantly increasing their long-term value to the organization.

✓ The Institute unites over 150,000 internal auditing professionals worldwide. Membership brings access to valuable resources, such as a dedicated resource library, a technical helpline and the latest published professional guidance. Access to these resources can bring significant benefits to an organization.

DOS AND DON'TS

DO

- Recognize that internal auditing is a progressive profession, the development of which is driven by clients' increasingly demanding needs.
- Take advantage of the Institute's commitment to help internal auditors to achieve their full potential through training and development. For example, the Institute offers a wide range of in-house, company-specific courses.

DON'T

- Don't interpret the code of ethics as simply a list of aspirations for internal auditors. The Institute demands the highest standards of professionalism from its members.
- Don't forget that, despite the best efforts of the Institute to ensure uniformity of standards across the profession worldwide, some individuals may benefit from extra employer support in view of the variations in business ethical standards across different countries and cultures.

MORE INFO

Books:

Pickett, K. H. Spencer. *The Internal Auditor at Work: A Practical Guide to Everyday Challenges.* Hoboken, NJ: Wiley, 2004.

Root, Stephen J. *Beyond COSO: Internal Control to Enhance Corporate Governance.* Hoboken, NJ: Wiley, 2000.

Articles:

Colbert, Janet L. "New and expanded internal audit standards." *CPA Journal* (May 2002). Online at: www.nysscpa.org/cpajournal/2002/0502/features/f053402.htm

Gavin, Thomas A., Richard A. Roy, and Glenn E. Sumners. "A corporate code of conduct: The internal auditor's role." *Managerial Auditing Journal* 5:2 (1990). Online at: dx.doi.org/10.1108/02686909010138412. (Also published in *Leadership and Organization Development Journal* 11:3 (1990): 32–40. Online at: dx.doi.org/10.1108/EUM0000000001152.)

Website:

Institute of Internal Auditors (IIA): www.theiia.org

Independence of the Internal Audit Function

DEFINITION

If an internal audit is to prove effective, the auditors must have complete independence to carry out the audit as they see fit and must be free from interference by executives. However, as the Institute of Internal Auditors (IIA) points outs:[1]

"The internal auditor occupies a unique position—he or she is 'employed' by management, but is also expected to review the conduct of management. This can create significant tension since the internal auditor's 'independence' from management is necessary for the auditor to objectively assess management's actions, but the auditor's 'dependence' on management for employment is clear."

With regard to independence, the IIA adds that:[2]

"The audit charter should establish independence of the internal audit activity by the dual reporting relationship to management and the organization's most senior oversight group. Specifically, the CAE [chief audit executive] should report to executive management for assistance in establishing direction, support, and administrative interface; and typically to the audit committee for strategic direction, reinforcement, and accountability. The internal auditors should have access to records and personnel as necessary, and be allowed to employ appropriate probing techniques without impediment."

Senior management should ensure that the internal audit department does not participate in activities that may compromise, or appear to compromise, its independence. These activities may include preparing reports or records, developing procedures, or performing other operational duties that are normally reviewed by auditors. To ensure that auditors are independent, they should be given the authority to:

- access all records and staff necessary to conduct the audit;
- expect from management a formal and timely response to significant adverse audit findings through the taking of appropriate corrective action.

The IIA adds that threats to independence must be managed at the individual auditor, engagement, functional, and organizational levels.

ADVANTAGES

- Having independent auditors ensures that an objective assessment of the risks facing an organization, and of the procedures in place to deal with these risks, can be carried out.
- The independence of internal auditors ensures that audits are effective in detecting and preventing fraud.
- Independence and objectivity are critical components of effective internal audit activity.

DISADVANTAGES

- There are no disadvantages of an independent internal audit function.

ACTION CHECKLIST

✓ Ensure that the chief audit executive (CAE) reports administratively to the chief executive officer (CEO) and not to the chief financial officer (CFO) or a similar officer who has a direct responsibility for systems being audited. Reporting to executives other than the CEO is not desirable as they can influence the internal audit work to be conducted in their area of responsibility, leading to a loss of independence by internal audit.

✓ The board or its audit committee should determine the CAE's performance evaluations and compensation.

✓ The CAE should report functionally for internal audit operations to the audit committee and for administration to the CEO.

✓ Ensure that the internal audit activity is free from interference in determining the scope of internal auditing, performing work, and communicating results.

✓ Establish the independence and the authority of internal audit staff by detailing this in a formal document such as an internal audit charter.

DOS AND DON'TS

DO

- Ensure that there is adequate consideration of audit reports.
- Ensure appropriate action on audit recommendations.
- Make sure that the CAE communicates directly with the board, has regular private meetings with the board, and habitually attends and participates in audit committee meetings.

DON'T

- Don't allow internal auditors to assume operating responsibilities.
- Don't allow internal auditors to draft procedures for, design, install, or operate systems.

- Don't let internal auditors audit activities they previously performed until a reasonable amount of time has elapsed, for example, two years.

MORE INFO

Books:

Harrer, Julie. *Internal Control Strategies: A Mid to Small Business Guide*. Hoboken, NJ: Wiley, 2008

Moeller, Robert R. *Brink's Modern Internal Auditing: A Common Body of Knowledge*. 7th ed. Hoboken, NJ: Wiley, 2009.

Rittenberg, Larry E., Karla M. Johnstone, Audrey A. Gramling, and Bradley J. Schwieger. *Auditing: A Business Risk Approach*. 7th ed. Mason, OH: South-Western Cengage Learning, 2010.

Website:

Institute of Internal Auditors (IIA): www.theiia.org

NOTES

1 Fraser, J., and Lindsay, H. "20 questions directors should ask about internal audit." IIA Research Foundation, 2004. Online at: www.theiia.org/iia/download. cfm?file=2927 [PDF].

2 IIA. "How does internal auditing maintain its independence and objectivity?" Online at: www.theiia.org/theiia/about-the-profession/internal-audit-faqs/?i=1084

Internal Audit Charters

DEFINITION

An internal audit charter is a formal document approved by the audit committee. It should be developed by the chief audit executive and agreed at the highest level of the organization. Standards published by the Institute of Internal Auditors (IIA) require that there be an internal audit charter, but there is no fixed requirement for what it should contain. At a minimum, the IIA standards require a charter to define the purpose, authority, and responsibility of the internal audit function. A charter establishes internal audit's position within an organization and authorizes it to access records, personnel, and physical property that are relevant to internal audit work. It can be used, for example, by an auditor when a manager in a remote part of the business questions the auditor's need to access particular documents, computer records, or personnel. A charter is particularly useful in large organizations but it is important to remember that such situations can also occur in smaller organizations.

The IIA refers to the need for a charter but does not provide specific guidance on what it should contain. IIA Standard 1000 says:[1]

"The internal audit charter is a formal document that defines the internal audit activity's purpose, authority, and responsibility. The internal audit charter establishes the internal audit activity's position within the organization, including the nature of the chief audit executive's functional reporting relationship with the board; authorizes access to records, personnel, and physical properties relevant to the performance of engagements; and defines the scope of internal audit activities. Final approval of the internal audit charter resides with the board."

ADVANTAGES

- A charter can be used in a positive fashion to describe the aims of internal audit.
- It can also be used to defend the audit against hostile managers or staff.

- A charter compels departments that need to be audited to cooperate with the auditor. Without this charter or similar authority, managers might not see the need for an audit and might refuse the auditor's requests.

DISADVANTAGES

- Such a formal document might not be necessary in a small organization.

ACTION CHECKLIST

✔ Develop a precise definition of internal auditing. This should be formally worded and include the objectives of the internal audit function. It may be possible to use the definition outlined by a body such as the IIA.

✔ Ensure that the charter makes it clear that internal audit engagements will cover the following four areas: reliability and integrity of financial and operational information; effectiveness and efficiency of operations; safeguarding of assets; and compliance with laws, regulations, and contracts.

Here is a suggested checklist for use in formulating an internal audit charter. The charter should:

✔ detail the purpose, authority, and responsibility of the internal audit function, together with the scope of its activities;

✔ establish internal audit's position within the organization;

✔ define the nature of the assurance services that will be provided by internal audit;

✔ include a definition of internal auditing;

✔ define the nature of the assurance services that will be provided by internal audit;

✔ authorize access to records, personnel, and physical property relevant to the performance of engagements;

✔ specify a periodic review of internal audit performance and of the charter itself;

✔ be approved by the audit committee.

DOS AND DON'TS

DO

- Ensure that the role of the internal audit function is clearly set out and that it is distinguished from management's responsibilities. Management should, for example, be responsible for establishing procedures to prevent fraud, while the auditors should be responsible for establishing the effectiveness of those procedures.
- Ensure that the charter is simple and unambiguous.
- Make sure that senior management supports the charter or serious problems could ensue.
- Keep the charter short and to the point.

DON'T

- Don't forget to revisit the charter periodically to ensure that it remains relevant to the organization's needs.

MORE INFO

Books:

Moeller, Robert R. *Brink's Modern Internal Auditing: A Common Body of Knowledge*. 7th ed. Hoboken, NJ: Wiley, 2009.

Pickett, K. H. Spencer. *The Internal Auditing Handbook*. 3rd ed. Chichester, UK: Wiley, 2010.

Website:

Institute of Internal Auditors (IIA): www.theiia.org

NOTES

1 IIA. "1000—Purpose, authority, and responsibility." Online at: tinyurl.com/65dspxb

Internal Control Frameworks: COSO, CoCo, and the UK Corporate Governance Code

DEFINITION

In auditing and accounting, internal control is defined as a process that is designed to help an organization to accomplish specific goals or objectives.

Organizations can choose from a number of internal control frameworks. The "Internal control—Integrated framework" published by the Committee of Sponsoring Organizations of the Treadway Commission (COSO) is a widely used framework in the United States and around the world. It was initially published in 1992 "to address key challenges presented by an increasingly complex business environment and help organizations worldwide better assess, design, and manage internal control." The COSO framework defines internal control as a process, effected by an entity's board of directors, management, and other personnel, that is designed to provide "reasonable assurance" regarding the achievement of objectives in the following categories:

- effectiveness and efficiency of operations;
- reliability of financial reporting;
- compliance with applicable laws and regulations.

COSO describes internal control as consisting of five essential components. These components, which are subdivided into 17 factors, include:

- the control environment;
- risk assessment;
- control activities;
- information and communication;
- monitoring.

The CoCo (criteria of control) framework was first published by the Canadian Institute of Chartered Accountants in 1995. This model builds on COSO and is thought by some to be more concrete and user-friendly. CoCo describes internal control as actions that foster the best result for an organization. These actions, which contribute to the achievement of the organization's objectives, focus on:

- effectiveness and efficiency of operations;
- reliability of internal and external reporting;
- compliance with applicable laws and regulations and internal policies.

CoCo indicates that control comprises: "Those elements of an organization (including its resources, systems, processes, culture, structure, and tasks) that, taken together, support people in the achievement of the organization's objectives."

The UK Corporate Governance Code (formerly the Combined Code) was developed by the UK authorities in the early 1990s and last updated in 2010. The Code is principles-based and includes guidelines for best practice. All companies with a Premium Listing on the London Stock Exchange are required to report on how they have complied with the Code and to provide an explanation where they have not.

ADVANTAGES

- Effective internal controls provide a reasonable assurance, but not a guarantee, that an organization's objectives will be met.
- In a large organization, a focus on internal controls should encourage greater standardization of processes.
- Implementing effective internal controls does not necessarily involve extra costs.

DISADVANTAGES

- Internal control cannot ensure that objectives will be met.

ACTION CHECKLIST

✔ Check local legislation. In some countries effective internal control is mandatory, and failure to meet these requirements may result in penalties.

✔ Establish a process for reporting internal control deficiencies, with serious matters reported immediately to top administration and governing boards.

DOS AND DON'TS

DO

- Ensure that all personnel receive a clear message from top management that control responsibilities must be taken seriously.
- Ensure that internal control systems are monitored through a process that assesses the quality of the system's performance over time.
- Be aware that internal control systems change over time, and the way in which controls are applied may evolve. Ensure that new personnel are fully trained in processes and that management knows whether the internal control system continues to be relevant and able to address new risks.

Core Principles • Checklists

DON'T
- Don't forget that there is no such thing as a perfect control system.

MORE INFO

Books:

Hall, James A. *Accounting Information Systems*. 6th ed. Mason, OH: South-Western Cengage Learning, 2008.

Leitch, Matthew. *Intelligent Internal Control and Risk Management: Designing High-Performance Risk Control Systems*. Aldershot, UK: Gower Publishing, 2008.

Moeller, Robert R. *Sarbanes–Oxley Internal Controls: Effective Auditing with AS5, CobiT, and ITIL*. Hoboken, NJ: Wiley, 2008.

Reports:

Canadian Institute of Chartered Accountants (CICA). "Guidance on control." 1995.

Committee of Sponsoring Organizations of the Treadway Commission (COSO). "Internal control—Integrated framework." Online at: www.coso.org/IC-IntegratedFramework-summary.htm

Financial Reporting Council (FRC). "The UK corporate governance code." June 2010. Online at: www.frc.org.uk/corporate/ukcgcode.cfm

Websites:

Canadian Institute of Chartered Accountants (CICA): www.cica.ca

Committee of Sponsoring Organizations of the Treadway Commission (COSO): www.coso.org

Financial Reporting Council (FRC; UK): www.frc.org.uk

Institute of Internal Auditors (IIA): www.theiia.org

QFINANCE

The International Organization of Supreme Audit Institutions (INTOSAI) and Their Congress (INCOSAI)

DEFINITION

The International Organization of Supreme Audit Institutions (INTOSAI) is an umbrella organization for external government organizations. INTOSAI provides a framework for supreme audit institutions (SAIs) to promote development and transfer knowledge, as well as helping to improve government auditing around the world. The professional standing, professional reputations, and influence of SAIs in their own countries are greatly enhanced by being members of INTOSAI.

INTOSAI's motto is *experientia mutua omnibus prodest* (mutual experience benefits all), and the organization prides itself on the exchange of experience, findings, and insights among its members. Such exchanges enable government auditing to progress using new developments.

As a nonpolitical organization, INTOSAI operates independently and autonomously. It is nongovernmental, but maintains a special consultative status with the Economic and Social Council of the United Nations (see www.intosai.org/blueline/upload/globalboardmeeting.pdf, p.13).

INTOSAI was the brainchild of Emilio Fernandez Camus, president of the SAI of Cuba, and the international organization was founded in 1953. The first INTOSAI Congress in Cuba was attended by 34 SAIs. In 2008, INTOSAI had 189 full members and three associate members.

There are several regional working groups, all of which promote the goals of INTOSAI in their own region, thereby providing members in the region with opportunities for professional and technical cooperation. In 2008, the following seven regional working groups were recognized by the INTOSAI Governing Board: Latin American and Caribbean, African, Arabian, Asian, Pacific Association, Caribbean, and European.

There are committees within INTOSAI that deal with member issues such as preparing standards and guidelines for government auditing practice. By the nature of their work, committees have a balanced representation of members from INTOSAI, and also receive clear direction from the governing board.

Working groups are formed when specific technical issues, such as privatization and environmental audits, need to be addressed as a result of themes and recommendations raised at the International Congress of Supreme Audit Institutions (INCOSAI), INTOSAI's congress. Specific guidance and best practices are usually published as result of the deliberations of a working group. Any member of INTOSAI can join any working group.

Task forces are a fourth type of group and are formed by INCOSAI or the INTOSAI Governing Board, as required. Task forces attend to issues of significant interest to many of the members of INTOSAI, and are dissolved when the tasks for which they have been set up are completed. Task forces aim to have a balanced representation of members of INTOSAI.

INCOSAI is composed of all the members, and holds meetings every three years, where all members can exchange experiences, discuss issues, and pass recommendations. The INCOSAI is chaired by the host SAI. Participants include representatives of the United Nations and the World Bank, members of SAIs, and other international organizations.

The last Congress was held in Mexico in 2007, where the key themes were, first, management, accountability, and audit of public debt, and, secondly, performance evaluation systems based on universally accepted key indicators.

MORE INFO

Websites:
INTOSAI: www.intosai.org/en
INTOSAI Development Initiative: www.idi.no

Key Competencies for Internal Auditors

DEFINITION

Internal auditors work in many organizations in the public and private sectors. They can either be trained while working or will possess an internal audit or accountancy qualification before applying for an internal audit position. However, other qualifications can also be useful as the work is varied, challenging, and draws on a broad range of skills.

However, there is a range of key competencies that are required if internal auditors are to carry out their function effectively. These will vary depending on the seniority of the auditor. The requirement in terms of qualifications varies from country to country. In the United Kingdom, for example, an internal auditor is likely to hold the Chartered Institute of Internal Auditors Diploma in Internal Audit Practice (PIIA) or equivalent. Senior internal auditors should hold the Institute's Advanced Diploma in Internal Auditing and Management (MIIA) or equivalent.

According to the UK government,[1] an internal auditor should have the following competencies.

- Understands the principles of the identification, assessment, and management of risk, including that arising from the extended enterprise nature of organizations.
- Is able to identify and critically evaluate the elements of governance and risk management in an organization.
- Is aware of and understands the organization's risk management strategy.
- Understands the relationship of risk management to corporate governance.
- Is able to review and provide advice and recommendations on the implementation of the risk management strategy.
- Understands the organization's high-level objectives, how these are funded, and key related risks.
- Identifies and understands how operational objectives link into the higher-level objectives.
- Understands the relationship between internal audit and risk management, including the choice of roles available to internal audit depending on the risk maturity of the organization and its possible impact on corporate governance.
- Understands the specific risks related to operational activities and is able to contribute to the review of risks in operational areas.
- Is able to relate the organization's risk appetite to the appropriateness of controls and is able to undertake reviews to assess their effectiveness and report to management accordingly.
- Understands the principles of performance measurement and output targets designed to deliver objectives.

ADVANTAGES

- Possessing key competencies enables internal auditors to do their job effectively.
- Possession of these competencies helps internal audit staff to gain the confidence and respect of senior management and of other staff they come into contact with. This is important if they are to carry out their professional duties effectively.

DISADVANTAGES

- Inevitably there will be costs involved in ensuring staff have the correct training and skills.

ACTION CHECKLIST

✓ Ensure that your internal auditors have a continuing commitment to learning. Business and technology are ever-changing, as are the political and regulatory environments in which a business operates.

✓ Before developing a training and development plan, ensure that training and development are linked to the organization's goals as well as those of personnel.

DOS AND DON'TS

DO

- Assess the competency level of each internal auditor, identify the gaps that need remediation, and develop an individual development plan for each internal auditor.
- Ensure that internal audit staff have an ability to manage projects and to work on their own initiative.
- Link the key competencies required by an internal auditor with your organization's personal development and appraisal systems.
- Ensure that internal audit staff have good written and verbal communication skills and are capable of interacting with senior management.

DON'T

- Don't forget to conduct a post-audit assessment, which should look at a variety of issues, including scoring auditors against key competencies.

MORE INFO

Books:

IIA Research Foundation. *Core Competencies for Today's Internal Auditor*. Altamonte Springs, FL: IIA Research Foundation, 2010.

Moeller, Robert R. *Brink's Modern Internal Auditing: A Common Body of Knowledge*. 7th ed. Hoboken, NJ: Wiley, 2009.

Pickett, K. H. Spencer. *The Internal Auditing Handbook*. 3rd ed. Chichester, UK: Wiley, 2010.

Website:

Chartered Institute of Internal Auditors (UK and Ireland): www.iia.org.uk

NOTES

1 Assurance, Control and Risk Team/PSG Competency Framework Working Group. "Government internal audit competancy framework." HM Treasury, March 2007. Online at: www.hm-treasury.gov.uk/d/gov_internalaudit_competencyframework.pdf

Key Components of a Corporate Risk Register

DEFINITION

Most large enterprises have a procedure for managing corporate risks. The procedure is intended to identify, record, and communicate risks in terms of their comparative importance to the company. The corporate risk register also forms the basis for reporting risk issues in the annual report. The information is usually stored in a central register, catalog, or inventory of risks. This should contain information suitably sorted, standardized, and merged for relevance to the appropriate level of management. Its key function is to provide management, the board, and key stakeholders with significant information on the main risks faced by the business. Every risk in the register should have the following features: opening date, title, short description, probability, and importance. A risk might also have a dedicated manager responsible for its resolution.

A risk register should help management to:
- Understands the principles of the identification, assessment, and management of risk, including that arising from the extended enterprise nature of organizations.
- Is able to identify and critically evaluate the elements of governance and risk management in an organization.
- Is aware of and understands the organization's risk management strategy.
- Understands the relationship of risk management to corporate governance.

However, a risk register is often out of date, incomplete, or inconsistent when selecting the appropriate controls and countermeasures for each risk. Many companies, therefore, use outside risk consultants. These consultants, working in conjunction with company staff, are better able to take an objective view of risks, assess their relative importance, and assign priorities.

ADVANTAGES

- A corporate risk register provides management and the board with important information on the main risks faced by the business.
- The register allows management to identify and prioritize risks, ensuring that risks with the greatest probability or the greatest potential loss are handled first.

DISADVANTAGES

- If risks are improperly assessed and prioritized, they can divert resources that could be used more profitably.
- Unless it is competently maintained and updated, the risk register may not be comprehensive or consistent, leading to unrecognized risks.
- The risk information may not be presented in a logical and unbiased form and, as such, can unintentionally mislead.

ACTION CHECKLIST

✓ Thoroughly check the risk register against any potential business risk you might foresee and compare similar companies' risk registers.

✓ Research your market and make sure that you have analyzed the consequences of any risks upon your own business.

✓ Encourage an atmosphere of openness about the kinds of risks facing the organization. Some risks are obvious, but managers of individual business units may sometimes know more about hidden risks. Only by fully understanding risks can you attempt to counteract them.

DOS AND DON'TS

DO

- Seek the advice of specialist strategic risk advisers. Risk management is very complex. Experts from specialist risk management companies can help devise customized risk registers to protect against potential problems.
- Keep in mind the distinction between risk and uncertainty. Risk can be measured by using the formula: Impact multiplied by Probability.
- Quantify and differentiate between risks that are merely the cost of doing business and those that might have an impact on objectives.

DON'T

- Don't make the error of failing to check the risk register thoroughly for inconsistencies.
- Don't believe that you can totally cover every risk your business could face.
- Don't rely on single controls and countermeasures for each risk.

MORE INFO

Websites:

American Institute of Certified Public Accountants (AICPA): www.aicpa.org

KnowledgeLeader: www.knowledgeleader.com

The Key Components of an Audit Report

DEFINITION

An audit is the examination and verification of an organization's financial statements and records. Audits provide independent and impartial opinion as to whether the information is presented objectively. Most organizations—privately held businesses, publicly owned corporations, and nonprofit organizations—have to prepare financial reports, which are audited. These reports assist owners and managers to make decisions, and help to show the company's financial status to stockholders, employees, regulators, and the public.

When reviewing an audit report on a company, key questions include: What is the source of its revenue? Where, and on what, does it spend its income? How much profit is it earning?

The answer lies in the company's financial statements, and, by law, all public companies have to make these statements freely available to everyone.

These financial statements can be broken down into two key components: the profit-and-loss statement (or income statement) and the balance sheet.

The profit-and-loss statement tells us whether the company is making a profit. It indicates how revenue is transformed into net income. Profit-and-loss statements cover a period of time—usually a year or part of a year.

The balance sheet is a snapshot of a business's financial health at a specific moment in time—usually the close of an accounting period. A balance sheet shows assets, liabilities, and stockholders' equity/capital. Assets and liabilities are divided into short-term and long-term obligations. The balance sheet does not show the flows into and out of the accounts during the period. A balance sheet's assets should equal liabilities plus owners' equity.

There are two kinds of audit: internal and external.

Internal audits ensure that the management of the business is meeting internal goals such as productivity, quality, compliance controls, consistency, and cost, as well as external goals such as customer satisfaction and market share.

External audits are carried out by outside auditors, who do not have any ties to the organization or its financial statements. The outside auditor checks the financial statements prepared by management for balance, and also to see whether the company is adhering to professional standards and Generally Accepted Accounting Principles (GAAP).

ADVANTAGES

- External audits improve understanding of underlying business trends and provide an objective opinion as to whether the information is presented fairly.
- Internal audits let managers know whether a business can expand or needs to adopt a more conservative approach. Can it deal with the normal ebbs and flows in revenue, or should it take immediate steps to bolster cash reserves?
- Internal audits focus on processes within the business, and can identify and help to analyze trends, particularly in the area of receivables and payables, i.e. is the receivables cycle lengthening? Can receivables be collected more aggressively? Is some debt uncollectible?

DISADVANTAGES

- Results sometimes depend on the accounting methods used. Measuring and reporting give management considerable discretion and the opportunity to influence an audit's results.
- Internal audits are not always carried out rigorously and the figures may not reflect the true financial position of the company. Salaries for internal audit staff are paid for by the organization. This can lead to questions about objectivity.

ACTION CHECKLIST

- ✔ Carefully analyze any profit-and-loss statements for differences during the reporting period. Anomalies might be due to seasonal or other variations, or may indicate deeper problems.
- ✔ When reviewing internal audits, be prepared to be involved in a long and detailed process of analysis. Some areas will need clarification by experts.
- ✔ Check which GAAP are used in the internal audit of the business in which you are interested.
- ✔ Internal audits are not infallible. If you are unsure about specific areas or numbers, don't hesitate to ask for clarification.

DOS AND DON'TS

DO
- Make sure that you take the time and effort to analyze the audit. If in doubt, consult an independent auditor.
- Use your judgment when reviewing internal audits; results do not always tell the whole story.

DON'T
- Don't assume that all audits truly reflect a company's financial position; they only reflect the auditor's opinion.

MORE INFO

Books:

Cardwell, Harvey. *Principles of Audit Surveillance*. Reprise ed. Philadelphia, PA: R. T. Edwards, 2005.

Switzer, Susan. *Internal Audit Reports Post Sarbanes – Oxley: A Guide to Process Driven Reporting*. Hoboken, NJ: Wiley, 2007.

Wealleans, David. *The Quality Audit for ISO 9001:2000: A Practical Guide*. 2nd ed. Aldershot, UK: Gower Publishing, 2005.

Websites:

American Accounting Association (AAA): aaahq.org

Institute of Internal Auditors (IIA): www.theiia.org

The Role of the Audit Committee

DEFINITION

The audit committee is an operating committee that deals with financial reporting and disclosure of the financial situation of a company. Since the Sarbanes–Oxley Act of 2002, the committee's role has become essential to a company's financial wellbeing. Depending on the size of a company and whether it is private or public, the audit committee is composed of three to six members with financial, accounting, and auditing experience.

The role of an audit committee is varied. The committee reviews the internal auditors' report and makes recommendations to the board of directors based on its findings. It also reviews the chairman's statement of internal control of a company.

The audit committee performs a reporting and accounting role by overseeing external auditors, reviewing their report and management letter.

Another important role of the audit committee is to assess the risk management of a company by reporting directly to the executive board of a company on the effectiveness of the risk management arrangements and making recommendations. For this the audit committee will familiarize itself with the risk management procedures of a company, review any corporate governance statements, and assess the internal and external audit reports of the company.

Each member of the audit committee should declare any potential conflict of interest that may arise out of the business of the company. In order to be able to fulfill their role, members of the committee must have a good understanding of the company's objectives and priorities. Ideally, the members as a group should bring expertise to the audit committee in various disciplines such as finance and law and in the industry in which the company operates. They must have a clear picture of their appointment, including duration and time commitments. The members must also understand how their individual performance will be reviewed.

ADVANTAGES

- An audit committee is an oversight body that is independent of management.
- An audit committee sets standards in respect of governance, risk management, and controls.
- An audit committee helps a company to assess the state of its business and to put in place measures to improve and develop it.
- It performs a reporting and accounting role as well as assessing the risk management of a company.

DISADVANTAGES

- Getting the right expertise to serve on an audit committee can be difficult.
- Setting appropriate terms of reference and giving the committee sufficient authority to be effective can be problematic.
- An audit committee is another corporate overhead.

ACTION CHECKLIST

✔ An audit committee should have an independent chairman and comprise an appropriate mix of people, skills, and experience relevant to company operations. Appointees should include nonexecutive directors and independent members.

✔ The committee should have a charter (terms of reference), a code of conduct, and a register of members' interests. Institute a procedure for dealing with conflicts of interest.

✔ There should be a thorough process for appointing committee members.

✔ The full audit committee should meet regularly, with a written agenda that is distributed in advance.

✔ Agenda items should address key governance matters of the company.

✔ Written records (minutes) should be kept of audit committee meetings.

✔ Consider an evaluation process to assess the effectiveness of the audit committee.

✔ The audit committee should meet with representatives of external and internal auditors at least once a year without management being present.

✔ The audit committee should prepare an annual report for the board of directors on governance, risk management, controls, and fraud.

DOS AND DON'TS

DO

- Review the chairman's statement regarding the internal control of a company.
- Submit the internal auditors' annual report to the audit committee for their consideration.
- Review the external auditors' report and management letter.
- Implement the recommendations made by the audit committee.
- Periodically monitor reports on risks.
- Make sure that the corporate objectives of the company are mapped against risks.

DON'T

- Don't ignore the findings of the audit committee or any recommendations it may make.
- Don't make decisions solely on financial grounds that may endanger the impartiality of audit committee have regard to the reputation of the members of the audit committee and their professionalism.

MORE INFO

Books:

Ruppel, Warren. *Not-for-Profit Audit Committee Best Practices*. Hoboken, NJ: Wiley, 2006.

Verschoor, Curtis C. *Audit Committee Essentials*. Hoboken, NJ: Wiley, 2008.

Articles:

Bugalla, John, Janice Hackett, Mary Lynn McPherson, and Kristina Narvaez. "Audit committees monitor control functions, risk committees provide oversight of a strategic function." *BoardMember.com* (November 2010). Online at: tinyurl.com/6gkojc3

George, Nashwa. "The role of audit committees in the public sector." *CPA Journal* (August 2005). Online at: www.nysscpa.org/cpajournal/2005/805/essentials/p42.htm

Report:

Australian National Audit Office (ANAO). "Public sector audit committees." February 2005. Online at: tinyurl.com/6fo5xwz

Websites:

BoardMember.com: www.boardmember.com

Institute of Chartered Accountants in England and Wales (ICAEW): www.icaew.com

Institute of Internal Auditors (IIA): www.theiia.org

New York State Society of CPAs (NYSSCPA): www.nysscpa.org

Sarbanes–Oxley: Its Development and Aims

DEFINITION

The Sarbanes–Oxley Act is a US federal law that was enacted in response to several major corporate and accounting scandals, such as those affecting Enron and WorldCom, which involved large-scale internal fraud. These scandals damaged confidence in US financial markets. A variety of complex factors created the conditions and culture in which the fraudulent activities were able to flourish undetected for a number of years, including conflicts of interest and incentive compensation practices. The analysis of their complex and contentious root causes contributed to the passage of the bill in 2002. The Act was named after Senator Paul Sarbanes and Representative Michael G. Oxley. It is also known as the Public Company Accounting Reform and Investor Protection Act of 2002 and is often referred to as Sarbanes–Oxley, Sarbox, or SOX.

The act imposes high standards of accountability and transparency on the boards and management of all US publicly listed companies and public accounting firms. The legal framework established a new, quasi-public agency, the Public Company Accounting Oversight Board (PCAOB), which has responsibility for the overseeing, registration, regulation, inspection, and disciplining of accountancy companies that carry out audits of public companies.

Beside the PCAOB, Sarbox covers issues such as auditor independence, corporate governance, assessment of internal control, enhanced financial disclosure, analysts' conflicts of interest, corporate tax, and corporate fraud. There are 11 legislative sections for this purpose, known as titles, which enable the imposition of additional corporate board responsibilities as well as criminal penalties. The Securities and Exchange Commission (SEC) has the power to implement rulings on requirements to comply with Sarbanes–Oxley.

There remains much disagreement over whether Sarbox has been a useful piece of legislation. Although the Act has helped to restore public confidence in the US capital markets and has strengthened corporate accounting controls, there is also evidence to suggest that it has displaced business from the United States to the United Kingdom, where regulations for the financial sector are less overbearing. In the United Kingdom, the nonstatutory Combined Code of Corporate Governance, monitored by the Financial Services Authority, is similar to Sarbox but has a lighter touch.

As the capital markets are global, Sarbox has also affected non-US companies cross-listed in the United States. Companies based in countries with poor regulation have benefited from better credit ratings by complying with Sarbox, despite the cost. Companies in countries that have a strong regulatory regime already benefit from adequate transparency, so the cost of compliance with Sarbox is less. Either way, companies that choose to be cross-listed on other exchanges, such as the London Stock Exchange, benefit from better credit ratings anyway. Studies comparing new foreign listings on both the US and UK exchanges between 1995 and 2006 showed that Sarbox had no real impact on the listing preferences of large foreign companies for the main exchanges. However, since Sarbox was enacted there is evidence that small foreign companies choosing between Nasdaq and the London Stock Exchange's Alternative Investment Market are less likely to opt for the US listing. It is thought that this is due to the higher costs associated with compliance with Sarbox. Certainly, the Alternative Investment Market has enjoyed spectacular growth since Sarbox was enacted, and this cannot be put down to coincidence alone.

Legislation or regulation similar to Sarbanes–Oxley has been introduced in Canada, Japan, Australia, South Africa, France, Germany, and Italy, ensuring that tighter antifraud controls have been brought into play in most major markets.

MORE INFO

Books:

Anand, Sanjay. *Sarbanes–Oxley Guide for Finance and Information Technology Professionals*. 2nd ed. Hoboken, NJ: Wiley, 2006.

Bainbridge, Stephen M. *The Complete Guide to Sarbanes–Oxley: Understanding How Sarbanes–Oxley Affects Your Business*. Avon, MA: Adams Media, 2007.

Marchetti, Anne M. *Sarbanes–Oxley Ongoing Compliance Guide: Key Processes and Summary Checklists*. Hoboken, NJ: Wiley, 2007.

Website:

Catalog of US Government Publications: catalog.gpo.gov. Search for "sarbanes oxley."

Understanding Internal Audits

DEFINITION

The Institute for Internal Auditors (IIA) defines internal auditing as "an independent, objective assurance and consulting activity designed to add value and improve an organization's operations." An internal audit "helps an organization accomplish its objectives by bringing a systematic, disciplined approach to evaluate and improve the effectiveness of risk management, control and governance processes."

The following comprise a set of guidelines for initiating an internal audit:

- Clarify guidelines and expectations with management (for example, purpose, timing, scope).
- Set up an audit committee and, with its help, develop an audit charter.
- Consider an appropriate budget and staffing model.
- Formulate reporting responsibilities for the internal audit function.
- Initiate a risk assessment, with management and audit committee involvement.
- Develop an internal audit plan in response to the risk assessment.
- Determine staffing requirements.
- Carry out the audit plan, including a monitoring and follow-up system.
- Update the risk assessment plan as circumstances change.
- Enhance and modify the audit function to meet the organization's changing needs.

If an evaluation of internal controls is to be effective, the audit function should be properly financed. When making staffing decisions, companies should look at their risk profiles. A business facing a significant number of risks or particularly complex risks will require various types of specialist expertise. A chief audit executive heads most internal audit departments, with specialist support staff.

ADVANTAGES

- Internal audits improve understanding of underlying business trends by giving independent objective financial information.
- Internal audits let managers know if a business can expand or needs to pull back, if it can deal with the normal revenue ebbs and flows, or if it should take immediate steps to boost cash reserves.
- Internal audits can identify and help to analyze trends, particularly in the areas of receivables and payables. For example, is the receivables cycle lengthening? Can receivables be collected more aggressively? Is some debt un-collectable?

DISADVANTAGES

- Results sometimes depend on the accounting methods used. Measuring and reporting give management considerable discretion and opportunity to influence results.
- Internal audits are not always rigorously carried out, and figures may not be a true reflection of the financial position of the company.
- Salaries for internal audit staff are paid for by the organization; this can lead to bias.

ACTION CHECKLIST

✓ When reviewing internal audits be prepared to be involved in a long and detailed process of analysis where some areas will need clarification by experts.

✓ Check which Generally Accepted Accounting Principles (GAAP) are used in the internal audit of the business area or country in which you have an interest.

✓ Internal audits are not infallible. If you are unsure about specific areas or numbers, don't hesitate to ask for clarification.

DOS AND DON'TS

DO

- Make sure that you take the time and effort to analyze the internal audit and, if in doubt, consult an external expert.
- Use your judgment when reviewing internal audits; numbers do not always tell the whole story.

DON'T

- Don't leave out the boring bits; number crunching is not always effortless or interesting, and often it is tempting to skip parts. Sometimes, however, the truth lies in the detail.

MORE INFO
Websites:
HM Treasury (UK): www.hm-treasury.gov.uk
Institute of Internal Auditors (IIA): www.theiia.org
US Department of the Treasury: www.treasury.gov

What Is Forensic Auditing?

DEFINITION

Forensic auditing is a blend of traditional accounting, auditing, and financial detective work. Technology has an increasingly important role to play, with complex data analysis techniques employed to help flag areas that warrant further investigation.

Forensic auditing offers a toolset that company managers can use to help detect and investigate various forms of white-collar financial impropriety and inappropriate or inefficient use of resources. As company structures and controls become ever more complex, so too does the scope for employees with specialized knowledge of the way control systems work to bypass them. In the past, various forms of auditing have been employed after a major control breach has come to light, but executives are now increasingly looking at forensic auditing to help identify vulnerabilities in financial control.

ADVANTAGES

- Forensic auditing strengthens control mechanisms, with the objective of protecting the business against financial crimes, be they potentially catastrophic one-off events that could threaten the viability of the business, or smaller-scale but repetitive misappropriations of company assets over a number of years.
- Forensic auditing can play an important role for companies under review by regulatory authorities and can also be invaluable to ensure regulatory compliance. For example, forensic auditing can be useful in helping companies to ensure that their anti-money laundering procedures are both effective and robust.
- Forensic auditing can help protect organizations from the long-term damage to reputation caused by the publicity associated with insider crimes. A forensic audit also provides a sound base of factual information that can be used to help resolve disputes, and can be used in court should the victim seek legal redress.
- Forensic auditing can improve efficiency by identifying areas of waste.
- Forensic auditing can help with the detection and recording of potential conflicts of interest for executives by improving transparency and probity in the way resources are used, in both private and public entities.

DISADVANTAGES

- A poorly managed forensic audit could consume excessive amounts of management time and could become an unwelcome distraction for the business.
- Forensic audits can have wide-ranging scope across the business. Under certain circumstances, the scope of the audit may need to be extended, with a corresponding increase in the budget.
- Some employees can interpret a proactive forensic audit as a slight on their integrity, rather than as a means to improve control procedures for the benefit of the business.

ACTION CHECKLIST

- ✓ Understand your risks, routes to their potential exploitation, and the tools available to detect abuses, fraud, or wastage.
- ✓ Analyze numerical data, comparing actual costs against expected costs.
- ✓ Investigate possible reasons for inconsistencies.
- ✓ Consider whether covert detection techniques might be more appropriate when investigating cases of possible fraud. Higher-profile full forensic audits can deter future fraud but could also reduce the likelihood of witnessing the culprit carrying out a fraudulent act.
- ✓ External auditing specialists with extensive experience of complex forensic audits can offer industry-specific experience, auditing management expertise, and advanced interviewing techniques. A combination of these external specialists and companies' internal accountants/auditors can achieve shorter audit timescales and lower levels of disruption to the business.

DOS AND DON'TS

DO

- Remember that well-resourced forensic auditing processes can help to identify misreporting at many levels of an organization.
- Bear in mind that regular proactive forensic audits can help businesses to ensure that their processes stay robust.

(Continued overleaf)

DO (*cont.*)

- Be prepared to widen the scope of a forensic audit to ensure maximum effectiveness.
- See forensic auditing as a continuous process, rather than a one-off event. On completing one audit, restarting the process could uncover something relevant that was previously overlooked.
- Be prepared to share the findings of the forensic audit with other areas of your company, and take into account industry best practice to improve efficiency and combat fraud.

DON'T

- Don't lose sight of the objective of a forensic audit. The cost of a forensic audit can be high, but the potential cost of not undertaking an audit and implementing its findings can be even higher.
- Don't fall into the trap of overlooking the importance of the "forensic" element of the audit. With the results of such a process deemed suitable for inclusion in legal proceedings, the high potential costs of the forensic audit process could easily be recovered from dispute resolution or higher levels of loss recovery.

MORE INFO

Book:

Cardwell, Harvey. *Principles of Audit Surveillance*. Reprise Edition. Philadelphia, PA: R.T. Edwards, 2005.

Articles:

Brannen, Laurie. "Top of mind: Is a forensic audit in your future?" *Business Finance* (June 2007). Online at: businessfinancemag.com/article/top-mind-forensic-audit-your-future-0601

Roberts, Marta. "Fraud fight in the Wild West." *Security Management* 48:11 (November 2004).

Websites:

American Institute of Certified Public Accountants (AICPA): www.aicpa.org

Institute of Chartered Accountants in England and Wales (ICAEW): www.icaew.com

Institute of Forensic Accounting and Investigative Audit (IFAIA; India): www.ifaia.org

Checklists
In Practice

Adopting an Internal Audit Capability Model

DEFINITION

An internal audit capability model (IACM) provides a framework for assessing the quality, impact, and cost-effectiveness of an internal audit activity. It also identifies the fundamentals needed for effective internal auditing and describes the levels and stages through which internal audit activity can develop and improve processes and practices. The Institute of Internal Auditors (IIA) produced an "Internal Audit Capability Model for the Public Sector" in 2009, for example, which can be used in public-sector organizations, and others are available, with some service providers producing IACMs.

The IIA model consists of five progressive capability levels, each describing the characteristics and capabilities of an internal audit activity at that level. Implementing repeatable and sustainable processes at one level provides the foundation on which to progress to the next. The levels are as follows.

Level 1. Initial. No sustainable, repeatable capabilities; dependent on individual efforts.

Level 2. Infrastructure. Sustainable and repeatable internal audit processes.

Level 3. Integrated. Internal audit and professional practices uniformly applied.

Level 4. Managed. Internal auditing integrates information from across the organization to improve governance and risk management.

Level 5. Optimizing. Internal auditing learns from inside and outside the organization for continuous improvement.

At Level 1, the least advanced, the internal audit infrastructure and its institutional capability are undeveloped. There may be isolated single audits, but the results are dependent on the skills of individuals. Internal auditing is ad hoc and unstructured. On reaching the most advanced level, the internal audit activity is a learning organization with continuous process improvements and innovation.

ADVANTAGES

* An IACM can assist users to develop an internal audit strategic plan, as well as to develop an effective internal audit function.
* The model can be used as a self-assessment and continuous improvement tool for internal audit activities by audit committees, senior management, and legislators to evaluate the need for and the type of internal audit activity appropriate to their organization or jurisdiction. The model could also be used by national, regional, and local legislative auditors as a source of benchmarks.

DISADVANTAGES

* As with any self-assessment process, the results obtained from the model are dependent on the supply of objective and accurate information.
* An internal audit activity might, for example, assess itself at a higher capability level than actually applies because the participants are not fully aware of professional practices.
* Implementing the model can be time-consuming and costly, particularly for a small organization.

ACTION CHECKLIST

✓ Participants in the IACM need to understand the structure and underlying principles of the capability model.

✓ The chief audit executive and the internal auditors must be committed to the exercise and its results, and should develop an action plan for improvement.

✓ Management needs to support and clarify the purpose of using the IACM, explaining how it will improve the capability of staff members and the potentially positive implications for their career development.

DOS AND DON'TS

DO

- Ensure that the team includes at least one person skilled in conducting internal or external assessments of an internal audit activity and another person who has responsibility for making improvements to the activity.
- When implementing the IACM, take into account organizational factors such as corporate governance, culture, internal control systems, and human resource capacities.

- Communicate the results by identifying strengths and areas for improvement and by formulating an action plan for the development of internal auditing.

DON'T

- Don't ignore the fact that internal auditing capabilities cannot outpace the maturity of the organization that they support. To reach the higher levels will need advanced enterprise risk management strategies and practices.

MORE INFO

Books:

Chambers, Andrew, and Graham Rand. *The Operational Auditing Handbook: Auditing Business and IT Processes.* 2nd ed. Hoboken, NJ: Wiley, 2010.

Institute of Internal Auditors Research Foundation. *Internal Audit Capability Model (IA-CM) for the Public Sector.* Altamonte Springs, FL: IIA Research Foundation, 2009.

Moeller, Robert R. *Brink's Modern Internal Auditing: A Common Body of Knowledge.* 7th ed. Hoboken, NJ: Wiley, 2009.

Swanson, Dan. *Swanson on Internal Auditing: Raising the Bar.* Cambridge, UK: IT Governance, 2010.

Auditing Information Technology and Information Systems

DEFINITION

The benefits of information technology (IT) are accompanied by a need to manage the complexities, risks, and challenges that come with it. Auditing IT and information systems involves auditing an organization's hardware, software, and data organization and processing methods to ensure quality control and security. It certainly does not involve the popularly held belief that it amounts to merely counting computers. Even the smallest companies are dependent on IT systems, and in order for an organization to take full advantage of the IT system at its disposal it is vital that any system can be controlled and is reliable. Moreover, fraudsters can exploit IT systems, so it is vital these systems are secure and that safeguards have been implemented to detect and deter fraud. Data protection legislation also requires that data are secure and remain confidential. According to the Institute of Internal Auditors, some of the more obvious results of information system failures include reputational damage, placing the organization at a competitive disadvantage, and contractual noncompliance.

ADVANTAGES

- Paying attention to the challenges involved in establishing and maintaining an IT system can prevent waste of money and resources, loss of trust, and reputational damage.
- Timely involvement by internal auditors can help to assure that problems are identified and solved at an early stage.
- IT auditors can serve as a bridge between individual business units and the IT function, point out previously unidentified risks, and recommend controls for enhancing outcomes.
- An IT audit can identify IT weaknesses that could be exploited by a fraudster or which could compromise compliance with data protection laws.

DISADVANTAGES

- Carrying out an IT audit and ensuring that staff have the necessary training can be time-consuming and costly (although not doing so can be far more costly).

ACTION CHECKLIST

✓ Develop an IT audit plan. This can help chief audit executives and internal auditors to understand the organization and how IT supports it, to define and understand the IT environment, to identify the role of risk assessments in determining the IT audit universe, and to formalize the annual IT audit plan.

✓ Develop an "audit checklist" to ensure that the auditors focus on areas and issues of concern.

DOS AND DON'TS

DO

- Make sure that your IT audit staff receive the latest technology and training, given the rapid pace of development in the IT world.
- Consider external IT auditors if the necessary skills are not available inhouse.
- Make sure that your staff are aware of all the legal requirements regarding data protection.

DON'T

- Don't carry out IT internal audits at fixed times. If staff know the timing of audits, they may adjust the way they use their IT resources, giving an inaccurate impression of their effectiveness, efficiency.

MORE INFO

Books:

Cascarino, Richard E. *Auditor's Guide to Information Systems Auditing.* Hoboken, NJ: Wiley, 2007.

Champlain, Jack J. *Auditing Information Systems.* 2nd ed. Hoboken, NJ: Wiley, 2003.

Wright, Craig, Brian Freedman, and Dale Liu. *The IT Regulatory and Standards Compliance Handbook: How to Survive an Information Systems Audit and Assessments.* Rockland, MA: Syngress Publishing, 2008.

Article:

Bayuk Jennifer. "Information systems audit: The basics." *IT World* (May 26, 2009). Online at: www.itworld.com/security/68365/information-systems-audit-basics

Websites:

Chartered Institute of Internal Auditors (UK and Ireland): www.iia.org.uk

Institute of Internal Auditors (IIA): www.theiia.org

Avoiding Conflict of Interest in Internal Audits

DEFINITION

Every year a company undergoes an external audit and will also undertake a program of internal auditing. Using external auditors to carry out internal audit work can lead to a conflict of interest. A conflict of interest may also occur when an internal auditor has a personal or professional involvement or association with the area that is subject to the audit.

There are two essential elements that apply to ensure that such conflicts of interest are avoided: independence and objectivity. *Independence* can be achieved by having an appropriate written internal audit charter that ensures the independence of auditors. The chief audit executive should report directly to the audit committee. Also, it is advisable that internal auditors do not have any operational responsibilities. The independence of an internal auditor appointed by the management of a company may be called into question if he or she is involved in reviewing the conduct of the management.

The *objectivity* element is ensured by the professionalism of the internal auditors. This is achieved by having a well-written and implemented internal audit charter. Recruiting and appointing the right internal auditor is essential. Maintaining good professional relations between the internal audit function and management is also extremely important. A good management team will be interested in a good audit process that will objectively highlight any positive or negative aspects of the way a company is managed. An internal auditor has a professional and ethical obligation to disclose any involvement on his or her part in an activity that could give rise to a conflict of interest.

The same firm should never be appointed to do both the internal audit and the external audit. Using different audit firms will not only avoid a conflict of interest but will provide independent opinions and reports that the management and shareholders can use to assess the business of the company.

ADVANTAGES

- Having an independent external audit helps an organization to assess the state of its business and to put in place measures to improve and develop it.

- Making sure that internal auditors are not involved in operational responsibilities avoids potential conflicts of interest.

DISADVANTAGES

- External auditors are expensive, but trying to cut costs by using the same auditors for both internal and external audits can lead to conflicts of interest and may in the end increase costs.
- In certain circumstances, a company will be required to change its external auditor after a fixed period and avoid using the same audit company for both internal and external audit work.

ACTION CHECKLIST

✓ Carefully assess your options for internal and external auditors. Obtain as much information from as many sources as you can before appointing auditors.

✓ Consider a selection bidding process and examine each bid carefully before making a decision.

DOS AND DON'TS

DO

- Establish good communication between management and auditors.
- Avoid conflicts of interest by choosing separate internal and external auditors.
- Encourage internal auditors to disclose any involvement in activities that might give rise to conflicts of interest.
- Consider reputation: a more expensive external auditor may offer better value for money in the medium to long term.

DON'T

- Don't make decisions that endanger the impartiality of an audit solely on the basis of financial considerations.
- Don't appoint internal auditors that have had management functions in the company.

MORE INFO

Books:

Pastor, Joan. *Conflict Management and Negotiation Skills for Internal Auditors.* Altamonte Springs, FL: Institute of Internal Auditors Research Foundation, 2007.

Porter, Brenda, Jon Simon, and David Hatherly. *Principles of External Auditing.* 3rd ed. Chichester, UK: Wiley, 2008.

Articles:

Fan, Joseph P. H., and T. J. Wong. "Do external auditors perform a corporate governance role in emerging markets? Evidence from East Asia." *Journal of Accounting Research* 43:1 (March 2005): 35–72. Online at: dx.doi.org/10.1111/j.1475-679x.2004.00162.x

Wang, Kun, and Zahid Iqbal. "Auditor choice, retained ownership, and earnings disclosure for IPO firms. Further evidence." *International Journal of Managerial Finance* 2:3 (2006): 220–240. Online at: dx.doi.org/10.1108/17439130610676484

Websites:

Chartered Institute of Internal Auditors (UK and Ireland): www.iia.org.uk
Institute of Internal Auditors (IIA): www.theiia.org

Cosourcing Internal Audits

DEFINITION

The internal audit departments of even the largest organizations cannot afford to employ the technical and expert resources required to meet all the requirements that they are likely to encounter at all times. By using cosourcing, organizations can tap into specialized skills that are not available inhouse. Cosourcing gives organizations access to world-class, global internal audit resources and capabilities, along with access to state-of-the-art technology, and it allows for the redeployment of staff to core activities. Moreover, it can cut costs (by not employing specialist staff on a full-time basis). Recruiting internal audit staff of sufficient caliber can also be time-consuming and recruitment costs are invariably loaded upfront, while mistakes in recruitment are expensive to reverse. Buying in expertise to assist with a particular assignment can therefore be a sensible alternative.

Cosourcing has become increasingly popular as the internal auditing function develops beyond its traditional role and provides information to management to assist its decision-making, as well as protecting organizations against risk and improving control systems. Under cosourcing, a service provider is contracted to assist the inhouse team with specific projects, such as supply chain efficiency or IT risk management. Costs are partially fixed and partially variable. Cosourcing can also be useful where extra internal audit resources are required or where internal audit staff vacancies remain unfilled for a long time.

ADVANTAGES

- Gives an organization access to auditors with specialist skills.
- Enables an organization to top up its internal audit resources.
- Can provide immediate access to resources that help the company to adjust to changing business conditions.
- Can cut costs: businesses can call on skills when they need them and gain access to world-class resources without investing heavily to develop those resources inhouse.
- Exposes internal staff to alternative practices, tools, training, and processes.
- Risks reside with an inhouse manager.
- Fewer employee shortages.
- Greater knowledge of company business, objectives, risks, systems, and culture.
- Greater flexibility.
- Fewer conflicts of interest.
- More direct control over quality of work.
- Corporate knowledge is retained.
- Can provide training for future managers.
- Critical mass makes inhouse internal audit department viable and sustainable.
- Skills transfer to inhouse employees from service providers.
- Cost-effective.

DISADVANTAGES

- It is not always possible to gain access to auditors specializing in a specific technical topic because they are in such high demand.
- Gaining access to a specialist auditor may be an even bigger problem if an organization is not located in a major business market.
- Service providers cost more than inhouse staff.

ACTION CHECKLIST

✓ Take time to make sure that you choose the right service provider. Some firms may be motivated by profit and seek to take on as much work as possible and get it completed as quickly as possible. Other firms are more interested in building a long-term relationship and in gaining future assignments. It is also important to look for firms with a history of success in similar assignments in your industry.

✓ Carefully assess the audit plan and staff capabilities to identify gaps that can be filled by cosourcing. The cosourcing contract should directly address the missing skills and should be for a minimum of three years to build relationships, trust, and consistency.

✓ Implement specific guidelines and procedures, including a communication plan that embraces open and honest communication with rapid resolution of problems and clarification of doubtful issues.

DOS AND DON'TS

DO

- Insist that services are provided by certified internal auditors, and for IT audits by certified information systems auditors.
- Insist that audits are conducted in accordance with the International Standards for the Professional Practice of Internal Auditing issued by the Institute of Internal Auditors.
- Require a minimum level of qualifications and experience from service providers so that you are not assigned inexperienced graduates who you end up training.
- Require CVs for the service provider staff who will do the work and do not allow them to be replaced without your written authorization.
- Provide an induction for the service provider staff.
- Establish matrices and scorecards to evaluate potential providers in terms of cultural compatibility, industry experience, and knowledge of the organization's business.
- Ensure that knowledge transfer takes place so that a department retains specialist knowledge internally for future uses of that information—for example, for revising a procedure, a policy, or a process.
- Use the organization's report format and not that of the service provider.
- Have an inhouse quality assurance process for the work and work papers, and do not just rely on the service provider's procedures.
- Insist that work papers are reviewed and retained by the organization.
- Evaluate the outsourced group's performance on an engagement-by-engagement basis and also on a yearly basis.

DON'T

- Don't hire a firm simply on the basis that they offer the cheapest deal.
- Don't forget to establish monitoring procedures and means of evaluating whether the service provider has met your requirements.
- Don't forget to actively manage the service provider.

MORE INFO

Books:

Kagermann, Henning, William Kinney, Karlheinz Küting, and Claus-Peter Weber (eds). *Internal Audit Handbook: Management with the SAP®-Audit Roadmap.* Berlin: Springer, 2008.

Pickett, K. H. Spencer. *The Internal Auditing Handbook.* 3rd ed. Chichester, UK: Wiley, 2010.

Rittenberg, Larry E., Karla Johnstone, and Audrey A. Gramling. *Auditing: A Business Risk Approach.* 8th ed. Mason, OH: South-Western/Cengage Learning, 2011.

Creating a Comprehensive Audit Committee Evaluation Form

DEFINITION

After the revelation of corporate fraud at Enron and evidence of management largesse at Tyco early in the new millennium, a lack of investor confidence in the veracity of some corporate earnings reports and questions over the integrity of some leading global executives sparked demands for dramatic improvements in global corporate governance. In the United States, the Sarbanes–Oxley Act (2002) required reforms to corporate governance practices, including the establishment of auditing and related attestations, ethics, and independence standards. Pressure grew elsewhere in the world for companies to tighten their corporate governance standards to meet the rising expectations of stockholders, to whom company boards and audit committees ultimately answer.

Given the elevated demands made by stockholders, activist investors, investment analysts, regulators, and journalists, many companies have sought to stay ahead of the curve by implementing formal measures to help verify the effectiveness of audit committees. Indeed, New York Stock Exchange proposals for improved listing standards have included the suggestion that companies should instigate formal evaluation processes for the entire board and for the board's major committees, not least the audit committee.

There are many different approaches to ensuring audit committee effectiveness. The evaluation form method has rapidly gained favor, although this is most effective as part of a broader program that includes processes to secure the independence and objectivity of members. In general terms, the scope of the audit committee should encompass the full range of the company's activities, rather than simply amounting to a box-ticking exercise relating to compliance with existing regulations.

ADVANTAGES

- Self-evaluation measures such as the evaluation form can help audit committee members focus on ways to improve existing processes.

- The evaluation form approach enables interested parties to provide a frank assessment of the audit committee's effectiveness on an anonymous basis.
- This method also provides a forum for participants to raise issues that members of the audit committee themselves may not have considered.

DISADVANTAGES

- Given the differences between company cultures and practices, no standard approach will consistently deliver major improvements in the effectiveness of all audit committees. However, the evaluation form can be a useful means of gauging the views of internal stakeholders.
- The approach is only truly effective if the form is compiled in a way that elicits unbiased feedback from participants. Phrasing questions to prompt responses that the compilers favor is certain to undermine the process.

ACTION CHECKLIST

✔ Agree on the evaluation process to be used and identify an individual to be charged with the overall responsibility for its coordination.
✔ Consider the main elements of the evaluation form, such as organizational factors, the overseeing of the reporting process, and routes to possible improvement. The evaluation form can then be compiled, inviting participants to grade the effectiveness of all aspects of the committee and its activities.
✔ Determine how communication should be handled with the main audit committee and other relevant individuals, such as the board chairman, independent auditor, and in-house legal heads.
✔ Give the evaluation forms to all relevant parties, and then compile the results. Compare the results from different categories of participants to determine how perceptions of the audit committee's effectiveness vary between different areas of the business.

DOS AND DON'TS

DO

- Maximize the effectiveness of this approach by carrying out the process annually.
- Leave space on the evaluation form for participants to add further comments on issues that may not have been considered when creating the form.
- Obtain the advice of company legal experts on how the results of the evaluation process should be recorded and filed.

DON'T

- Don't regard the evaluation form as merely a means of demonstrating compliance with existing industry regulation. To do so could mean missing out on a real opportunity to improve the effectiveness of the audit committee.
- Don't use this evaluation approach as the sole means of improving the effectiveness of the audit committee. Rather, use this method of internally driven improvement in conjunction with other industry-wide best-practice methods to provide an externally driven element for further improvement.

MORE INFO

Book:

Verschoor, Curtis C. *Audit Committee Essentials.* Hoboken, NJ: Wiley, 2008.

Articles:

Braiotta, Louis, Jr. "Corporate audit committees: An approach to continuous improvement." *CPA Journal* (July 2002). Online at: www.nysscpa.org/cpajournal/2002/0702/dept/d074802.htm

Smith, L. Murphy. "Audit committee effectiveness: Did the blue ribbon committee recommendations make a difference?" *International Journal of Accounting, Auditing and Performance Evaluation* 3:2 (2006): 240–251. Online at: dx.doi.org/10.1504/IJAAPE.2006.010303

Websites:

American Institute of Certified Public Accountants (AICPA) provides an audit committee toolkit: www.aicpa.org

KPMG's Audit Committee Institute: www.kpmg.com/aci

Establishing a Framework for Assessing Risk

DEFINITION

Instituting a framework for identifying risks (or opportunities), assessing their probability and impact, and determining which controls should be in place can be critical to achieving the company's business objectives. Identifying and proactively addressing risks and opportunities helps businesses to defend themselves. Debt rating agencies and regulators are also increasingly stipulating that companies institute risk-identifying frameworks.

Enterprise Risk Management (ERM) is a name given to the structures, methods, and procedures used by organizations to identify and combat risk. The setting up and monitoring of ERM is typically performed by management as part of its internal control activities, such as appraisals of analytical reports or management committee meetings with relevant experts to make sure that the risk-response strategy is working and that the objectives are being achieved.

Once the risks have been identified and assessed, management chooses a risk-response approach. This may include:
- Avoidance: Leave risky activities.
- Reduction: Lessen their probability or impact.
- Share or insure: Diminish risk by transferring or sharing.
- Accept: In response to a cost–benefit analysis, take no action.

The most widely used ERM frameworks are COSO (from an organization that prepares audit-related reports) and RIMS (Risk and Insurance Management Society). Both use methods for identifying, analyzing, responding to, and scrutinizing risks or opportunities within the internal and external settings of the business.

ADVANTAGES

- ERM allows an enterprise to identify and prioritize the risks that might be facing the organization.
- An improved understanding of the risks—both systemic and non-systemic—facing businesses can help in contingency planning for when the unexpected happens.
- Robust identification of risks can protect businesses from events that might otherwise threaten the viability of the entity.

DISADVANTAGES

- Protracted risk-framework evaluation could be counterproductive if the fruitless pursuit of perfection leaves the company exposed to the very risks it hoped to avoid.
- Evaluating risks depends on judgments, estimates, and interpretation. Risks are often intangible issues that might be highly relevant but cannot be easily measured.

ACTION CHECKLIST

✓ Overcome resistance to the introduction or upgrading of risk frameworks by ensuring that the board and managers are conscious of the fact that it is in everyone's interest to be aware of business risks.

✓ Encourage an open environment when establishing a risk framework. Some risks are obvious, but stakeholders or managers of individual business sectors may sometimes know more about hidden risks.

✓ Engage key business stakeholders and managers in the evaluation of risks and when seeking the best resolutions for those risks.

DOS AND DON'TS

DO

- Regularly update risk-assessment frameworks, as these can help to keep management informed of the constantly changing business environment and its risks.
- Spell out in clear terms the risks that the organization may be facing, their probability, and their potential impact.

DON'T

- Don't take risks for granted; just because a risk has been the same in the past, there is no guarantee that it will be the same in the future. Only by fully understanding the risks and updating risk frameworks can you counteract the dangers.
- Don't get bogged down by risk frameworks. Risk is sometimes a natural and acceptable part of doing business.

In Practice • Checklists

MORE INFO
Websites:
American Accounting Association (AAA): aaahq.org
Society of Actuaries (SOA): www.soa.org

QFINANCE

Internal Auditing and Doing Business in Foreign Countries

DEFINITION

As companies increasingly expand abroad, chief audit executives face a host of new and unexpected challenges. Operating abroad in unfamiliar political environments exposes businesses to new types of risks and complexities, which can threaten business performance. These risks can range from differences in regulatory and compliance practices to those that violate domestic law, such as the US Foreign Corrupt Practices Act 1977, as well as political risks. When investing in a foreign country, the latter can be just as important as economic factors in the decision-making process.

Any company operating abroad, but particularly in emerging markets, needs timely, accurate, and objective assessments of the political and economic environment. Though management is responsible for the identification, continuing assessment, and management of political, legal, commercial, and economic risk events, internal auditing can play a role by evaluating the overall effectiveness of these processes. If management is failing to take areas such as political risk into account, this should be highlighted by the internal auditor, while political and other risks needs to be a key consideration in internal auditing's risk assessment, whether or not management is addressing this risk on a formal basis.

If management's risk assessment does include political and other risks, the internal auditor should evaluate the findings of management's risk assessment and its impact on the internal audit plan. Internal auditors should gather objective information about risk events, factor this information into their risk-based audit planning activities, and communicate the audit findings to the audit committee and management.

ADVANTAGES

- Assessing the risks of investing and operating in a foreign country is vital if that investment is to prove successful and to avoid violating laws in the company's domestic market.
- Auditing foreign investment risks across a number of markets enables an investor to gauge which markets are likely to prove most fruitful.
- Auditing foreign investment risks helps investors to identify potential pitfalls and take preventive action.

DISADVANTAGES

- Auditing foreign investment risks can prove time-consuming and costly.
- A company will have to train key members of staff to undertake internal audit activities and they will have less time to spend on other revenue-generating activities.

ACTION CHECKLIST

✓ Investing in foreign countries opens a business to new risks. Internal auditors need a solid grasp of how political, economic, and commercial factors can affect a business. Internal auditors need a solid grasp of how political factors affect corporate governance and regulatory compliance in addition to operating performance and bottom-line earnings.

✓ Use specialist risk analysts to get an independent assessment of the risks of operating in a foreign county. Relying on local sources alone can be risky since their views may be skewed by local news reports, and they may seek to promote personal interests through, for example, the expansion of operations under their own control.

✓ Corruption is a particular threat in developing countries. Transparency International's Corruption Perceptions Index ranks almost 200 countries by their perceived levels of corruption, as determined by expert assessments and opinion surveys.

DOS AND DON'TS

DO

- Monitor rapid economic growth, instability, or deterioration, increasing levels of foreign investment, and major changes in government leadership.
- Monitor changes in regulations or trade agreements that may affect the organization.

(Continued overleaf)

In Practice • Checklists

DO (*cont.*)

- Monitor social unrest and major security issues and ensure that the risks they pose are adequately addressed. Remember that political risk assessments are inherently more subjective than economic analysis and are thus more vulnerable to bias.

DON'T

- Don't forget that political risk events are difficult to measure and quantify, or that they are rarely assessed and incorporated into audit plans by internal auditors or addressed by other corporate functions.

MORE INFO

Books:

Bishop, R. Doak, James Crawford, and William Michael Reisman. *Foreign Investment Disputes: Cases, Materials and Commentary.* The Hague: Kluwer Law International, 2005.

Brink, Charlotte H. *Measuring Political Risk: Risks to Foreign Investment.* Aldershot, UK: Ashgate, 2004.

Websites:

Economist Intelligence Unit: www.eiu.com

Political and Economic Risk Consultancy, Hong Kong: www.asiarisk.com

Transparency International Corruption Perceptions Index: www.transparency.org/policy_research/surveys_indices/cpi

Internal Auditing for Financial Firms

DEFINITION

In view of the recent global recession of 2009–10, when investments made by banks and financial institutions proved unsafe and almost triggered a financial meltdown that required strong input and investment by most democratic governments, the need for internationally regulated and well-audited financial institutions is greater than ever. Therefore, financial institutions have started to concentrate on rigorous internal audit processes undertaken by an internal audit team that conducts regular control self-assessments. This is a process in which management and staff analyze their roles and activities, and assess how efficient and effective their internal control procedures are.

Financial institutions should have an internal audit team that has a dual role of assessing whether the risks taken are appropriately managed and of making recommendations to consolidate the institution's controls. The internal audit team should be independent in its evaluation of the control systems within the organization.

The internal audit team must also assess and report on management's performance, analyzing and reporting on whether it has performed appropriately, effectively, and efficiently. The internal audit team needs to ensure that the financial institution has complied with all the procedures, standards, and policies imposed by the applicable laws and regulations. This is no mean task as the financial sector is complex and highly regulated.

The nature of the role means that internal auditors will not only gather and provide information, but that they will also help in the assessment and interpretation of that information as it pertains to the overall compliance and security of the organization, including the procedures that are in place to manage and control risk. The actual control of risk will in all probability be in the hands of specific risk managers, but the internal audit team will want to report on the effectiveness of the procedures involved and on executive management's relationship with the risk managers. One of the problems of the crash was the way in which the concerns of risk managers were sidelined by managements intent on boosting profits without regard, or without sufficient regard, to the risks that were being assumed.

ADVANTAGES

- Internal auditing of financial institutions improves their productivity.
- It assesses how investments have performed and helps to increase a firm's revenues.
- It should provide an insight into the performance of an institution and provide constructive criticism on what should be changed and how.
- It can help to prevent fraud and mismanagement.

DISADVANTAGES

- Regulations and laws are increasingly stringent and the cost of compliance is now a significant factor.
- Trained staff are required if the internal audit function is to perform its task effectively, and this too requires a substantial investment. An internal audit department is a pure "cost" to the company. However, not having a strong internal audit function exposes the company to fraud and to failures of control and compliance that could ultimately cost it everything—as spectacular cases such as Enron demonstrate.
- Line management can be resentful of the "braking" effect of a rigorous internal audit policy and an active internal audit department, blaming the latter for "undue caution" and for implementing time-consuming control procedures. This is not so much a disadvantage as a factor that requires handling by senior management.
- The internal audit function can only be as effective as it is allowed to be. It requires a board-level champion to maintain effectiveness.

ACTION CHECKLIST

✔ Study the relevant laws carefully. Compliance with regulations for the internal audit of financial firms is closely monitored.

✔ Ensure that the board of directors has reviewed the control systems and capital assessment procedures of the bank or financial institution.

✔ Ensure that the internal auditors have examined and evaluated the effectiveness of the internal control systems.

✓ See that the internal auditors have assessed the means of safeguarding assets.

✓ Review the internal audit analysis of operational efficiency.

✓ Ensure that the members of the internal audit team have no connection or conflict of interest with the financial sector they will investigate.

DOS AND DON'TS

DO

- Appoint the best possible team of internal auditors, ensuring that they have the capability and authority required to assess the financial state of the firm.
- Provide board-level support for the function to enable it to gain access to everything it requires to fulfill its role.
- Comply with all the laws and regulations governing the assessment and operation of financial institutions.
- Ensure that the integrity of the internal audit function is maintained at all times.

DON'T

- Don't ignore any constructive criticism made by the internal audit team.
- Don't cut costs by appointing low-caliber internal auditors—it could turn out to be a very expensive economy.
- Don't appoint auditors that have connections with personnel in the departments to be examined by the internal audit function.

MORE INFO

Books:

Bainbridge, Stephen M. *The Complete Guide to Sarbanes–Oxley: Understanding How Sarbanes–Oxley Affects Your Business.* Avon, MA: Adams Media, 2007.

Pickett, K. H. Spencer. *The Essential Handbook of Internal Auditing.* Chichester, UK: Wiley, 2005.

Regulatory Compliance Associates, Inc. *Bank Internal Audit: A Working Guide to Regulatory Compliance.* Austin, TX: Sheshunoff. Periodic updates via subscription.

Articles:

Anderson, Richard J., and David R. Albright. "Bank regulators now have put internal audit in their sights." *American Banker* (July 24, 2003). Online at: www.americanbanker.com/issues/168_144/-202175-1.html

Anon. "High performance auditing in banking." *Internal Auditor* (February 1996). Online at: www.highbeam.com/doc/1G1-18202725.html

Cahill, Edward. "Audit committee and internal audit effectiveness in a multinational bank subsidiary: *A case study*." Journal of Banking Regulation 7:1 (February 2006): 160–179. Online at: dx.doi.org/10.1057/palgrave.jbr.2340011

Websites:

Institute of Internal Auditors (IIA): www.theiia.org

MIS Training Institute (audit and information security training): www.mistieurope.com

Internal Auditing for Fraud Detection and Prevention

DEFINITION

Fraud protection is a key concern for businesses, and internal audits can play a major role in both detecting and preventing fraud. According to the Institute of Internal Auditors (IIA), for example, "internal auditors support management's efforts to establish a culture that embraces ethics, honesty, and integrity" and "they assist management with the evaluation of internal controls used to detect or mitigate fraud, evaluate the organization's assessment of fraud risk, and are involved in any fraud investigations." This is because, although it is management's responsibility to design internal controls to prevent, detect, and mitigate fraud, the internal auditors are "the appropriate resource" for assessing the effectiveness of the measures that management has implemented. Consequently, the IIA says that depending on directives from management, the board, audit committee, or other governing body, internal auditors can play a variety of consulting, assurance, collaborative, advisory, oversight, and investigative roles in an organization's fraud management process. Internal auditors are well placed to deter and detect fraud because they are highly proficient in techniques used to evaluate internal controls. These skills, "coupled with their understanding of the indicators of fraud, enables them to assess an organization's fraud risks and advise management of the necessary steps to take when indicators are present," concludes the IIA.

ADVANTAGES

- As a part of their assurance activities, internal auditors watch for potential fraud risks, assess the adequacy of related controls, and make recommendations for improvement. They can help also to benchmark statistics related to the probability of occurrence and consequences of fraud.
- Internal auditors are exposed to key processes throughout the organization and have open lines of communication with the executive board and staff. They are thus able to play an important role in fraud detection.
- Since internal auditors report directly to the board or governing body, they have the independence and objectivity necessary for them to undertake investigations of a sensitive nature.

DISADVANTAGES

- Although internal auditors may have a direct role in investigating fraud, they generally lack the expertise of professionals whose primary responsibility is detecting and investigating fraud.

ACTION CHECKLIST

✔ Consult the internal auditors on methods to ensure integrity within the organization and involve them in communicating or interpreting those methods. Internal auditors can also help to develop training related to integrity policies and fraud prevention and detection.

✔ Ensure that the internal auditors have key competencies for this work through specialized training and related experiences. They can also gain certification as fraud or forensic investigators.

✔ Ensure that the chief audit executive is responsible for responding to issues raised on ethics that may lead to detection of fraud.

DOS AND DON'TS

DO

- Establish a culture of integrity, as it is a critical component of fraud control. Executive management must set the highest levels of integrity as a benchmark.
- Ensure that you comply with IIA standards on this issue. In January 2009, for example, the IIA implemented a new standard making auditing for fraud mandatory for internal auditors.
- Make sure that your internal auditors consider using technology-based audit and other data analysis techniques in line with IIA standards.

DON'T

- Don't rely solely on internal auditors to root out and deter fraud. Simple procedures such as vetting employment candidates thoroughly can be highly effective and relatively cheap ways of preventing fraud.

In Practice • Checklists

MORE INFO

Books:

Pickett, K. H. Spencer. *The Internal Auditing Handbook*. 3rd ed. Chichester, UK: Wiley, 2010.

Rezaee, Zabihollah, and Richard Riley. *Financial Statement Fraud: Prevention and Detection*. 2nd ed. Hoboken, NJ: Wiley, 2010.

Vona, Leonard W. *Fraud Risk Assessment: Building a Fraud Audit Program*. Hoboken, NJ: Wiley, 2008.

Reports:

Coram, Paul, Colin Ferguson, and Robyn Moroney. "The importance of internal audit in fraud detection." Paper presented at AFAANZ Conference, July 2–4, 2006, Wellington, New Zealand. Online at: tinyurl.com/6fvsvxl [PDF].

IIA. "Internal auditing and fraud." December 2009. Online at: tinyurl.com/4vsycok

Websites:

Chartered Institute of Internal Auditors (UK and Ireland): www.iia.org.uk

Institute of Internal Auditors (IIA): www.theiia.org

Internal Auditing for Small and Medium-Sized Enterprises (SMEs)

DEFINITION

Internal audits can have a range of functions, from determining the financial health of an organization to looking at how efficient and effective it is. Internal audits can also assess the nonfinancial areas of an entity. However, small and medium-sized enterprises (SMEs) have particular needs in terms of internal auditing. The accounts of very small businesses, for example, are less complex than those of larger organizations, and they can neither afford, nor do they probably need, the services of qualified auditing professionals.

An internal audit can vary from encompassing all areas of a business to focusing on a very narrow and specific aspect of an enterprise's operations and systems. However, performing a successful small business audit is likely to involve examining various areas, including: cash flow, accounts receivable, accounts payable, quality, human resources, procurement, payroll, IT, and profitability. Auditing these areas helps to ensure that the small business is able to meet its main goal, which is to generate a profit.

As survival is the key requirement for any SME, understanding cash flow is essential. Auditing cash flow involves examining the receipts of the business and determining the sources from which they are derived. This will highlight key factors, such as dependence on a particular source or the volatility of receipts, and will reveal how much money is flowing in and out the business. Examining the accounts receivable highlights how long money is tied up before it is released for the business, and the results may prompt a revision of credit policy. Examining accounts payable will determine how much money is owed to suppliers, and such an examination should leave the managers better positioned to control cash flow. Examining quality, which involves looking at products, marketing, advertising, and the overall image of the business, as well as human resources, will highlight any problems in these areas. Examining profit enables a business to ensure that its assets and liabilities are correctly balanced, as well as whether a business is generating sufficient profit to justify the investment that has gone into it.

ADVANTAGES

- Performing an internal audit of a SME can provide assurance that it is operating as efficiently as possible, as it will highlight any problem areas that need to be addressed.
- Internal audits can also be used in a preventive fashion. An internal auditor may, for example, spot potential problems and risks in business operations, allowing management to take preemptive action that stops the potential problem from developing.
- Carrying out an audit can deter or detect fraud and other crimes. Knowing how many computers your company owns, for example, can protect against theft. A bigger risk in a small organization is likely to be inadequate controls when people perform multiple tasks.

DISADVANTAGES

- Carrying out an internal audit can be time-consuming, diverting key staff from core activities.
- Internal audit has a cost, and the benefits must outweigh the cost.

ACTION CHECKLIST

✓ The purpose of the audit should be discussed and agreed by the SME's management. The auditor should establish the audit's scope and objectives, as agreed with the relevant managers.

✓ Establish how frequently the audit should be carried out. The riskier units of a SME should be audited more frequently than other departments. They should also be audited more intensely.

✓ Policies and procedures should focus on continuously improving how work is performed. Management should review all organizational policies and procedures on an annual basis to ensure that they reflect the changing business environment.

✓ If, as the result of an audit, a SME's net income is found to be low, corrective strategies must be implemented in the affected areas to correct the problem and restore the business to financial health.

DOS AND DON'TS

DO

- Ensure that the person carrying out the audit is given the authority to act independently and produce results without fear or favor.
- Ensure that the internal auditor is given specific reporting guidelines, a time frame, and access to all files so as to avoid conflict within departments or among superiors.

DON'T

- Don't provide any unrequested or extraneous information. If you are unsure about the information and how it may relate to the audit, but the auditor has not specifically requested it, consult with the managers responsible for the internal audit first so that a decision can be made on how to proceed.

MORE INFO

Books:

Chadwick, Leslie. *Essential Finance and Accounting for Managers*. Harlow, UK: FT Prentice Hall, 2002.

Harrer, Julie. *Internal Control Strategies: A Mid to Small Business Guide*. Hoboken, NJ: Wiley, 2008.

Henschel, Thomas. *Risk Management Practices of SMEs: Evaluating and Implementing Effective Risk Management Systems*. Berlin: Erich Schmidt Verlag, 2008.

Internal Auditing for the Public Sector

DEFINITION

Governments and government departments in democratic societies are subject to internal audit. This is essential to assess whether the departments are run efficiently and provide good value for taxpayers' money.

The UK government's internal audit standards (HM Treasury, 2011) define internal auditing as an independent, objective assurance and consulting activity designed to add value and improve an organization's operations. Its scope is to help an organization to accomplish its objectives by bringing a systematic, disciplined approach to the evaluation and improvement of the effectiveness of risk management, control, and governance processes.

Internal auditors must be independent from the public sector that they audit in order to be able to provide impartial audit review and advice. This means that the process of appointing public auditors must be well regulated and impartial. Usually this is regulated by law; however, in the public sector the appointment of internal auditors is usually a decision for management or the audit committee.

The auditing process in the public sector has a wide remit. The scope of the internal audit work will usually focus on:
- reviewing the achievement of objectives;
- making sure decisions are properly authorized;
- assuring the reliability and integrity of information;
- promoting efficiency and effectiveness;
- safeguarding assets;
- assessing compliance with laws, regulations, policies, and contracts;
- reviewing the opportunities for fraud.

ADVANTAGES

- Internal auditing of public sector organizations and government departments is a necessary process that provides an insight into how the public sector is run.
- It provides an assessment of the resource budget estimates that in turn helps a government department to meet its published aims and objectives.
- It offers consultancy advice in the form of recommendations that management are free to accept or reject.

DISADVANTAGES

- Regulations and statutes can make the internal auditing of public sector departments lengthy and complicated.
- Since many departments are concerned with vital public services, subjecting them to internal audit can be disruptive and can create difficulties with line management if the function, objectives, and ultimately the benefits of internal audit are not understood by department personnel.
- Unless the internal audit function is properly trained, with a full understanding and appreciation of the department that is being audited, its judgments will be challenged by line management. Proper training is essential.

ACTION CHECKLIST

✓ Ensure that internal auditors are appointed in full compliance with the relevant legislation.
✓ Make sure that the auditors appointed have no connection or conflict of interest with the public sector they will investigate.

DOS AND DON'TS

DO

- Set up a transparent and clear process which the public can easily consult.
- Make sure that the principles of independence of public sector auditors, propriety of auditors, and providing good value for money are achieved.
- Make sure that the internal audit process is supervised by an independent watchdog such as the Audit Commission in the United Kingdom or equivalent.

DON'T

- Don't ignore the importance of public sector auditing. It may seem expensive, but it will provide value for money in the long term.
- Don't appoint auditors that have any connection with the public sector in question; otherwise the impartiality of the audit function will be put at risk.

MORE INFO

Book:

Keating, Lori. *Performance Auditing of Public Sector Property Contracts*. Aldershot, UK: Gower Publishing, 2011.

Articles:

Broadbent, Jane, and James Guthrie. "Public sector to public services: 20 years of 'contextual' accounting research." *Accounting, Auditing and Accountability Journal* 21:2 (2008): 129–169. Online at: dx.doi.org/10.1108/09513570810854383

Parker, Lee, and Graeme Gould. "Changing public sector accountability: Critiquing new directions." *Accounting Forum* 23:2 (June 1999): 109–135.

Reports:

Chartered Institute of Public Finance and Accountancy. "Code of practice for internal audit in local government in the United Kingdom 2006." Online at: tinyurl.com/6bx4q4h

HM Treasury. "Government internal audit standards." February 2011. Online at: www.hm-treasury.gov.uk/d/internalaudit_gias_0211.pdf

Websites:

Audit Commission (UK): www.audit-commission.gov.uk

MIS Training Institute (audit and information security training): www.mistieurope.com

International and Multinational Internal Auditing

DEFINITION

Internal audit activities are performed in diverse legal and cultural environments and within organizations that vary in purpose, size, and structure; and by persons within or outside the organization. These differences may affect the practice of internal auditing in each environment. Standards have been established by bodies such as the International Federation of Accountants (IFAC) to ensure that internal audits are carried out to the same high level across international boundaries. More than 100 countries have either adopted international standards on auditing (ISAs) issued by the IFAC or have declared their intent to do so in the future. ISAs, as well as international financial reporting standards (IFRSs), are endorsed by the World Bank, the International Monetary Fund, and other international institutions as the best-practice standards for corporate financial reporting.

ISAs are issued by the International Auditing and Assurance Standards Board (IAASB), an independent standard-setting body that operates under the auspices of the IFAC. The objective of the IAASB is to "serve the public interest by setting high quality auditing, assurance, quality control and related services standards and by facilitating the convergence of international and national standards, thereby enhancing the quality and uniformity of practice throughout the world and strengthening public confidence in the global auditing and assurance profession."

The growth of multinational businesses has increased pressure to harmonize international auditing standards. The auditing of multinational enterprises needs to take into account the rules in their home country, such as Sarbanes–Oxley in the United States. The internationalization of auditing has largely taken place within international audit firms. During the past few decades many local audit firms have merged into international groups.

ADVANTAGES

The benefits of international standards for auditing include the following.
- They give readers of audit reports confidence in the auditors' opinions.
- They provide greater assurance that accounting standards are being adhered to.
- They facilitate international financial comparisons.
- They assist in the flow of investment capital.
- Developing countries can use them as a basis for their own standards.

DISADVANTAGES
- Organizations have different auditing requirements, and a standardized approach may not suit every business or entity.
- It can be expensive for companies in developing countries to apply international standards, some of which may not be relevant or needed in their domicile.

ACTION CHECKLIST
✔ Ensure that your financial statements are prepared in line with international standards such as IFRSs.
✔ Make sure that you are aware of issues such as transfer pricing—the price setting for cross-border transfer of goods, services, and intangibles between associated parties. Errors in this area could result in double taxation involving foreign tax authorities.
✔ Intellectual property (IP) is another problematic area. The benefits of IP should lie with the owner, so it is important to establish both where the IP has been created and where it is legally owned.

DOS AND DON'TS
DO
- Be aware that tax authorities around the world are increasing their audit activities, and the need to meet international auditing standards has never been more pressing.

DON'T
- Don't forget that the responsibility for safeguarding the assets of the company and for the prevention and detection of fraud, error, and noncompliance with law or regulations continues to rest with management.

MORE INFO

Books:

Collings, Steven. *Interpretation and Application of International Standards on Auditing*. Chichester, UK: Wiley, 2011.

Dauber, Nick A., Anique Ahmed Qureshi, Marc H. Levine, and Joel G. Siegel. *The Complete Guide to Auditing Standards and Other Professional Standards for Accountants 2009*. Hoboken, NJ: Wiley, 2009.

Hayes, Rick, Roger Dassen, Arnold Schilder, and Philip Wallage. *Principles of Auditing: An Introduction to International Standards on Auditing*. 2nd ed. Harlow, UK: FT Prentice Hall, 2005.

Websites:

Chartered Institute of Internal Auditors (UK and Ireland) on international standards: tinyurl.com/5vsuhkl

International Auditing and Assurance Standards Board (IAASB): www.ifac.org/IAASB

International Federation of Accountants (IFAC): www.ifac.org

Preparing and Executing an Internal Audit Review

DEFINITION

An internal audit review is the systematic process of analyzing a firm's business and includes planning (also called a survey or preliminary review), fieldwork, an audit report and a follow-up review. The internal audit review is conducted to assess the firm's compliance with laws and regulations, efficiency of operations (process, procedures), and progress toward key goals (including preserving and enhancing assets). The main aims of the internal audit review are to assess business operations, review progress toward business objectives, determine the reliability of financial and other operations, ensure that legal and regulatory requirements are met, identify the effectiveness of risk management activities, and deter fraud.

An internal audit review is a legal requirement for many firms, especially those which are publicly traded. Regulations such as Sarbanes–Oxley have increased the demand for internal auditors. The review is undertaken annually by appointed internal auditors. In general, an internal audit review committee is established which reports to the board of directors and the CEO. Internal auditors are hired. Currently, the internal audit profession is unregulated; however, the Institute of Internal Auditors (IIA) publishes standards and has more than 150,000 members in 165 countries.

Each firm has a unique auditing process. Auditors usually begin the planning process by gaining a detailed understanding of the firm and the objectives of the audit. Audit objectives can include: an assessment of management; verification of internal control procedures; assessment of the ability to respond to urgent market needs and events; improving risk management in the company; and assessing the skills of employees of the company and its training program.

At the fieldwork stage internal auditors examine all divisions of the firm, and across finance management, risk management, internal compliance control, and procedures and operations.

Following the fieldwork, the internal auditors prepare an initial report summarizing their findings. The draft is read by the firm's leadership (e.g. CEO, board of directors) and is then finalized.

The final step, often one year after the audit report is completed, is a follow-up review. This review involves assessing the extent to which recommendations have been implemented.

ADVANTAGES
- An internal audit helps a firm to assess the state of its business.
- Internal audit reports can lead to solid suggestions for business improvement.
- Internal auditing helps to assess risk management policies and deter fraud.

DISADVANTAGES
- Internal auditing can be an expensive process, beginning with recruiting talented internal auditors with high levels of professional experience and qualifications. A third party may provide an interim internal audit.

ACTION CHECKLIST
✔ Recruit the right individuals as internal auditors. Obtain as much information from as many sources as you can before appointing these individuals. Consider the use of a third party for an interim internal audit.
✔ Communicate your business plans and aims to auditors.
✔ Allow the auditors transparency in examining documents and speaking with key staff.
✔ Implement the suggestions made in the auditing report.

DOS AND DON'TS
DO
- Invest in internal audit technology to improve the quality of the audit process.
- Establish good communication between management and internal auditors. This helps both with the audit process and with the implementation of recommendations. Even if an internal audit review is not a requirement for your firm, consider undertaking the process to assess and improve the business.

DON'T
- Don't underestimate the need for proper training of directors and employees in order to help them to fulfill their duties.
- Don't ignore the recommendations made in the final internal audit report as doing so could adversely impact your firm.

MORE INFO

Articles:

Dickhart, Gary. "Risk: Key to governance." *Internal Auditor* (December 2008). Online at:
www.entrepreneur.com/tradejournals/article/190852308.html

Smith, Philip. "IT skills for internal auditors." *Internal Auditor* (August 2008). Online at:
www.entrepreneur.com/tradejournals/article/183444840.html

Websites:

AuditNet example of an internal audit review for a university: www.auditnet.org/process.htm
Chartered Institute of Internal Auditors (UK and Ireland): www.iia.org.uk
Institute of Internal Auditors (IIA): www.theiia.org

Quality Assessment of Internal Audits

DEFINITION

Most countries have established standards that aim to improve the quality of internal auditing services. In the United Kingdom, for example, HM Treasury has established the Internal Audit Quality Assessment Framework (IAQAF), a tool for evaluating the quality of the internal audit service in an organization. HM Treasury says that the IAQAF is intended to: "facilitate identification of actions for continuous improvement; facilitate evaluation of progress with improvement plans; [and] provide an approach to both internal and external quality assurance reviews which is not 'tick box' and which goes beyond compliance with the Standards alone."

Internationally, best practice as set out by the Institute of Internal Auditors (IIA) requires an independent quality assessment of the internal audit function at least once every five years. The IIA has established a program related to the quality assurance process that is known as Standard 1300. The program is designed to enable an evaluation of the internal audit activity's conformance with the Definition of Internal Auditing and the Standards, and an evaluation of whether internal auditors apply the IIA's code of ethics. There are various requirements within Standard 1300. Standard 1312, for example, requires every internal audit department to undergo an external quality assessment at least once every five years by a qualified independent reviewer from outside the organization. The IIA also offers courses which help firms to meet quality assessment standards. Studies have found that the level of use of the Standards and compliance with the Standards varies from country to country.

ADVANTAGES

- Quality assessment monitors on a continuous basis the internal audit activity of a company.
- It helps the organization to comply with the IIA's internal auditing standards and code of ethics.
- It adds value and helps to improve an organization's objectives, activities, and business.

DISADVANTAGES

- Quality assessment of internal audit involves a process within a process, and therefore extra time and expense.

ACTION CHECKLIST

✔ Keep up-to-date with the rules and regulations that govern the internal audit process.

✔ Monitor the technology that is used in internal auditing and improve it to the best of the company's ability.

✔ Employ the best consultants you can afford to evaluate your internal audit process.

✔ Establish good communications between internal auditors, the management, and the reviewers.

DOS AND DON'TS

DO

- Prepare for the quality assessment by interviewing employees, monitoring procedures, and comparing results against written policies to identify inconsistencies and opportunities for improvement.
- Ensure that employees rely on established policy and procedures rather than following their own.
- Establish processes for updating policies and procedures and develop methods to train employees when modifications require training or retraining.

DON'T

- Don't ignore the need to assess the quality of your internal audit. A badly managed internal audit can harm the business by not unearthing serious failings in procedures.
- Don't skimp on appointing the right people to review your internal audit systems and processes.

QFINANCE

Best-Practice Approaches to Internal Auditing

MORE INFO

Books:

Palmes, Paul C. *Process Driven Comprehensive Auditing: A New Way to Conduct ISO 9001:2008 Internal Audits*. 2nd ed. Milwaukee, WI: ASQ Quality Press, 2009.

Pastor, Joan. *Conflict Management and Negotiation Skills for Internal Auditors*. Altamonte Springs, FL: Institute of Internal Auditors Research Foundation, 2007.

Articles:

Karapetrovic, Stanislav, and Walter Willborn. "Quality assurance and effectiveness of audit systems." *International Journal of Quality and Reliability Management* 17:6 (2000): 679–703. Online at: dx.doi.org/10.1108/02656710010315256

Marais, M. "Quality assurance in internal auditing: An analysis of the standards and guidelines implemented by the Institute of Internal Auditors (IIA)." *Meditari Accountancy Research* 12:2 (2004): 85–107. Online at: www.meditari.org.za/docs/2004vol2/85_107.pdf

Websites:

Chartered Institute of Internal Auditors (UK and Ireland): www.iia.org.uk

Institute of Internal Auditors (IIA): www.theiia.org

HM Treasury Internal Audit Quality Assessment Framework (IAQAF): www.hm-treasury.gov.uk/psr_governance_risk_iaqaf.htm

KnowledgeLeader resources for internal auditors and risk management professionals: www.knowledgeleader.com

In Practice • Checklists

QFINANCE

XBRL (eXtensible Business Reporting Language) and Internal Auditing

DEFINITION

XBRL (eXtensible Business Reporting Language) is a computer language for the electronic transmission of business and financial data. The goal of XBRL is to standardize the automation of business intelligence and thus create a global standard for sharing business information. XBRL uses tags to describe and identify each item of data in an electronic document. The tags allow computer programs to sort through data and analyze relationships quickly and generate output in various formats. Because the tags are standardized, analysis can be conducted across multiple documents from multiple sources, even if the text in the documents is written in different languages.

XBRL provides major benefits in the preparation, analysis, and communication of business information, and at a reduced cost. It provides standardized controls that can result in improved efficiency and effectiveness of audits. Filing financial statements in XBRL format has become a regulatory mandate for many companies in the world. In the United States, for example, the Securities and Exchange Commission ruled that as of June 2009 all public companies with more than US$5 billion in assets must report financials using XBRL. It is thus important that management and internal auditors understand the value it brings throughout the entire compliance and reporting process.

ADVANTAGES

- XBRL helps internal auditors by facilitating the migration from manual to automated processes in key activities.
- XBRL gives auditors the ability to more efficiently access and integrate data across an organization.
- XBRL allows the abstraction of business rules and controls that can be applied across a wide range of software applications.

DISADVANTAGES

- If inexperienced users create data for transmission, XBRL's complexity increases the opportunity for errors.
- Outsourcing the implementation of XBRL, as is done by many organizations, leads to increased costs. This undermines one of the main advantages of XBRL, which is to cut costs.

ACTION CHECKLIST

✔ Examine whether it is best to instruct your accountant, your auditor, or a specialist provider to convert your accounts to XBRL. Cost is clearly an important consideration, but the timescale may also be an issue.

✔ Send your report to third parties in Word or Excel format rather than as a PDF to make it easier for them to convert it to XBRL.

DOS AND DON'TS

DO

- Discuss XBRL with your audit advisors before purchasing any Word/Excel-based tagging solutions.
- Be aware that the initial setting up of XBRL can be costly. Unless a company has an automated tagging process, tagging XBRL data consumes hours of labor.
- Investigate all the numerous software products on the market for converting accounting reports to XBRL to find the one most suited to your organization.

DON'T

- Don't forget that XBRL data remain available at all times and thus require greater security to maintain their integrity.

MORE INFO

Books:

Coderre, David. *Internal Audit: Efficiency through Automation*. Hoboken, NJ: Wiley, 2009.

Deshmukh, Ashutosh. *Digital Accounting: The Effects of the Internet and ERP on Accounting*. Hershey, PA: IRM Press, 2006.

Hoffman, Charles, and Liv Apneseth Watson. *XBRL for Dummies*. Hoboken, NJ: Wiley, 2009.

Websites:

Chartered Institute of Internal Auditors (UK and Ireland): www.iia.org.uk

Institute of Internal Auditors (IIA): www.theiia.org

International Accounting Standards Board/International Financial Reporting Standards (IASB/IFRS) on XRBL: www.ifrs.org/xbrl/xbrl.htm

XRBL International: www.xbrl.org

XRBL UK: www.xbrl.org/uk

Index

Index